First published 2004
by Way Books, Campion Hall, Oxford,
OX1 1QS
www.theway.org.uk

Cover Design: Peter Brook SJ

Printed and bound by Antony Rowe Ltd, Eastbourne
British Library Cataloguing-in-Publication Data
A catalogue record for this book is available from
the British Library
ISBN 0 904717 24 0

CORNELIA CONNELLY
AND
HER INTERPRETERS

Judith Lancaster SHCJ

Way Books
Campion Hall, Oxford

CONTENTS

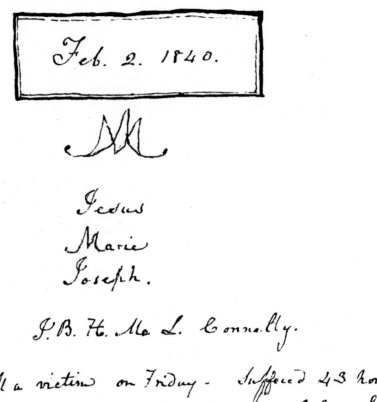

I. B. H. M. L. Connelly
Fell a victim on Friday – Suffered 48 hours
and was taken "into the temple of the Lord"
on the
Purification.

From Cornelia Connelly's Notebook,
recording the death of her two-year-old son, John Henry, 2 February 1840

FOREWORD

This book is not itself a religious biography but something else, something more subtle: a *study in* religious biography. It sets out to uncover the ways in which Cornelia Connelly's life has been transformed into a story by her biographers, and it teases out the various literary, spiritual and historical strands that can be identified in the different biographies. Dickens' Mr Gradgrind claimed that "Facts … facts alone are wanted in life." But "facts" are not neutral; what counts as a "fact" will always be conditioned by the questions that researchers are asking, and by what they regard as good answers. Thus this book concentrates on the questions and answers that influence the way each biographer constructs Cornelia's story. Each account of Cornelia is shaped by the biographer's own perspectives, arising as these do from her moment in history, from her personality, from her spirituality, from her assumptions about holiness, and from the way in which she herself lived and experienced religious life. Because Cornelia's life was spent in different settings, each yielding different kinds of material that do not easily fit together, biographers find it difficult to give a unified picture of her. And their attempts are interesting, not only for what they say about Cornelia, but also for what they reveal about themselves.

Cornelia's dramatic, scandalous story is fascinating, both in its own right and in how it has been interpreted subsequently. But this book also has wider applications. Any religious congregation uses its founder's story to promote or reinforce its traditional core values and assumptions, and to validate its changing self-understanding. Thus what is said in this book about Cornelia, her interpreters and their contexts raises questions not just for people interested in Cornelia herself, but for the understanding of consecrated life in general. More widely still, the different accounts of a woman who was successively a wife, a mother and a religious sister inevitably imply differing images of femininity and holiness. This study may thus reveal much about how women have understood themselves and their God over the last century and more.

Cornelia's biographers, with one exception, wrote as members of the congregation she founded, the Society of the Holy Child Jesus. Moreover, every member of the Society, living and dead, who has preserved and handed on and interpreted Cornelia's story and the Society's traditions has in some way contributed to what follows: without them this book would not have been possible. I thank especially those who have shared their views and experiences with me in many conversations. I am particularly grateful for the insights of Cornelia's living biographers, Radegunde Flaxman SHCJ, Elizabeth Mary Strub SHCJ, and Juliana Wadham. Their extensive research and thoughtful interpretation have made a major contribution to current knowledge and understanding of Cornelia. My respect for their scholarship is in no way diminished by those instances where my questions and answers differ from theirs.

The Society's leadership team generously provided me with the time and opportunity to complete this study. I thank both them and the members of the Society who have lived uncomplainingly in community with me during the years of composition.

This book first saw light of day as a PhD thesis, presented at Heythrop College, University of London and graciously examined by Professor Olwen Hufton and Dr Susan O'Brien. My two supervisores could not have been more helpful. Anne Murphy SHCJ embodied Cornelia's principle that "in training and teaching ... it is absolutely necessary to walk step by step, to teach line by line." Philip Endean SJ was unfailingly supportive and enthusiastic about the project. Helen Forshaw SHCJ, the Province and Society archivist, has answered all my queries not only with impressive efficiency but with ready humour and genuine interest. Helen was joined by Margaret Loran SHCJ, Jean Sinclair SHCJ and my sister, Helen Wellicome, in spending many hours on the tedious but essential task of proof-reading. And I am especially in debt to the Revs Joe Boland and Ian Tomlinson SJ, whose conviction about the importance of the project and my need to complete it acted as a constant spur. Finally I record my thanks to Elizabeth Lock and Philip Endean SJ at Way Books; they have been the best of editors.

Judith Lancaster SHCJ
February 2004

ABBREVIATIONS

CC   Writings of the Servant of God, Cornelia Connelly, Foundress of the Society of the Holy Child Jesus compiled for the Beatification and Canonisation Process (58 volumes).

D   Documentation Presented by the Historical Commission for the Beatification and Canonisation of the Servant of God, Cornelia Connelly, Foundress of the Society of the Holy Child Jesus (87 volumes).

(The original punctuation and spelling have usually been retained in quotations. Alterations have been made only in the interest of intelligibility.)

Chapter One

INTRODUCTION

This book sets out to explore a series of biographies of a woman whose extraordinary story arouses powerful reactions in most people who hear it: Cornelia Connelly, an American who died in England in 1879. But because we live today in a culture that values the visual as least as highly as the written text, I want to begin by looking, not at the details of her story, but at five pictures—glimpses of Cornelia at different moments in her life.

This, the earliest extant picture of Cornelia, is dated 1831, when she was 22, and probably marks her marriage in Philadelphia to Pierce Connelly, the curate of an Episcopalian parish. She has a complicated hairstyle and her dress looks expensive (a good deal of material has been needed for the sleeves and the bodice, and a shawl or wrap is draped over the balustrade behind her). But she wears no jewellery of any kind, no earrings, brooches, necklace or rings. She sits sideways-on to the artist, and has turned her head to gaze directly out of the painting. Her expression and body language are subject to conjecture: certainly her biographers have not been unanimous in their reading of them. But we know for sure that the young woman in this picture is deeply in love with a man who will eventually cause her a great deal of suffering.

This second drawing was executed between 1836 and 1837 whilst Pierce and Cornelia were resident in Rome, meeting senior clergymen, exploring classical ruins, learning Italian, appreciating art, and wining and dining with the English-speaking Catholic aristocracy. Yet it does not immediately communicate that here is a young wife, the mother of two small children, whose cultural and religious horizons are being rapidly expanded. Cornelia's face is only lightly sketched; it is the ornate mantilla-like veil, with its religious connotations, which dominates the picture. Whatever is happening in Cornelia's life at this time seems controlled and suppressed.

Some years later, about 1845, a portrait of Cornelia was painted, again in Rome, during her second stay in that city. The artist was a woman, a postulant at Trinità dei Monti, the Sacred Heart convent. Cornelia was living in seclusion at the convent with her youngest son, Frank, whilst Pierce explored his calling to the Roman Catholic priesthood, and whilst she herself contemplated the possibility of joining the Society of the Sacred Heart. She commissioned the painting for her children. It is unfinished, and one of

Cornelia's biographers, Mary Francis Bellasis, wrote on the back of a copy that it was "not like" Cornelia; nevertheless, it reveals something of the major changes that had taken place in her life since the last picture. Gone are the expensive dress of the wedding portrait and the ornate veil of her earlier Roman stay. In this picture she is wearing a plain black outfit with a small white collar and a very simple black veil; she is not presented as a wife and mother, but as an aspirant to religious life. Indeed, she seems to have intended this painting as something by which her children could remember her.

A later representation of the mature Cornelia shows her in the habit of the Society of the Holy Child Jesus, the religious congregation that she founded in 1846. This portrayal is immediately differentiated from the pictures we have already looked at because it is not a painting but a photograph, taken on the sands at Blackpool in 1874 whilst Cornelia was visiting her communities in north-west England. So, either Cornelia herself was interested in this new medium, or someone else prevailed upon her to sit for her photograph. This portrait of Cornelia as an older woman, her face marked by the events of her life, was used on the dust-cover of Marie Thérèse Bisgood's 1963 biography, where it was encircled in ivy, a symbol of fidelity.

Finally we have a photograph which was probably taken in St Leonards-on-Sea in 1877, a couple of years before Cornelia's death. Cornelia is looking into the middle distance, her right hand resting on a prayer book. The religious habit is more fully revealed, though we know that the silver cross round Cornelia's neck has been superimposed on the photograph: it was not adopted by members of the Society until after the founder's death. That in itself should give us pause for thought: looking even at a nineteenth-century photograph we cannot be sure that it has not been doctored, made to look as people wanted it to look.

All visual images, like written accounts, offer an interpretation of the subject; through these five pictures we have in some way already read Cornelia's life. Yet, as we look at drawings, paintings and photographs of Cornelia, we are seeing her through the lens of the person who created each image. A particular aspect of her personality, a particular moment in her life, is being called to the notice of the viewer and presented as significant. Portraiture, like biography, involves a three-way relationship between the subject, the painter or photographer or writer, and the viewer or reader. So questions asked of visual representations may validly be asked of written life accounts too. What aspect of the sitter is being emphasized? What assumptions about women, about nuns, are reflected in the picture? What are we being invited to believe about the subject? And why? Questions such as these lie at the heart of this examination of the biographies of Cornelia Connelly.

But before it is possible to address them, a brief outline of Cornelia's complex story must be provided. Aspects of the traditional account will be challenged in the chapters to come, but some grasp of the facts is necessary if the arguments that follow are to be appreciated. The extraordinary twists and turns of her life are not easily summarised, and sometimes beggar belief.

Cornelia Connelly (1809-1879)

Cornelia was born in Philadelphia on 15 January 1809, the daughter of Mary Swope Bowen, and Ralph Peacock, a Yorkshire-born property speculator who became an American citizen in 1797. Cornelia's mother, a Philadelphian of German descent, was a widow with two children at the time of her marriage to Ralph Peacock; her first husband, John Bowen, another Englishman, had owned a plantation in Jamaica. The Peacocks had a further seven children, of whom Cornelia was the youngest. Cornelia's father died when she was nine, and her mother died when she was fourteen; after that she lived with her half-sister, Isabella Bowen Montgomery.

In 1831, in spite of family opposition, Cornelia married Pierce Connelly, an Episcopalian minister, and the couple set up home in Natchez, Mississippi, where Pierce had accepted the rectorship of Trinity Church. Two of the Connellys' children were born in Natchez—Mercer in 1832, and

Adeline in 1835. By the time Adeline was born, Pierce was contemplating conversion to Catholicism, and in August 1835 he resigned his living.

The Connellys spent the next two years in Europe, mainly in Rome. Cornelia was received into the Catholic Church in New Orleans before they sailed, but Pierce waited until they reached Rome because, even at this stage, he was exploring the possibility of the Catholic priesthood for himself. In Rome they became friends with the Earl of Shrewsbury and his family. A third child, John Henry, was born in Vienna in 1837; and the Connellys, having lost a good deal of money in a US financial crisis, returned to Natchez later that year.

In the spring of 1838 they moved to Grand Coteau, Louisiana, at the invitation of the Jesuits. In this remote outpost, Pierce taught English at the Jesuit college, and Cornelia taught piano, singing and guitar at the Sacred Heart convent. Both Connellys received spiritual direction from members of the Jesuit community. A fourth child, Mary Magdalen, was born in July 1839 and died six weeks later. At the end of 1839 Cornelia joined the Sacred Heart nuns for the first three days of their retreat. She said that she was "converted" during this retreat, and that all other retreats in her life built on this experience.[1]

On 2 February 1840 the two-year-old John Henry died of burns. He had fallen into a vat of hot sugar, and Cornelia nursed him for 43 hours before he died. This event is perceived as seminal in Cornelia's spirituality.

On 13 October 1840, whilst Pierce was making an eight-day retreat, he told Cornelia that he was certain God was calling him to pursue priesthood in the Roman Catholic Church. Cornelia was four months pregnant. The Connellys agreed that, from that day forward, they would abstain from sexual intercourse—a promise they both agree was faithfully kept. Their fifth child, Frank, was born the following March, 1841.

Pierce left for Europe in May 1842, with Mercer (aged nine), who was to go to school in England, initially at Oscott and later at Stonyhurst, his fees being paid by Lord Shrewsbury. Cornelia and the two younger children remained at Grand Coteau. In April 1843 Pierce, in Rome, presented his request for matrimonial separation. He was informed that it could not be

---

[1] D63:65.

granted unless Cornelia gave her consent in person. In July, therefore, Cornelia left Grand Coteau to return to Philadelphia, where Pierce met her to accompany her to Europe.

Once they reached Rome, events moved much more quickly than the Connellys had anticipated. Their deed of separation was signed on 1 April 1844. On 9 April Cornelia entered the Sacred Heart Convent at Trinità dei Monti as a quasi-postulant, taking Frank with her. Adeline had already become a boarder at the school. On 1 May Pierce was admitted to minor orders.

Cornelia spent two years at the Trinità, but she was not happy, and by February 1845 she had informed those responsible that she could not enter the Society of the Sacred Heart. Nevertheless, on 18 June 1845, she made the vow of chastity that was required of her before Pierce could be ordained. His ordination and his first Mass took place in the convent chapel in July.

Throughout 1845 Cornelia was being encouraged by her spiritual director, John Grassi SJ, to make initial plans for the foundation of a religious community in the United States. Assisted by Pierce as well as by Grassi, Cornelia worked on outline Constitutions. However, in 1846, Lord Shrewsbury and Bishop Wiseman prevailed upon her to make her first foundation in England. Wiseman provided her with a large house (and three companions) in Derby, and Cornelia's congregation, the Society of the Holy Child Jesus, was established there in October 1846.

Pierce also came to England, as chaplain to Lord Shrewsbury. He was quickly dissatisfied with the arrangements made for Cornelia, and was frustrated that they were no longer free to meet regularly as they had done in Rome. He especially resented Wiseman's authority over his wife. Cornelia pronounced her vows in the Society on 21 December 1847. In mid-January 1848, Pierce, without reference to Cornelia, removed the children from their schools and took them to Europe, intending to use them as a means of gaining access to their mother and power over her.

When he returned to England in May, Pierce went to Derby, but Cornelia refused to see him unless he returned Adeline to her care. In December 1848, deeply disillusioned with the Roman Catholic Church and its priests and religious, he began legal proceedings in the Court of Arches with a view to reclaiming his conjugal rights over her. The case was found in his favour (though Cornelia immediately lodged an appeal). Ultimately, it was only lack of money that prevented him from pursuing his victory.

Pierce abandoned Catholicism and, after some time, returned to his practice of Episcopalianism, becoming the Episcopalian minister in Florence. In the early 1850s he wrote many vitriolic pamphlets and tracts, denouncing the evils of Roman Catholicism and broadcasting the intimate details of his and Cornelia's story. In 1851 he petitioned the House of Commons, pleading for the return of his wife, and asking that "all nunneries and monastic establishments may be suppressed and for ever prohibited by law."[2] He denied Cornelia contact with the children, and she was obliged to forfeit any influence she might have had over them.

Mercer, their eldest son, died of yellow fever in the USA at the age of 20, completely estranged from his mother. Adeline visited Cornelia only once in adult life. She never married, but lived with her father until his death in Florence in 1883 (four years after Cornelia). After Pierce died, Adeline returned to the practice of Catholicism. Frank never married either, though he cared for and educated his illegitimate daughter, Maria Cornelia, who subsequently married into the Italian aristocracy. Through her, Cornelia continues to have direct descendants. Frank, who shared his father's hatred of Catholicism, met his mother on only two occasions after early childhood, and, tradition has it, he accused her of loving the nuns more than she loved him. He became an artist and sculptor, dying in 1932.

In 1848 the Holy Child community (consisting of 18 women) moved from Derby to St Leonards-on-Sea in Sussex. The property they occupied there belonged to the Rev. Mr Jones. On his death the estate passed to Col. Charles Towneley, who established an educational trust in the care of the Holy Child sisters. The arrangements made by Towneley were inimical to the local parish, the priests and the bishops, and the ensuing dispute about the property dragged on for thirteen weary years. Cornelia's relations with the local community and with the hierarchy generally were seriously damaged; she was subject to ongoing verbal abuse and denigration, and was regularly denounced to Rome.

---

[2] Petition of Pierce Connelly, Clerk, to the House of Commons, 8 May 1851, final paragraph.

Gradually the Society began to expand. During the 1850s houses were opened in London, Liverpool, Preston and Blackpool; in 1862 the first sisters sailed for America; in 1863 the Society gained possession of the ruins of the Old Palace, Mayfield; and in 1869 the first house was established in France. Cornelia's vision was of a congregation devoted to the spiritual works of mercy; in practice, this came to mean a congregation primarily engaged in education, retreat giving and parish ministry. In 1863 her educational philosophy (quite far-seeing by comparison with the principles underlying most girls' education in England at this time) was encapsulated in her *Book of the Order of Studies in the Schools of the Sisters of the Holy Child Jesus*. This book, like many others, was produced on the convent printing press at St Leonards.

But Cornelia's relations with some of the significant early members of the Society were as problematic as her relations with the hierarchy. Emily Bowles, a gifted English convert, who had gone with Cornelia to Derby in 1846, left the Society over an acrimonious financial dispute. And Lucy Woolley, who had successfully maintained schools and communities in Preston for over twenty years, parted company with Cornelia on personal and constitutional grounds.

The constitutional history of Cornelia's congregation was no less complex and tortuous than her personal story. Cornelia had brought with her from Rome in 1846 the outlines of a rule based on the teaching of St Francis de Sales. This was the text with which Pierce and Grassi had assisted her. But it was by no means a finished document: throughout the rest of her life Cornelia continued to refine and modify the Constitutions of the Society. Almost as soon as she came to England, Ignatian spirituality and, more specifically, the *Spiritual Exercises*, became central to her approach.

By 1850 she understood that the Society needed the stability offered by ecclesiastical recognition, and Bishop Wiseman gave formal episcopal approval to the Constitutions. However, unknown to Cornelia, when Pierce took the children to the continent in 1848, he visited Rome and submitted constitutions for the Society, claiming to be its founder. These spurious constitutions continued to be a cause of confusion for the rest of Cornelia's life. When she took the Constitutions approved by Wiseman to Rome in 1854, the consultor could not separate this text from Pierce's, and sent a negative report back to the English hierarchy. For reasons never explained to Cornelia, Grant, the Bishop of Southwark, kept this report for ten years before he sent it to her, without comment, in 1864.

As the Society expanded, and especially once communities were established in the United States, something more than episcopal approval was needed for the Constitutions if the Society was not to disintegrate into a loose federation of communities under the authority of diocesan bishops. But Cornelia was blocked at every turn. Revised Constitutions, sent to Rome for submission to Propaganda Fide in 1864, remained in an unopened parcel at the English College for five years.

In Rome, between May and July 1869, Cornelia eventually made extensive revisions to the Constitutions, under the direction of Anselmo Knapen OFM, to bring them into line with the requirements of Propaganda Fide. But, before Propaganda would ratify these Constitutions, the signatures of all the professed sisters were required, indicating their approval. Cornelia, unwisely, sent the printed text by post to each community, presuming that the members of the Society would simply accept the revisions and append their signatures. However, the changes in the Constitutions were not well received; the Preston nuns, especially, created a grave crisis of confidence in the Society by forwarding their signatures to Cornelia without comment, and at the same time sending protests about Cornelia and about the Constitutions to Cardinal Barnabò, the prefect of Propaganda Fide.

Though a schism was averted, the ill feeling rumbled on, and Cornelia's authority, which had been based not on constitutional election but on good will, was necessarily weakened. Bishop Grant would never permit the calling of a general chapter, though a chapter was the only body which could legitimise authority within the Society. After Grant's death, his successor, Danell, also prevaricated about a chapter. When in 1874 a general chapter was finally held, Cornelia was elected superior general almost unanimously. But any security and stability that this might have brought was undermined by another, totally unexpected, act of Danell's. At this first chapter he presented the delegates with entirely new Constitutions written by himself with the assistance of his canonist, Philip Bosio SM. These constitutions named Danell as "Bishop Superior of the Institute" and drastically reduced the real authority of the superior general. They were imposed on the unwilling nuns for an initial three year period. Though they were modified to some extent at a second chapter in 1877, they were still in force when Cornelia died.

She died at St Leonards, aged 70, on 18 April 1879. Three of her five children had predeceased her. She had almost lost contact with her husband and her two remaining children, though she had loved them all passionately. And, at her death, the Society, for which she had sacrificed so much, and which she had directed for thirty-three years, had not yet regained the Constitutions that she had written for it.

Cornelia's Context

Women who entered active religious congregations in the nineteenth century were fully cognisant of current social issues—they often worked in areas of great deprivation, and fought tirelessly for improvement in education and health care provision. But, within their congregations, they consciously withdrew from "the world" and lived a curiously decontextualised, ahistorical existence. As, with one exception, the biographers we will examine were members of the congregation that Cornelia founded, they readily accepted this disjunction: Cornelia's context in the biographies is by and large the convent or, before that, her family, rather than the wider world in which she lived. It seems important, therefore, to fill this lacuna with a brief comment on the world which shaped her.

United States

When Cornelia was born in 1809, the United States was still new: the colonists had won their independence from Britain only in 1783. Her birthplace, Philadelphia, was no longer the nation's capital, as it had been between 1790 and 1800. But it was still a city of financial and cultural significance, which traced its tradition of religious liberty back to the Quaker William Penn. Her mother's family had lived in the city for several generations, but her father was a recent immigrant from England. Cornelia's more recent biographers, struggling with the lack of information about her childhood, call attention to the many learned institutions the city boasted, and argue that Cornelia would have had access to concerts, museums and libraries. (Certainly her three brothers were members of the Athenaeum of Philadelphia that was established in 1814.)

After her marriage in 1832, Cornelia lived for three years in Natchez, Mississippi, and then, after a period in Europe, she spent five years in Grand Coteau, Louisiana; but the influence of life in the southern States on Cornelia has been less fully explored than her Philadelphian origins. Mississippi had become a state only in 1817, and the people whom Cornelia met in Natchez were the wealthy owners of great cotton plantations worked by thousands of slaves. When the Connellys' first child was born, Dr Newton Mercer presented them with a slave as a christening gift. Slaves were not part of Philadelphian life (the census of 1820 numbers only three slaves in the whole city)[3] but Cornelia continued to own slaves until she left Grand Coteau in 1843. Nowhere does she pass any comment on slavery, though abolition was a live issue at this period. But both her own and her husband's brothers made fortunes in the south (George Connelly, for instance, was a cotton factor and, according to Cornelia, "very rich before the [civil] war"),[4] and their sympathies were with the Confederates.

In Natchez, Cornelia absorbed American Protestant culture; in Grand Coteau, the influence was almost exclusively French and Roman Catholic. Philippine Duchesne had brought the Society of the Sacred Heart to America in 1818, and their school at Grand Coteau had been established in 1821. French Jesuits founded St Charles College, close by, in 1836. Life for the Connellys in this isolated spot was almost as decontextualised as religious life: they seem to have spent a great deal of time in prayer and spiritual reflection, and to have made a number of retreats.

Rome

After their conversion to Roman Catholicism, and before moving to Grand Coteau, the Connellys left Natchez and spent two years in Europe, mostly in Rome. The American Connellys might be expected to have approved of the republican movements that were growing in Italy at this period, but of them they say nothing. Their response to Rome was not political; it was much more that of the British visitor on the Grand Tour, delighting in

---

[3] Helen McDonald SHCJ, "Cornelia's Life in the South" (unpublished paper, 2003).
[4] CC7:89.

classical art and culture. And their response to the Church was equally apolitical. They were perhaps a little overawed by the unfamiliar Catholic circle they entered in Rome, which seems to have been largely English and aristocratic: it included the Earl and Countess of Shrewsbury and their two daughters, Cardinal Thomas Weld, and Nicholas Wiseman, rector of the Venerable English College.

V. Alan McClelland describes Pio Nono in the 1850s as taking "regular walks among the people of Rome," and directing "attention to individuals as though the one before him were the only object of his care."[5] Easy access to the pope seems to have been a feature of the pontificate of Gregory XVI in the 1830s too. Gregory took a personal interest in the Connellys, and Cornelia saw him in private audience at least twice.

Rome provided an intense introduction to an increasingly centralised form of Catholicism for the newly converted couple; and it contrasted strongly with the life they were to embark upon in the anti-Catholic Britain of the 1840s and 1850s.

Britain

When the Connellys arrived in Britain in 1846, the "No Popery" that "was deep in the English psyche"[6] had been stirred again by the parliamentary controversy surrounding the award of a government grant to the seminary at Maynooth. And it would be inflamed further, both by Irish immigration after the famine, and by the restoration of the Roman Catholic hierarchy in 1850. The national outcry at Wiseman's triumphalist pastoral letter, 'From without the Flaminian Gate', is well documented.

The religious atmosphere of Britain at this period was highly charged. The Oxford Movement of the 1830s had strengthened high church practices within Anglicanism and brought a flood of distinguished converts to Roman Catholicism. With this came both the encouragement of nuns and convents, and a reaction of horror against them. Within the Church of England, Puseyites were founding sisterhoods; and within Roman

---

[5] V. Alan McClelland, "The Formative Years, 1850-92," in *From Without the Flaminian Gate: 150 Years of Roman Catholicism in England and Wales*, edited by V. Alan McClelland and Michael Hodgetts (London: Darton, Longman and Todd, 1999), 4, 3.

[6] A. N. Wilson, *The Victorians* (London: Hutchinson, 2002), 69.

Catholicism, a confident revival, the Second Spring, was being actively assisted by congregations of religious women, and was encouraged both by Italian missionaries like Dominic Barberi and by converts like Newman.[7] These developments aroused fear and opposition too; the Evangelical MP, Charles Newdegate, went so far as to introduce a Religious Houses Bill in the Commons in 1851, pressing for the registration and inspection of convents. Though this bill did not become law, Edna Hamer nevertheless suggests that nuns may have been the most persecuted group of women in Britain in the mid-nineteenth century.[8]

Outside the convent, the people whom Cornelia and her congregation hoped to serve were living in a rapidly changing world. For the working class, the industrial revolution had brought Poor Laws and Poor Relief in its wake—the greatly feared workhouse. Cholera and typhoid were rampant, and not only in overcrowded slum dwellings. 1848, a year of revolution in Europe, saw Chartist demonstrations in Britain. There were continuing demands for the extension of the franchise, and the beginnings of a women's movement. The British Empire was expanding; Prince Albert was preparing for the Great Exhibition of 1851; and science and technology seemed to be offering a path to a bright tomorrow. The need for education, for the schools that Cornelia's congregation would establish, had never been greater.

Cornelia crossed many boundaries, coming under a wide variety of social, cultural, philosophical and theological influences in different parts of the world. She was an intelligent woman, not formally educated, but ready to absorb—or to reject—the attitudes and opinions of others. However, she was not politicized, and her views were seldom articulated; they have to be inferred from her writings and decisions.

But her earliest biographers largely ignored the world which shaped her, and the religious, cultural and geographical distances that she travelled,

---

[7] Newman's romantic dream of a "second spring" for Roman Catholicism has been reassessed by modern historians who point to the limitations of its clergy-dominated, ultramontanist ecclesiology. Nevertheless, women religious at this period provided a huge number of Catholics, new and old, with education and catechetical instruction, with nursing care and social assistance of all kinds. See Anne Murphy SHCJ, "Old Catholics, New Converts, Irish Immigrants: A Reassessment of Catholicity in England in the Nineteenth Century," *Cherwell Papers,* 1/3 (San Diego, 1993).

[8] Edna Hamer, *Elizabeth Prout 1820-1864: A Religious Life for Industrial England* (Bath: Downside Abbey, 1994), 142.

beyond noting that Cornelia was an American, and therefore significantly "other" in nineteenth-century England. For these biographers, her context was their own—the subculture of religious life—with a momentum, meaning and value other than that of "the world" from which they had consciously withdrawn.

The Biographers

Cornelia's life as wife, mother and religious founder was extraordinary by any standards, so it is not surprising that a number of people have written her story; certainly more biographies seem to have been written of her than of other comparable figures. Her life is not easily categorized, and it does not fit comfortably into stereotypes of any kind. (She was, for instance, still married when she founded her congregation, and she took her five-year-old son with her to the convent.) So her biographers' choices and decisions in their construction of her life story cannot have been unthinking, and they may consequently be more revealing of underlying assumptions than those of biographers whose subjects were more conventional.

This study is based on the conviction that the neutral telling of a life story is not possible, that the arrangement, expression and presentation of biographical material can never be entirely value-free. All biography is necessarily selective and interpretative; consequently, it is revelatory of the biographer as well as of the subject. From this premise, this book sets out to examine how and why the biographies of Cornelia differ. What are the authors' attitudes and intentions? Do their historical and cultural contexts, their personalities and personal preferences, colour their telling of the story? Do the biographies reflect differing world-views, theologies, spiritualities and assumptions about holiness? Are the biographers, consciously or unconsciously, using Cornelia's story to promote or validate a particular model of religious life, a particular view of the Society that she founded? Finally, it asks whether a biographer writing today, and conversant with contemporary biographical strategies and with the principles underlying contemporary Christian feminist spirituality, might provide a substantially different reading of the story.

Seven major accounts of Cornelia's story have been written in English since her death in 1879. The first biographer began her work in 1879, just weeks after Cornelia's death; the most recent published her text in 1991.

Maria Joseph Buckle SHCJ (1822-1902) spent years collating *Materials Collected for a Life of Cornelia Connelly*, which survives today as an unpublished typescript, dated 1886. The work of the second biographer, Mary Francis Bellasis SHCJ (1842-1927), entitled *Life of the Mother Foundress, SHCJ* and dated 1919, is also an unpublished typescript.

The first printed biography, *The Life of Cornelia Connelly, 1809-1879* (London: Longman, Green & Co), was published anonymously in 1922 by "A Member of the Society." The author was Mary Catherine Gompertz SHCJ (1880-1963), and her text remained the only published account of Cornelia's life until Juliana Wadham, a young married woman, brought out *The Case of Cornelia Connelly* (London: Collins) in 1956. In 1963, on the eve of the Second Vatican Council, Marie Thérèse Bisgood SHCJ published *Cornelia Connelly: A Study in Fidelity* (London: Burns & Oates).

The sixth biography considered here is not a discrete text; it is the biographical section of the *Informatio*, which is the first volume of the *Positio for the Canonisation Process of the Servant of God, Cornelia Connelly (née Peacock) 1809-1879*.[9] It was published by the Society of the Holy Child Jesus in Rome in 1987, the work of Elizabeth Mary Strub SHCJ. Finally, the most recently published biography, *A Woman Styled Bold: The Life of Cornelia Connelly 1809-1879,* written by Radegunde Flaxman SHCJ, was published in London in 1991.

Susan O'Brien has proposed four main phases in the development of the active women's congregations that were founded in considerable numbers in the nineteenth century: from *c.*1800 to the 1890s; from the 1890s to 1914; from the First World War to the middle 1960s; and from the middle 1960s to *c.*1990.[10] How was Cornelia's story retold in each of these periods? How far did the concerns of the moment influence the way in which it was told? Did the Society experience the need for a new biography, a different telling of the founder's story, each time it entered a new phase of its existence? And, as the story was told afresh, did it reflect and reinforce the Society's changing understanding and presentation of itself? Because

---

[9] A *Positio* and an *Informatio* form part of the documentation submitted to the Sacred Congregation for the Causes of Saints in support of a candidate's canonisation. A *Positio* is a summary of all the documentation available about the candidate, and an *Informatio* presents the evidence for the candidate's sanctity.

[10] Susan O'Brien, "Women Religious: Historical Past—Future Perspective" (a talk given to the Assembly of the British Province of the Sisters of Notre Dame, August 1994).

Cornelia's story is complex, multi-faceted, many-stranded, her biographers had many choices to make about emphasis, interpretation and omission. And though some of the choices will have been deliberate and well-considered, others will have been unreflective and unconscious.

Cornelia's story, therefore, does not cease with her death; from 1879 onwards it assumes a significance of its own, almost distinct from her life as she lived it. In the biographies we meet Cornelia the text rather than Cornelia the person. Through the narratives of the seven biographers we are given different perspectives on Cornelia, and "Different accounts … relay different truths."[11] Central to this study is the conviction that our knowledge and understanding of Cornelia is enriched and enhanced by the multiple presentations of her in the biographies. But, in order to appreciate and evaluate each retelling, a grasp of the context and intentions of the authors is necessary. Whatever we can discover of the motivations and assumptions of the biographers will contribute to our understanding, because a biography reveals not just the subject—Cornelia—but also the narrator of the story.

The narrators too are potential subjects, with their own life stories which impinge on, intertwine with, and develop through their relationship with Cornelia and their account of her history. The details of their stories are integral to the history of the biographies, and are presented in the chapters that follow. Nevertheless, it is important to acknowledge that these narrators are independent individuals; and so they are briefly introduced here.

Maria Joseph Buckle, one of the earliest members of Cornelia's congregation, was a thoroughgoing Victorian, with an unswerving conviction as to the superiority of the Empire and of all things English, and an unquestioning acceptance of women's restricted social status. Her struggle to reconcile these views with her presentation of the American Cornelia is evident in her text, as are her ultramontane views on ecclesiology and spirituality.[12] Her scrupulosity and consequent emphasis on the virtue of obedience colour her interpretation of her subject.

---

[11] Judy Long, *Telling Women's Lives: Subject, Narrator, Reader, Text* (New York: New York UP, 1991), 2.

[12] Ultramontanes valued and promoted authority within the Church, especially the centralised authority of the papacy. The movement culminated in the definition of papal infallibility at the First Vatican Council in 1870.

Mary Francis Bellasis' father was an eminent parliamentary lawyer who became a Catholic at the time of the Oxford Movement. His children enjoyed a lively and liberal home life and education. This background influenced his daughter's presentation of Cornelia: she approached her biography through her sense of family, as a spiritual daughter of the founding mother. As will be seen, much important material about Cornelia would have been lost without Bellasis' intervention.

Mary Catherine Gompertz was a daughter of British India, who had been a pupil in the school at St Leonards before entering the Society. She was considered intellectually gifted, and was among the first women educated to university level by the Society. Her biography, the first published life, was written with a view to the introduction of the cause of Cornelia's canonisation.

Juliana Wadham differs from Cornelia's other biographers: she was not a member of the Society, but a married woman in her late twenties who was expecting her fourth child as she completed her text—though this distinctive perspective does not colour the biography as much as might be expected. Her interest in Cornelia had been aroused when she was a pupil in the Society's schools during the Second World War.

Marie Thérèse Bisgood entered the Society immediately after the First World War and, despite the fact that her biography did not appear until 1963, her personal style was such that she might well be described as Cornelia's Edwardian biographer. She was a woman of fine sensibilities, who had already written a number of articles on Cornelia and completely revised Gompertz' text before she came to write her own biography. Although she wrote on the eve of the Second Vatican Council, her life of Cornelia is used to validate tradition rather than to promote *aggorniamento*.

Elizabeth Mary Strub is a Californian, the first American biographer of Cornelia. She had just completed ten years as superior general of the Society when she was asked to prepare the *Informatio*, part of the documentation presented in defence of the cause of Cornelia's canonisation. Though her text is constrained by the requirements of the Sacred Congregation, her theological education and her experience of religious life in the post-Vatican II Church enabled her to approach Cornelia's story in a fresh way.

Radegunde Flaxman, Cornelia's most recent biographer, is a convert to Catholicism who entered the Society in the 1950s. She was caught up in the re-examination of the Society's founding charism that followed Vatican II. She had studied Cornelia's educational philosophy, and had had responsibility for the formation of new members, before being elected to the Society's general council. After she came out of office, she spent ten years in Rome studying all the available primary sources on Cornelia's life, before finally producing a new biography.[13]

The purpose of this introduction has been twofold: first to provide a brief account of Cornelia's complex life story, so that the chapters that follow need not be littered with too many cumbersome explanations; and secondly to introduce her biographers and to raise questions that might be asked of them.

With the exception of Juliana Wadham, a young wife and mother, all Cornelia's biographers have been members of the Society she founded, and none was young when she embarked upon her work. None of them seems to have *chosen* to be a biographer. They are "official" biographers, appointed to the task by the most senior members of the Society. So an examination of their work may be expected to uncover opinions, attitudes and assumptions that reflect the received views held in the Society at the time of writing. But before a detailed study of the biographies themselves is undertaken, I shall outline something of the biographical and spiritual framework within which I shall approach them.

---

[13] Because, in a work of this length, only a limited number of texts can be explored satisfactorily, a decision has been taken to restrict discussion to full length biographies of Cornelia that have been written in English. The most important text that is thereby excluded is a life of Cornelia written in French by Marie Osmonde de Maillé SHCJ. *Cornelia Connelly, Fondatrice de la Societé du Holy Child Jesus (1809-1879)* was first published in Paris by Librairie Plon in 1931; a revised edition, *Du Mariage au Cloître*, was published in Paris in 1962 by Editions France Empire.

Three other significant texts are also excluded, on the grounds that they are not strictly biographies. They are *The Spirituality of Cornelia Connelly: In God, For God, With God* by Caritas McCarthy SHCJ, and *The Priesthood and Apostasies of Pierce Connelly* by D. G. Paz (both published in 1986 in Lewiston, Michigan by The Edwin Mellen Press); and *Cornelia Connelly's Work in Education, 1848-1879*, the doctoral thesis of John Marmion, submitted in the University of Manchester in 1984, and printed in facsimile by UMI Dissertation Information Service (Ann Arbor, Mi) in 1987. Though these texts are not discussed, reference is made to them and the insights of their authors are drawn upon.

Chapter Two

FRAMING THE QUESTIONS

The significance of the telling and retelling of individual life stories down the centuries cannot be exaggerated. W. B. Yeats wrote: "We may come to think that nothing exists but a stream of souls, that all knowledge is biography."[1] And Kenneth Woodward, towards the end of his study of sainthood in the Catholic Church, suggests that story is central not just to religion, but to human self-understanding generally:

> Throughout this book I have stressed the centrality of stories to the process of the making of saints. I have done so because man [*sic*] is essentially a storytelling animal. We understand ourselves, if at all, as characters in a story, and it is through stories that we come to understand others, including saints.[2]

Christianity, like other religious traditions, has always recognised the importance of story for the understanding and communication of its message; Sam Keen goes so far as to suggest that "telling stories is functionally equivalent to belief in God."[3] Within Christianity, stories have spiritual and theological significance; and this study explores the link between the presentation of a story and the author's Christian understanding and intention.

Cornelia Connelly lived during the nineteenth century, and so the facts of her life are not like some medieval legend, "facts" with which a storyteller or theologian can make free because they are no longer verifiable. The facts are accessible to any researcher in a substantial collection of primary documents. Yet, even in the century and a quarter since her death, a series of biographers, through subtle changes of emphasis, through omission and interpretation, has presented us with a

---

[1] Quoted in Leon Edel, *Writing Lives: Principia Biographia* (New York and London: W. W. Norton & Company, 1984 [1959]), 20.
[2] Kenneth Woodward, *Making Saints: Inside the Vatican: Who Become Saints, Who Do Not and Why* … (London: Chatto and Windus, 1991), 391-392.
[3] Quoted in John Navone SJ, *Seeking God in Story* (Collegeville, Mn: Liturgical, 1990), 233.

series of Cornelias. This is noteworthy in itself, and all the more so when
the biographers' shared purpose in writing is acknowledged—their
conscious intention of demonstrating Cornelia's holiness. Only Juliana
Wadham did not begin with the presupposition that Cornelia was holy, and
even in her biography the question of Cornelia's holiness and saintliness is
central.

    Throughout Christian history, hagiographical literature has played a
significant part in shaping assumptions about women's holiness, and the
Cornelian biographies are part of this tradition. This book explores the
extent to which the biographers' understanding of Christianity, of holiness
and of women influences their structuring of her story, before asking
whether a different portrait of Cornelia would be retrieved from the
primary documents by a consciously unhagiographical author. Such an
evaluative study is necessarily interdisciplinary, involving both biographical
interpretation and spiritual awareness.

Nineteenth- and Twentieth-Century Biography

In England, the beginnings of biography proper are dated from the late-
seventeenth and early-eighteenth centuries, when Izaak Walton and John
Aubrey began writing the lives of poets and other literary figures. In
October 1750, Samuel Johnson published a seminal essay on biography in
the *Rambler*,[4] in which he argued for more rigorously honest lives, for
accounts which would reveal something of the person behind and beneath
the "extrinsic." This interest in the private and personal life of the
individual, "the inner man," was a part of that cultural shift which found its
full flowering in late-eighteenth-century romanticism.[5] In the 250 years
since then, interest in the subject's inner life has remained central to
biography, but understanding of what the inner life consists in has changed
out of all recognition. For the Victorians, the inner life was largely a matter
of religious convictions and sensibilities and of the acquisition and practice
of virtues, but by the late-twentieth century, when the influence of Freud

---

[4] Samuel Johnson, *Rambler*, 60 (13 October 1750). Text downloaded from the internet, where it had been typed
from an 1826 edition of the *Rambler* essays, printed in three volumes by Thomas Tegg, London.
[5] See Edel, *Writing Lives*, 37.

was all-pervasive, it had popularly come to mean an exploration of people's unconscious and subconscious minds and, often, of their secret sexual lives.

Virginia Woolf claims that by the nineteenth century biography had emerged, "fully grown and hugely prolific," and yet was still "the most restricted of all the arts."[6] As two of Cornelia's earliest biographers were Victorians, Woolf's strictures about nineteenth-century biography are of some relevance. Her argument that Victorian biographies, in spite of their length, seldom presented a full picture of the individual, is particularly pertinent. During this period, the tone of biographies was laudatory rather than revelatory, and the outcome, Woolf says, was fundamentally unsatisfactory. Because the widow or friends of the subject breathed down the biographer's neck, insisting that less flattering incidents and traits be glossed over or omitted, a "perfect" but unreal image of a model of rectitude was invariably constructed:

> And thus the majority of Victorian biographies are like the wax figures now preserved in Westminster Abbey … effigies that have only a smooth superficial likeness to the body in the coffin.[7]

If, as Woolf claims, this smoothing down and polishing up was characteristic of nineteenth-century biography in general, we may expect to find it heavily employed by writers who were consciously intent on demonstrating the holiness—even the perfection—of their subject. And, internal evidence suggests, Cornelia's first biographers were women of their time, who saw no reason to question or abandon the practices and assumptions of Victorian culture.

So, the warts-and-all biography was a twentieth-century phenomenon: it was not until that time that the biographer "won a measure of freedom … [and] could hint that there were scars and furrows on the dead man's face."[8] The person who did most to bring about the shift was Lytton Strachey, who "might be called the father of 'psychobiography.'"[9] Strachey shocked his

---

[6] Virginia Woolf, "The Art of Biography," in *The Crowded Dance of Modern Life: Selected Essays: Volume Two* (London: Penguin Books, 1993), 144.

[7] Woolf, "The Art of Biography," 145. It is perhaps worth commenting that the great novels of the nineteenth century explore inner experience in something of the way that biographies do today.

[8] Woolf, "The Art of Biography," 145.

[9] Edel, *Writing Lives*, 143.

contemporaries with his ironic portraits of Victorian worthies; he reacted against the conventional biographical smoothing and polishing, and delighted in highlighting the human inconsistencies and ambiguities of his subjects.

Leon Edel is convinced that twentieth-century developments in anthropology, the social sciences and most significantly psychology, have completely transformed both the form of biography and the expectations of its readers, because "we understand so much more now about behaviour and motivation"[10]:

> Today … neglect of psychoanalytic psychology means the neglect of a very large area of modern human knowledge. I would go so far as to say that biographies which do not use this knowledge must henceforth be reckoned as incomplete: they belong to a time when lives were entirely "exterior" and neglected the reflective and inner side of human beings.[11]

Certainly, the psychobiography has flourished during the closing decades of the twentieth century; even biographers who do not share Edel's enthusiasm for psychoanalysis have been influenced by the general trend. Today there is an expectation that biography will examine the subject's personal development and general motivation, and that it will explore the context of a person's life—those places, people, circumstances and events which helped to form him or her. Moreover the modern biography has to be more than a neat presentation of the subject from birth to death. A person's story may well begin long before birth, with an exploration of parental experiences and influences, and continue long after death, with a discussion of the changing nature of their reputation and significance for subsequent generations.

Cornelia's story, like every other, offers the possibility of multiple beginnings and endings. Her biography might begin in Philadelphia, where she was born, or in Yorkshire, which her father (who died before he was 50) did not leave until he was 22 or 23 years old, or in Jamaica, where her mother lived with her first husband. It might end in St Leonards, where she died, or with an examination of her continuing influence on the Society she

---

[10] Edel, *Writing Lives*, 27.
[11] Edel, *Writing Lives*, 145.

founded, or with the memories, less frequently explored, of her family and descendants. Anyone writing her life today will have to weigh the options.

Biography is a developing genre, and so someone writing Cornelia's life today might also choose to circumvent the problems inherent in the attempt to present her life tidily, whole and entire, by focusing on the detailed examination of just one specific aspect of her life, or by the close study of a brief period. This approach to the biographical task reflects the postmodern interest in the particular perspective rather than the comprehensive judgment, and it is increasingly recognised as a valid biographical method.[12] Even within this format, however, biographers will need to be alert to the significance of their relationships with both the subject and the reader.

Relationship between Biographer and Subject

Interest in psychology led Edel and others to an understanding of motivation, which they applied not only to the inner life of the subjects of biography, but also to the intentions and attitudes of biographers: they realised that the relationships between biographers and their chosen subjects were more subtle and complex than had previously been acknowledged. Biographer-subject relationships, and in particular the effect of the biographers' personalities, interests and contexts upon their construction of Cornelia's life, are explored in detail in the following chapters.

In the nineteenth century it was assumed that a biographer could maintain a totally distanced, cool and objective stance towards the subject, and so produce an unbiased, accurate and definitive life. Today it is commonly acknowledged that the biographer's own issues, interests, attitudes and assumptions are writ large across the account of another person's life. In fact, students of the genre now see the relationship between author and subject as a central factor in any biography; they stress the problems arising from emotional involvement, and note the biographer's ongoing temptation to confuse self with subject, or even to produce autobiography disguised as biography:

---

[12] Perhaps the first example of this form was Alethea Hayter, *A Sultry Month* (London: Faber and Faber, 1965). See also Richard Holmes, *Dr Johnson and Mr Savage* (London: Hodder and Stoughton, 1993) and Penelope Hughes-Hallett, *The Immortal Dinner* (London: Viking, 2000).

The relation of the biographer to the subject is the very core of the biographical enterprise. Idealization of the hero or heroine blinds the writer of lives to the meaning of the materials. Hatred or animosity does the same. But most biographies tend to be written in affection and love. If there ensues an emotional involvement on the part of the biographer he or she must be reminded that love is blind.[13]

Similarly, Dee Garrison writes:

Biographical interpretation reveals a peculiarly reciprocal relationship between author and subject. The biographer is visible in the selection of documents and testimony, in the intuitive choice of a quote or incident to move along the story, and, above all, in the choice to write this particular life and not another.[14]

And Lois Rudnick:

A few biographers … have revealed the subjective, partial, and context-bound nature of biography, thereby demonstrating the importance of our paying attention to the writer, the writer's narrative voice, and the dialogue that is established between biographer and subject.[15]

The questions raised by these modern scholars must be asked of Cornelia's biographers. Were they, in some sense, in love with their subject? Did idealization of Cornelia blind them to different possible interpretations of their material? What do they reveal about themselves by their choice of incidents and quotations to move the story along? What is the nature of their dialogue with Cornelia? As Elinor Langer says, biography "is the story of one life as seen by another, with both always growing and changing."[16]

---

[13] Edel, *Writing Lives*, 14. Virginia Woolf was well aware of this emotional entanglement. On completing her life of Fry, she wrote in her diary: "I feel very much in his presence at the moment; as if I were intimately connected with him: as if we together had given birth to this vision of him: a child born of us." (Virginia Woolf, *A Writer's Diary* [New York: Harcourt Brace, 1954], 326-327, 25 July 1940, quoted in Harvena Richter, "The Biographer as Novelist," in *Essaying Biography: A Celebration for Leon Edel*, edited by Gloria G. Fromm [University of Hawaii Press: Honolulu, 1986], 63-64.)

[14] Dee Garrison, "Two Roads Taken: Writing the Biography of Mary Heaton Vorse," in *The Challenge of Feminist Biography*, edited by Sara Alpern, Joyce Antler, Elisabeth Israels Perry and Ingrid Winther Scobie (Urbana & Chicago: University of Illinois Press, 1992), 68.

[15] Lois Rudnick, "The Male Identified Woman and Other Anxieties: The Life of Mabel Dodge Luhan," in Alpern and others, *The Challenge of Feminist Biography*, 118.

[16] Quoted in Kathryn Kish Sklar, "Coming to Terms with Florence Kelley: The Tale of a Reluctant Biographer," in Alpern and others, *The Challenge of Feminist Biography,* 19.

In biography, then, the biographer as well as the subject is encountered. And the biographers are going to be especially visible when, as here, several biographies of the same person are examined; the differences between the accounts will reveal the biographers' contexts, motivations and assumptions. Whilst the facts remain unchanged, each biographer presents a subtly different view of Cornelia. "Biographers are active agents .... They create their subjects from a particular angle of vision and with a particular set of strategies that help determine the outcome."[17]

Relationship between Biographer, Subject and Reader

A biography, however, is not a private encounter between author and subject: the reader is also caught up in the relationship. Examining the biographies of Cornelia, it is clear that they are not all addressed to the same readership, and that the authors' assumptions about their readers influence their selection and presentation of material. A brief glance at the seven principal biographies reveals that the earliest of them were addressed exclusively to members of the Society of the Holy Child Jesus, the congregation that Cornelia founded; the first printed biography assumed a Roman Catholic readership; and a biography addressed to the general public did not appear until the 1950s.

The first biographer, Maria Joseph Buckle, wrote explicitly for other members of Cornelia's congregation. She assumed a good deal of shared understanding with her readers, her text being very much an *apologia* for the foundress, written explicitly to convince the other sisters of Cornelia's holiness. Mary Francis Bellasis wrote out of this context too, though Herbert Thurston SJ, whom she consulted, encouraged her to tone down her references to "our Mother" in the interests of a wider readership. Catherine Gompertz, author of the first printed life, states that her intention is to provide material for a possible canonisation process; her assumed readership, though wider than members of the Society alone, was exclusively Roman Catholic. Juliana Wadham's 1956 life was the first written explicitly for the general public. Marie Thérèse Bisgood's biography was published after Wadham's, but its true antecedent was that of Gompertz,

---

[17] Rudnick, "The Male Identified Woman," 118.

and it retreats into the more restricted, convent-focused world of her SHCJ predecessor. Elizabeth Mary Strub was writing within the context of the canonisation process, and her format is constrained by canonical regulations and by her knowledge of the expectations of her ecclesiastical readership. Radegunde Flaxman's life, by far the most thoroughly researched, is the first by a member of Cornelia's Society to be addressed to the general reader, and yet Flaxman cannot entirely free herself from the hagiographical temptation to edify, and to justify or explain away Cornelia's faults and limitations.

In biography, as in all other literary composition, the reader is crucial: "Texts do not say anything—unless someone reads them."[18] Through the act of reading, the world behind the text (the author's intentions and methods of construction) and the world within the text (the life of the subject) encounter the world in front of the text (the reader, with all his or her assumptions, attitudes, questions and responses), where the author and subject are interpreted and judged.

This was well understood in the nineteenth century, at least by novelists: Trollope and Thackeray and, perhaps most famously, Charlotte Brontë ("Reader, I married him") never lost sight of their readers, and often addressed them directly. Through this device they drew the reader into a privileged relationship with the author, and encouraged "emotional identification rather than critical detachment."[19] It is part of the storyteller's art to engage emotions, and this is as true in biography as in fiction.

All theories of reading explore the relationship between reader, text and author, but concepts of the reader—and explicitly of the female reader—have not remained static. In the nineteenth century, when the first of the texts considered in this study was written, the woman reader was presumed to be "mentally passive and accepting of what she consumes."[20] She was judged to be without critical acumen, a *tabula rasa* on which the author's views could be indelibly imprinted. And, therefore, she had to be protected, her reading censored and controlled:

---

[18] Annelies van Heijst, *Longing for the Fall*, translated by Henry Jansen (Kampen: Kok Pharos, 1995), 64.

[19] Kate Flint, *The Woman Reader, 1837-1914* (Oxford: Clarendon, 1993), 22. Flint is, in fact, discussing paintings when she makes this observation, but it is equally applicable to novels.

[20] Flint, *The Woman Reader*, 15.

> Very many commentators … in the nineteenth century … addressed
> themselves to questions of what women should read, and what they should
> be protected against reading; how they should read; where and when they
> should indulge in this occupation.[21]

During the twentieth century, as women's educational opportunities
increased, discussion of the specifically female reader waned. Influenced by
new and increasingly pervasive psychological insights, those who commented
on reading noted the reader's tendency to turn all texts into autobiographies—
a parallel to the temptation, observed by Leon Edel, for biographers to write
their own lives into those of their subjects. In his study of the history of
reading, Alberto Manguel calls attention to this constant self-identification:

> The Canadian essayist Stan Persky once said to me that "for readers, there
> must be a million autobiographies," since we seem to find, in book after
> book, the traces of our lives. "To write down one's impressions of *Hamlet* as
> one reads it year after year," wrote Virginia Woolf, "would be virtually to
> record one's own autobiography, for as we know more of life, so
> Shakespeare comments upon what we know."[22]

It is beyond the scope of this book to enter into a full philosophical
analysis of the act of reading. But as we examine the different approaches
and intentions of Cornelia's biographers, it is important not to lose sight of
the reader. The reader's reaction influences the text itself. Cornelia's story
frequently elicits a strong emotional response from the reader because it is
so radically other and foreign to most readers' own experience, social
situations and value systems. A wholly text-centred approach, in which the
reader is viewed as no more than "a neutral decoder … subordinate to the
text,"[23] is patently unsatisfactory. The relationship between reader and text
is subtle and interactive:

> Reading is not a passive, receptive event but an active, imaginative
> construct. The reader takes the initiative in putting her imagination to
> work. This act of imagination is not unrestrained but bound to the text
> …. The text plays a double role: it stimulates the imagination but restrains

---

[21] Flint, *The Woman Reader*, vii.

[22] Alberto Manguel, *A History of Reading* (London: HarperCollins, 1996), 10.

[23] van Heijst, *Longing for the Fall*, 66.

> it as well. It gives rise to introspection but it is also the manifestation of an alterity that is not to be reduced to the reader .... The reader can make a contribution to the construal of context and significance. She can read her own context into the text so much that she misses indications that reveal an entirely different context ... [or she] can encounter a new view of reality.[24]

Van Heijst's argument is particularly apposite when the text in question is a biography. For the biographer too is a reader—a reader of the subject's life and of the primary documentation. In biography, therefore, a complex three-fold relationship is entered into. First there is the lived experience of the subject, and, in the primary documentation, interpretation of that experience by the subject herself and by her contemporaries. Then there is the biographer's reading—selection and interpretation and emphasis—influenced by her values and intentions. Finally the readers bring their own attitudes and questions to the text.

With so much interpretation intervening between the present-day reader and the original events, the question arises as to whether an authentic encounter with the subject is possible. An examination of the different biographers' intentions and contexts can provide a clearer grasp of their varying perspectives on the subject; but whether an encounter with the "real" Cornelia can be achieved remains debatable. The facts of Cornelia's life allow for a wide variety of presentations—with an emphasis on her fidelity, for example, as in Bisgood's study, or on her boldness, as in Flaxman's. They can be written up primarily as the edifying life of the founder of a congregation, as the first biographers presented them, or with an eye to a woman caught in a dramatically disastrous relationship with a man, as Wadham saw her. All these perspectives hold truths about Cornelia; as we reread her story, we need to take account of their cumulative effect.

The Form of the Genre: Is Biography Fiction?

In nineteenth-century biographies "the distanced, authorial voice ... provides the illusion that the life actually was as it is presented."[25] Today this illusion is recognised for what it is. All stories are constructs; a biography is the *story* of a life—and, by and large, lives are not lived in neat story shapes.

---

[24] van Heijst, *Longing for the Fall*, 64.
[25] Rudnick, "The Male Identified Woman," 118.

Rather, the biographer is engaged in a creative act, a crafting and arrangement of material from the subject's life into a form that is pleasing and intelligible in the biographer's own context.[26] So biography is now understood as an open genre, an investigative art: biographies are not statements of unchallengeable truth, but interpretations of facts, arrangements of events. And facts are always open to reinterpretation; events are always open to rearrangement.

Today, no biography is considered definitive; there is always the possibility, not so much that new information about the subject will be uncovered, as that a new biographer will offer fresh insight. The biographer is a conduit, connecting the reader to the subject. But the presence of biographers within their texts, the power they exercise over the presentation of the life, is often overlooked. Edel comments: "Readers of biographies tend to take for granted the facts given them; they do not seem to be aware that there has been an act of composition."[27] And Lois Rudnick suggests that most readers are really looking for fact presented with all the panache of fiction:

> Biographers have to deal with contradictory expectations from their readers, for whom the goal of a good biography is to provide a true and convincing portrayal of a life while reading like fiction.[28]

So significant is the biographer's role in composing and arranging the facts of the subject's life that biography has sometimes been described as a form of fiction. Dee Garrison points out that the biographer must employ "the techniques of the novelist":

> One must shape and order the evidence, deal with flashbacks, develop believable characters, dramatize crucial moments, and analyze human relations … [29]

Edel, whilst acknowledging the biographer's role as a creative composer, categorically opposes this view: "Novelists have omniscience. Biographers

---

[26] Richard Holmes' exploration of biography opens with the words, "Look back, and the past becomes a story." See *Sidetracks: Explorations of a Romantic Biographer* (London: HarperCollins, 2000), 3.

[27] Edel, *Writing Lives*, 38.

[28] Rudnick, "The Male Identified Woman," 132.

[29] Garrison, "Two Roads Taken," 67.

never do." [30] But Virginia Woolf is more exercised, more ambivalent. She wrote over a dozen essays on the genre, struggling especially with the tension between what she called the "granite" of fact and the "rainbow" of fiction in biography. [31]

For Woolf, facts are sometimes antithetical to truth, "if by 'truth' one means the essence of [the] subject's personality which the biographer tries to capture—an achievement reached by manipulation [of material] rather than a simple presentation of the truth." [32] Fictional forms can enhance the truth. "This appears the direction in which biography as a whole is headed," writes Harvena Richter, "a movement towards fictional modes [and] a quest for the mystery of the personality ...." [33]

Edel, too, argues that communication of personality is more important than chronological exactitude. He believes that the biographer's task is to identify those themes and patterns which provide the key to the subject's sense of self:

> In structure a biography need no longer be strictly chronological, like a calendar or datebook. Lives are rarely lived in that way. An individual repeats patterns learned in childhood, and usually moves back and forward through memory .... [So] the task and duty of biographical narrative is to sort out themes and patterns, not dates and mundane calendar events. [34]

This focus on themes and patterns, on the biographer's choice of key ideas which seem to unify and synthesize the subject's life, highlights the complexity of the biographical enterprise. The effective biographer must simultaneously employ the scholar's research skills, the novelist's creative use of form, and the autobiographer's self-awareness: she must remain rigorously true to her sources, creative and imaginative in her presentation of them, and conscious of her own subjective biases.

---

[30] Edel, *Writing Lives*, 15.

[31] Woolf developed the image in her essay "The New Biography," in *Collected Essays*, volume 4, edited by Leonard Woolf (London: Hogarth, 1967), 231-235. Harvena Richter, "The Biographer as Novelist," in Fromm, ed., *Essaying Biography*, 61, quotes her discussion of "The biographer whose art is subtle and bold enough to present that queer amalgamation of dream and reality, that perpetual marriage of granite and rainbow."

[32] Richter, "The Biographer as Novelist," 60. Today Woolf's confident assumption that the "essence" of a person can be captured by a biographer would be questioned. The self is very elusive.

[33] Richter, "The Biographer as Novelist," 70.

[34] Edel, *Writing Lives*, 29-30.

The biographical project is further complicated by the fact that "Life as it happens fails often to have a recognisable pattern."[35] People's lives are messy and full of unfinished business; their attitudes and choices are inconsistent and self-contradictory. This truth was faced neither by the medieval hagiographer, whose task was to present an exemplar of virtue perfectly practised, nor by the nineteenth-century biographer, who was creating a model of social rectitude. But in today's post-Strachey, post-Freud context, biographers deliberately highlight the complexities, the inconsistencies and the contradictions in their subjects' lives, comfortably acknowledging "how hard it was for any of our subjects to lead lives that we would have considered totally admirable, for they, like us, could never fully escape the culture in which they lived."[36]

Feminist Approaches to Biography[37]

In the final chapters of this book, I shall consider questions which might concern a feminist biographer of Cornelia. Feminist biographers are as alert as any other biographer to the issues that have been outlined above: the complexities of the form, the significance of the writer-subject relationship, the consciously postmodern conviction that all biography is provisional. And, in company with other modern biographers such as Leon Edel, they apply a hermeneutics of suspicion to their source materials.[38] But they also address issues of content which have not been adequately explored in male biography: mother-daughter relationships, female friendships, public and private spheres, the details of everyday life.[39]

The approach of Anglo-American feminist biographers lies at the opposite end of the spectrum from that of hagiographers. Where the

---

[35] Mary Heaton Vorse, quoted in Garrison, "Two Roads Taken," 75.

[36] Alpern and others, *The Challenge of Feminist Biography*, Introduction, 11.

[37] These approaches to biography are not exclusively feminist: similar attitudes can be discerned in the pre-feminist writing of Leon Edel, for instance. This section simply attempts to outline approaches to biography—used by many — which feminist scholars have valued, explored and developed.

[38] Edel did not use the phrase "hermeneutics of suspicion," but he certainly understood the concept, frequently exploring the differences between what he called "the figure *in* the carpet" and "the figure *under* the carpet." His image was taken from tapestry (via Henry James' short story), and he suggested that the figure under the carpet was often the very obverse of that which appeared in the carpet, and that the biographer's task was to discover the concealed figure. See for instance Edel, *Writing Lives*, 163-164.

[39] The attitudes explored here are, by and large, those of Anglo-American feminists who have generally shown a preference for socio-political readings.

hagiographers polished and honed the facts of a life to produce a picture of perfection, feminist biographers not only acknowledge but emphasize the complexities, self-contradictions, inconsistencies and ambivalence which they encounter in their subjects. Lois Rudnick, for instance, explains:

> In my biography, I attempt to create a coherent picture at the same time that I try to remain true to the ambiguities and complexities of a woman who was viewed by herself and others from myriad and contradictory angles of vision.[40]

In taking this approach, feminist biographers are consciously challenging the traditions of the genre. Rudnick argues that biography has been "one of the most Western and male-dominated of genres," not merely because "the subjects traditionally chosen" have been male, but because male biographers have consistently shaped their subjects' lives to "adumbrate the myth of the individuated heroic—or antiheroic—self."[41]

Feminist biographers seem to have little interest in constructing a heroine, or even in focusing on an individual in isolation; they attempt to create a picture of a contextualised woman, exploring all that has influenced and formed her, all that has shaped her personality—family relationships and social and political conditions as much as psychological development. If anything, psychological analysis and interpretation are given less emphasis than other factors. In many cases, and certainly in Cornelia's, an explicitly psychoanalytic approach is not possible, at least in Freudian terms, because so little is known about the subject's childhood. So, feminist scholars prefer to explore the external influences on the growth and development of the subject:

> Feminist scholars, especially, favour social and historical explanations over psychological ones. If one psychological theme emerges from feminist biographers' work, it is a focus on the natural growth of personality, shaped

---

[40] Rudnick, "The Male Identified Woman," 134. This is not exclusively a feminist view. James McClendon writes similarly, outside the feminist context: "But we know that our convictions, though tenacious, *do* sometimes change, that style can both be acquired and modified, that the total vision by which one lives can sometimes be made over again." (James W. McClendon, *Biography as Theology: How Life Stories Can Remake Today's Theology* [Philadelphia: Trinity Press International, 1990 (1974)], 17.)

[41] Rudnick, "The Male Identified Woman," 118.

by the changing passages of life as much as by dominant traits and motivations.[42]

In the same way, Susan Ware stresses the potential importance of apparently trivial personal events, and the effect that these can have on public achievements. Again, she seems to favour exploration of the details of everyday life over psychological interpretation:

> … one of the most important contributions of women's history to the craft of biography may be its emphasis on personal lives and their impact on public accomplishments. This is not necessarily a call for more psychological interpretations or psychobiographies, however. Rather, it asks for attention to the ordinary daily lives of our subjects. Whom you share your bed with and how you pay your bills do have an impact on events beyond the household. This insight applies to both men and women but is more salient for women achievers. Women who lived the kind of public life worthy of historical treatment almost inevitably had to make decisions and sacrifices that had potentially profound effects on their personal lives. In charting a woman's public achievements, we need to pay special attention to both the benefits and costs of such personal choices.[43]

Observations such as this explain why gender is a central issue in feminist biography: historically, just being a woman has involved the individual in a whole series of crucial "decisions and sacrifices" and "personal choices" which would not have exercised her—or at least would not have concerned her biographer to the same extent—had she been a man. How good a mother was she? Did she put career before children? Did she succeed in being effective in both the public and the private sphere? There is no counterpart to these questions in the biographies of male achievers, though it would make for a fuller, more rounded exploration of their lives if there were.

Feminist biographers, recognising "that the private life is no less real or important than the public one,"[44] have consciously expanded the biographical enterprise by exploring both, and seeking a balance between

---

[42] Garrison, "Two Roads Taken," 67-68.

[43] Susan Ware, "Unlocking the Porter-Dewson Partnership: A Challenge for the Feminist Biographer," in Alpern and others, *The Challenge of Feminist Biography*, 61.

[44] Garrison, "Two Roads Taken," 77.

them. They have turned this gender trap into a biographical asset. In the same way, they have used their understanding of their own subjectivity and partial vision to advantage. They reject the "once-presumed objectivity of biography"[45] and openly acknowledge their attachments and biases, arguing that this self-awareness makes them better scholars and better biographers. "The solution to the dilemma of subjectivity is to be acutely aware of it."[46]

Feminist biography is overtly partial and subjective ("a subjective portrait of the subject from a particular angle of vision"); it acknowledges the influence of the biographer's own life history on the construction of the biography ("our attitudes, perceptions and feelings toward the subject"); and it accepts that all biography is necessarily provisional, unfinished ("For we bring to our chosen genre the feminist challenge of creative indeterminacy—the continuous possibility of enriching and transforming our own—as well as our subjects'—lives").[47]

To apply these principles to an examination of Cornelia Connelly's life is a worthwhile task, at least for members of the congregation which she founded, precisely because engaging with her afresh opens the possibility that we will be changed ourselves, as our perception of her is changed:

> Puzzling out the narrative of another woman's life, we recognise dimensions of her character to which she herself is blind and consequently discover new dimensions and possibilities in ourselves .... We have challenged the illusion of objectivity and given up the arrogance of believing that we can, once and for all, get our foremothers right. Second readings thus come with the territory of feminist biography. For only by telling new stories and telling our stories anew can we glimpse the truths that emerge not once and for all but all in their own good time.[48]

We must expect that the application of feminist principles to the Cornelian sources will provide us with a less coherent, more ambiguous and complex picture of her than has previously been drawn—an unfinished portrait. But these principles can also enrich our study of the earlier

---

[45] Rudnick, "The Male Identified Woman," 119.

[46] Garrison, "Two Roads Taken," 68.

[47] Rudnick, "The Male Identified Woman," 137.

[48] Jacquelyn Dowd Hall, "Lives Through Time: Second Thoughts on Jessie Daniel Ames," in Alpern and others, *The Challenge of Feminist Biography*, 155.

biographies, enabling us to understand their partial and subjective approaches more clearly, and to explore the subtle differences behind their apparent similarities.

Hagiography and Women's Holiness

Any historical study of the place of women in the Church—especially one concerned with issues surrounding women's holiness—will be faced with questions about hagiographical literature, a genre constructed from a particular mix of theology and biography. Current feminist scholarship in both disciplines is deeply suspicious of the presentation of women within hagiography; it queries the validity and purpose of presenting women as "perfect," and castigates the deliberate construction of a life story to illustrate a virtue or point a moral.

Holiness

In the Judaeo-Christian tradition the holy has frequently been defined as the thing or person set apart for God; and within Christianity holy persons have been presented as set not only apart from but also above others, exemplars to be admired and imitated in the pursuit of private virtue and personal perfection. But this is not the only tenable theology of holiness. Contemporary women writers, alert for the problems raised by dualism, connect holiness with wholeness and wholesomeness. Elizabeth Stuart calls for "a daring theology of sainthood," with which she associates "nourishing and flourishing ... resistance and solidarity."[49] Rather than employing the term "holiness" at all, she suggests, "feminists would probably prefer 'wholeness' or 'subversive female presence.'"[50] Sara Maitland describes the holy person as a risk-taker: "Holiness must manifest itself in a growing freedom, and increasing sense of adventure .... [A] true sense of joyful adventure ... is the mark of holiness."[51] These definitions and approaches are obviously as applicable to men as to women. But Christian feminist writers have reached their stance on holiness by rejecting previous generations' assumptions about women's holiness in particular—

[49] Elizabeth Stuart, *Spitting at Dragons: Towards a Feminist Theology of Sainthood* (London: Mowbray, 1996), 119.
[50] Stuart, *Spitting at Dragons*, 108.
[51] Sara Maitland, "Saints for Today," *The Way*, 36/4 (October 1996), 276, 277.

assumptions which today seem inappropriate and unacceptable, if not downright unhealthy. It is out of their reflection on the ways in which women have been presented within the tradition that feminist scholars have come to argue for more challenging, energizing, and life-giving models of holiness for all.

Issues of Women's Holiness

Hagiography is littered with stories of women who seem to have been admired for only "partly living."[52] But a more robust tradition also exists. Jane Tibbets Schulenburg calls attention to this contradictory state of affairs, and the reasons for it, in her study of women saints between the sixth and twelfth centuries. On the one hand, she says, "The women saints of the Middle Ages were transgressors, rule-breakers, flouters of boundaries"; on the other, "with the new 'privatised' domestic saint or the obedient, subservient wife-saint, for example, the Church attempted to popularise and promote passive virtues for women."[53]

To explore the history of women's holiness, to attempt to retrieve what has been forgotten or suppressed, is clearly a legitimate task in Christian spirituality; it is not merely an "exercise in archaeological hagiography,"[54] but rather an attempt to identify the "usable past,"[55] which can then become a basis of hope for both women and men in the present and for the future. This view is not, however, shared by the most radical feminists. Mary Daly, for instance, takes a diametrically opposite stance, in her usual trenchant language:

> Surviving, moving women can hardly look to the masochistic martyrs of sadospiritual religion as models. Since most patriarchal writing that purports to deal with women is pornography or hagiography (which amount to the same thing), women ... are trying to break away from these "mouldy" models ...[56]

---

[52] T. S. Eliot, *Murder in the Cathedral* (London: Faber and Faber, 1953 [1935]), 19. The Chorus say "We do not wish anything to happen/ Seven years we have lived quietly/ Succeeded in avoiding notice/ Living and partly living."

[53] Jane Tibbets Schulenburg, *Forgetful of Their Sex: Female Sanctity and Society, Ca. 500-1000* (Chicago and London: University of Chicago Press, 1998), 3-8.

[54] Woodward, *Making Saints*, 251.

[55] A phrase attributed to Letty Russell, but used and developed by Monika K. Hellwig in *Christian Women in a Troubled World* (1985 Madeleva Lecture in Spirituality) (New York and Mahwah: Paulist, 1985), 17 following.

[56] Mary Daly, *Gyn/Ecology: The Metaethics of Radical Feminism* (London: Women's Press, 1991 [1979]), 14.

Nevertheless, the argument explored here is that a retrievable female tradition exists within spirituality, and that, patriarchy notwithstanding, it is possible to connect with our foremothers in the faith and learn from them. But the attempt to examine the history of women's holiness comes up against serious problems almost before it has begun:

> The saints honoured in the Church to date have been predominantly male: on the present liturgical calendar, 73% of the saints celebrated are men, 27% women, if one counts Mary once; of the saints canonised in this century [the 20th] to the end of Paul VI's pontificate, 79% have been clergy, 21% lay, of whom an even smaller percentage are women.[57]

"This official silence about the history of women's holiness [is] a socio-political function of the androcentric world-view that takes the humanity of men to be paradigmatic and normative." It highlights the need "to retrieve the hidden history of holy women and to present it free of stereotypical distortions of the feminine," in order to provide "impetus for mature adult personhood for women as well as men."[58]

But the truth has to be faced that for 2000 years women have been consistently marginalised in the Christian Church, and under-represented in positions of influence and authority. Because they threatened the established male order, they were presented in largely negative terms:

> Viewed as exercising profoundly threatening, transgressive, or disturbing roles, such women were seen as the dangerous "other"; they needed to be contained, marginalised, or punished. The daring, defying conduct, or acts of insubordination of these women thus served as a convenient arsenal of negative role models for ecclesiastical writers.[59]

In every respect the lives of Christian women have been circumscribed and interpreted by men—the dominant group within the Church—and the

---

[57] Elizabeth A. Johnson, "Saints and Mary," in *Systematic Theology: Roman Catholic Perspectives*, volume 2, edited by Francis Schüssler Fiorenza and John P. Galvin (Minneapolis: Fortress, 1991), 163. Other surveys (see, for example, that quoted by Philip Sheldrake, *Spirituality and History* [London: SPCK, 1991], 70) give slightly different figures, but the differences are minimal.

[58] Johnson, "Saints and Mary," 163.

[59] Schulenburg, *Forgetful of Their Sex*, 2. Cornelia Connelly, it can be argued, suffered from the same kind of discrimination in the nineteenth-century English Church.

spiritual tradition has been a tradition of maleness.[60] Men established the
norms of spiritual growth and development, of sanctity and sinfulness, and
women reinterpreted their experience in terms of the established (male)
categories. This is true even in the ranks of the saints: it was men who
determined what constituted holiness in women and which women were
holy.

In 1978 when the calendar of the Alternative Service Book of the
Church of England was revised, only one of the twenty post-Reformation
British people allotted an annual day, Josephine Butler, was a woman.
Questioned about this obvious lacuna, Margaret Hewitt, chairman (*sic*) of
the revision committee for the new calendar, stated:

> Women appear in relatively small numbers in the ranks of the sanctified,
> since up to very recent times in the West, it was more difficult, and certainly
> less acceptable for women than men to distinguish themselves in society
> without attracting odium. Hence it was arguable that behaviour which was
> held to imply sanctity in men only appeared as insanity when engaged in by
> women and was recorded as such by their contemporaries.[61]

The dualistic theology of sexuality that underlies much female
sainthood, the ways in which sainthood reduces real women to two-
dimensional ideals, and the hierarchical power constructs inherent in the
whole process of canonisation are now routinely challenged in women's
writing. As Stuart says: "There can be no doubt that the theology of
sainthood and the politics of canonisation have been deployed against self-
affirming women for centuries."[62] But Christian women abandon the
tradition at their peril:

> Catholic women cannot simply turn away from the images and cult of the
> saints without paying the price of alienation from ourselves and from our
> particular Christian tradition and community. [If we do so] we are in danger

---

[60] Sheldrake, *Spirituality and History*, 51: "To say that women's religious experience was caged within a male theology
is more than to note that the theological teaching was for so long dominated by men. Although, theoretically,
theology was *a priori*, in practice the categories and tone expressed a male mentality."

[61] General Synod, *Report of Proceedings* (1987), volume 1, 146, quoted in Richard Symonds, *Far Above Rubies: The
Women Uncommemorated in the Church of England* (Leominster: Gracewing, 1993), 2. Schulenburg makes the same
point about medieval women saints, writing that "there frequently existed only a very fine line separating
contemporary notions of "sanctity" from perceptions of aberrant or deviant modes of behaviour."

[62] Stuart, *Spitting at Dragons*, 8.

of leaving these religious images of women in command and control of Catholic women's psyche, not to mention in the command and control of the male hierarchy which interprets their meaning for women.[63]

Hagiography and Canonisation

Part of the difficulty of confronting "the images and cult of the saints," and particularly of the women saints, is that once they were canonised and their stories were written, over and over again "self-affirming women" ceased to be people and became two-dimensional ideals, examples of virtues to be imitated or moral lessons to be learnt. The written texts of the saints' lives acquired a power of their own, quite independent of the real existence of the women behind the stories. In the Church, "it is hardly an exaggeration to say that the saints *are* their stories … making saints is a process whereby a life is transformed into a text."[64] Stuart draws attention to the ways in which this process has been disempowering, not only for the saint in question but for all who have been influenced by her story:

> The individuality of the woman [saint], her own personhood, is lost beneath the "ideals" and her life is then used to encourage other women to reduce their lives and possibilities to these [same] narrow … ideals.[65]

So, any attempt to meet the women who have been canonised—and the holy women who have not been canonised—during the Christian centuries, any attempt to retrieve and reread their stories, immediately encounters not only the gulf which separates our time from theirs, but the stereotypical manner in which their stories have been told. We are faced with disentangling the stories from the didactic or hagiographical purposes for which they were written (the authorial assumptions that the life stories were made to bear). And, almost always, we are reading lives of women which were written by men.

To meet our foremothers in the faith, to gain some knowledge of the holiness of their lives, it is necessary not only to understand something of

---

[63] Elisabeth Schüssler Fiorenza, *Discipleship of Equals* (London: SCM, 1993), 40-41, quoted in Stuart, *Spitting at Dragons*, 44.

[64] Woodward, *Making Saints*, 18.

[65] Stuart, *Spitting at Dragons*, 21.

their context, of the times in which they lived, of "the cultural relativity of sanctity,"[66] but also to be aware of the history of hagiography, of the different intentions that biographers have had in presenting these stories:

> We cannot be holy, until we have learned to see and understand a history of holiness, and to see it in relation to the political and social realities of its different times. … More: in order to understand and examine such holy lives we also need an understanding of the history of representation, of the writing about the saints, of hagiography.[67]

A glance at the history of holiness and canonisation reveals that in the first millennium of the Church's history, saints were usually proclaimed spontaneously by the people among whom they had lived. Gradually, between the fifth and tenth centuries, bishops took control of emerging cults, and the naming of saints became an ecclesiastical function.[68] The pope became officially involved in the process in the tenth century (the canonisation of Ulrich of Augsburg in 993 being the first authenticated case of papal validation),[69] and by the thirteenth century the right to name saints was restricted to the papacy.[70] Since then canonisation has become an increasingly complex and formalised procedure in the control of cardinals and the pope—an act of those at the apex of the hierarchical pyramid.

One consequence of this centralisation is that those in authority have been able to use the individuals whom they accepted for canonisation as a way of embodying the dominant ideology and theology.[71] In the Church the criteria that determine who and what is judged to be holy have not been unchanging—but neither have they often been openly and clearly articulated. They are unexamined assumptions determined by historical, social, cultural and ideological factors, and they are the assumptions of the people who are powerful. When the Church canonises someone it necessarily does so in the context of the current church agenda.[72]

---

[66] Schulenburg, *Forgetful of Their Sex*, 2.

[67] Maitland, "Saints for Today," 278.

[68] Woodward, *Making Saints*, 65.

[69] Woodward, *Making Saints*, 65.

[70] See Johnson, "Saints and Mary," 147.

[71] Stuart, *Spitting at Dragons*, 29.

[72] Describing the beatification of Maria Goretti in 1947, Woodward writes (*Making Saints*, 123): "In an address that was reported in newspapers throughout Europe, the pope [Pius XII] used the occasion to denounce those in the

In the late-nineteenth and early-twentieth centuries, for instance, saints were named against a background of growing secularism in Europe, where an increasingly educated working class was encountering the alternative world-view presented by socialism and being attracted to it. The Church reacted by becoming more centralised and insular (developing its own press, education system, voluntary organisations), and by naming as saints those who would reinforce obedience to its authority and loyalty to the pope.[73] At the beginning of the twenty-first century, the Church is in a very different place—aware of the world beyond Europe, of pluralism, of postmodern thinking, of ecumenism, of feminism, of many other current concerns. And in naming saints it responds to, or reacts against, these different factors.

In every age, those who canonise, and those who tell and retell the stories of the canonised and the holy, are usually (perhaps inevitably) engaged—consciously or unconsciously—in promoting a particular view of holiness, a view which enhances and reinforces the agenda of the powerful in the current social, political and spiritual circumstances of the Church. Religious biographers, like all writers of lives, have traditionally sought out themes and images to make sense of the subject's life and draw together different moments and experiences into a cohesive whole. Often the key they chose, the unifier, was the current perception of what constituted holiness, and the subject's life was shaped to fit this predetermined model. Walter Brueggeman speaks of a tendency to "trim and domesticate" stories "to accommodate regnant modes of knowledge [and] to enhance regnant modes of power."[74] And Philip Sheldrake writes:

> It does not seem unfair to reflect upon the Christian tradition in terms of those who seek to control, produce and then dispense spirituality and those who are made into the recipients of spiritual bequests that originate with others. This is an issue of power: who has it, how it is used (whether

---

movie industry, the fashion industry, the press, the theatre, and even the military, which had recently conscripted women, for corrupting the chastity of youth."

[73] Stuart (*Spitting at Dragons*, 63), commenting on the canonisation of Joan of Arc, writes: "It was political expediency, fear of communism and a desire to encourage movements against communism that led to her canonisation in 1920."

[74] Walter Brueggeman, *The Bible and Postmodern Imagination: Texts Under Negotiation* (London: SCM, 1993), vii. He quotes Karl Marx, "The ruling ideas of each age have ever been the ideas of its ruling class."

consciously or not) and what the effects are, in different contexts, on those who are, at different times, a spiritually dependent underclass.[75]

At least until the Second Vatican Council the process of canonisation, and the hagiography which accompanied it, presented the "spiritually dependent underclass" with saints who were set apart from them and above them by virtue of their closeness to God, saints who were as near perfect as it was possible for human beings to be. Any suggestion of weakness or failure was justified or explained away.

This remoteness and unreality have made the whole company of saints less accessible to many post-conciliar Catholics. (Stuart quotes Dorothy Day's plea: "Don't call me a saint! I don't want to be dismissed so easily!")[76] A model of sainthood for today must involve communion and solidarity; we need saints with whom we can identify, who share our common humanity, our common struggle, our common weakness, whose example in victory and defeat is liberating and encouraging for us. We need saints who can be "models for confronting oppressive regimes, for treasuring the dignity and rights of the dispossessed and deprived, for daring to contradict current values"[77]; saints whose holiness has some relevance to the lives which people currently lead.

Yet the process of canonisation still seems to take little account of this. Documents presented in support of a cause for canonisation deliberately and overtly downplay any faults or weaknesses; such are the demands of the system. Margaret Press, describing the beatification in 1995 of Mary MacKillop, the Australian founder of the Sisters of St Joseph, notes:

> Try as one may to promote human weakness as part of the candidate's reality, faults are buried under the sheer weight of positive testimony, each hint of weakness being accounted for by a worthy motive.[78]

This, she argues, is not in harmony with the outlook or the needs of the late-twentieth century:

---

[75] Sheldrake, *Spirituality and History*, 215.

[76] Stuart, *Spitting at Dragons*, 36. However, the cause of Day's canonisation is currently in process.

[77] Margaret Press, "Sanctity, Images and Stories," *The Way*, 36/4, (October 1996), 321.

[78] Press, "Sanctity, Images and Stories," 318.

Today, our ways of reading saints' lives have changed, as have standards of research and presentation. Contemporary readers of serious works are likely to have moved towards a critical stance, if not as far as deconstruction .... Those books which continue the tradition of recording only what is edifying, meeting the curial expectations of orthodoxy, perfection and popular veneration, are no longer the norm.[79]

Feminist Religious Biography

Biographies that fit Press' criteria, deconstructing the traditional presentation of holy women as models of perfection and presenting more rounded and fully human figures, are increasingly available. The work of Caroline Walker Bynum, who has read the lives of medieval women saints against the grain of their presentation by their original male clerical biographers, has been of particular importance.[80] Ruth Harris has examined the construction of the Lourdes phenomenon and has retrieved a refreshingly different portrait of Bernadette, and feminist studies of both Teresa of Avila and Thérèse of Lisieux have been undertaken.[81] What might be involved in a similar re-presentation of Cornelia is explored in chapters seven and eight.

In this chapter I have sought to establish the framework within which the biographies of Cornelia are to be examined. This book deals first with the biographers themselves, and with the unexamined assumptions that underlie their interpretation and presentation of Cornelia's story. The biographies are considered as windows onto the worlds in which they were written, hinting at the contemporary concerns that led to specific selection and emphasis. Their seven readings of the same story may be expected to reveal, through what is written into and out of the life, what is emphasized and what downplayed, the (conscious and unconscious) assumptions and biases about women and about holiness that have been current since Cornelia's death in 1879.

---

[79] Press, "Sanctity, Images and Stories," 318.

[80] See, for instance, Bynum's retrieval of the nuns of Helfta in *Jesus as Mother* (Berkeley and Los Angeles: University of California Press, 1982), and her study of the religious significance of food to medieval women, *Holy Feast and Holy Fast* (Berkeley and Los Angeles: University of California Press, 1987).

[81] Ruth Harris, *Lourdes* (London: Allen Lane, 1999); Thérèse Taylor, *Bernadette of Lourdes* (London: Burns and Oates, 2003); Alison Weber, *Teresa of Avila and the Rhetoric of Femininity* (Princeton: Princeton UP, 1990); Constance Fitzgerald, "The Mission of Thérèse of Lisieux," *The Way Supplement*, 89 (Summer 1997), 74-96.

Cornelia is, at one and the same time, a candidate for canonisation in the Roman Catholic Church, and one of those "self-affirming women" whom Stuart suggests have been ill served by the theology of sainthood and the politics of canonisation. This tension is neatly summarised by Woodward:

> Of all the historical causes to reach the congregation since the reform of 1983, none is more arresting than the case of Mother Cornelia Connelly, founder of the Society of the Holy Child Jesus. Certainly it is one of the most delicate and complicated to confront the congregation's judges .... [T]here was serious concern among the saint-makers that the life of this extraordinary woman would, if made known through canonisation, scandalise Catholics of the late-twentieth century. After all, the Church has never before canonised a nun who was married to a priest.[82]

Then, only two paragraphs later, Woodward allows us to hear the very different voice of Elizabeth Mary Strub, the first woman, he says, ever to prepare the historical documentation required by the Sacred Congregation for the Canonisation of Saints:[83]

> I think you'll see that Cornelia speaks to every woman who has suffered from ruptured personal relationships through divorce, alienation of children, and so on. In this sense she really is a very contemporary woman. A saint for our times.[84]

Quite apart from questions about Cornelia's sanctity, Woodward believes that her life would present problems to any biographer:

> [She] is not a conventional candidate for sainthood. Theology aside, her life appears to be so relentlessly episodic that it challenges even the most adroit biographer's effort to find a coherent thread.[85]

If this is the case, then the threads that her biographers, at different periods, have succeeded in finding may be revealing not only of Cornelia but of the

---

[82] Woodward, *Making Saints*, 252. Schulenburg's comments on women as "the dangerous 'other'" should not be forgotten.

[83] In fact Strub was bringing to completion work largely carried out by Ursula Blake SHCJ.

[84] Woodward, *Making Saints*, 253.

[85] Woodward, *Making Saints*, 253.

biographers themselves and of their criteria for holiness. The next chapter, therefore, gives a historical overview of the biographies.

Chapter Three

CORNELIA'S CANARIES: A HISTORY OF THE BIOGRAPHIES

The image of the biographer as a canary—more specifically as a miner's canary—is taken from Virginia Woolf. In an essay in the *Atlantic Monthly* of April 1939, she noted that the facts of a person's life "are not like the facts of science—once they are discovered, always the same." Rather, "They are subject to changes of opinion, [and] opinions change as the times change." Biographers, conscious of this, must avoid the clichéd approach to the writing of a life, "the old chapter headings—life at college, marriage, career," and "seek the true features of the human face ... the real current of the hero's existence."

> Thus the biographer must go ahead of the rest of us, like the miner's canary, testing the atmosphere, detecting falsity, unreality, and the presence of obsolete conventions. His sense of truth must be alive and on tiptoe.[1]

The story of those who went "ahead of the rest of us" in Cornelia's case—an account of the evolution, history and interconnection of the biographies—provides an insight into the ambivalent relationship between the Society of the Holy Child Jesus and its extraordinary founder. Her life was not easily told; and the scandal that surrounded her proved a stumbling block to the acceptance of the Society and its works within the English Church. So, initial enthusiasm for a biography immediately after her death was followed by a long period when her story was suppressed, even within the Society. How biographies were eventually written, the themes that the seven major biographers chose to emphasize, and the models of holiness that preoccupied them, are detailed in this chapter. A study of the

---

[1] Woolf, "The Art of Biography," 149. Current biographical theory eschews the notion that "the true features" and "the real current" are ever likely to be identifiable.

biographies is in effect a study of attitudes to the founder and of understandings of holiness among members of the Society during the last 150 years.

Maria Joseph Buckle: *Life of Cornelia Connelly*, 1886

The second Superior General of the Society, Angelica Croft, was a member of the General Council at the time of Cornelia's death; she had held various positions of authority in the Society and was known to be Cornelia's own choice for a successor. Cornelia died on 18 April 1879; on 14 May, Croft wrote a long letter to Cornelia's brother-in-law, John Connelly, giving him details of her final illness and death and responding gratefully to his offer of information about the Connellys' family life:

> With regard to sending the valuable letters which you possess, I can only say that you can not do us a greater service, as we are trying to collect materials from all parts to help us in writing the details of our beloved Mother's most beautiful and remarkable life—which we know however cannot be published in Mr Connelly's life time. You may judge therefore how very valuable every document and every—even the simplest details of her early life will be and as we have no friend, excepting yourself to apply to in America, your letter came as a ray of hope or I should rather say, a ray of light to lead us to our possible channel from which we might glean the information we so much want. The Sister who is most engaged in the work has sent you a few little notes of inquiry intended for your kind consideration.[2]

"The Sister … most engaged in the work" was Maria Joseph Buckle, whose life of Cornelia, a typescript in eight volumes, was begun in 1879 and completed in Neuilly, France, in 1886. When the typescript was included in the material presented to the historical commission for the cause of Cornelia's canonisation, it was entitled *Materials Collected … for a Life of Cornelia Connelly*, which gives a fair description of the contents; Buckle makes no claim to having written a polished biography.

Buckle's first volume is consciously introductory, containing her own general observations, judgment and summing up of Cornelia's personal qualities and her spirituality. Buckle informs the reader that her work has

---

[2] D76:25-26. Punctuation as in original.

been undertaken "in holy obedience," that it is "only a beginning" and that it must be supplemented "by others who will aid me in the task of collecting materials."[3] She is conscious of the partial and limited view she has brought to her task, and judges this an unsatisfactory approach to biography. Her biographical ideal is impartiality: "We can only ... endeavour to place the story of her life as impartially as we are able before our readers ...."[4]

The rest of Buckle's biography is a collection of primary source materials which she transcribes, edits and comments upon; sometimes she even censors them. She organizes and arranges chronologically the large collection of family letters and papers provided by Pierce's brother, John Connelly; Cornelia's own spiritual notebooks; information gleaned from conversation with Cornelia's daughter, Adeline; the recollections of other members of the Society; and her own lived experience and personal knowledge. From the account of the founding of the Society onwards, her writing becomes increasingly specific, entering into minute detail about people, places and events, and to a certain extent fusing, indeed confusing, her own experience with Cornelia's.

Not only in the biography, but also in the extant chapters of her personal reflections, Buckle asserts her belief in Cornelia's holiness, even going so far as to envisage the possibility of her beatification:

> The first priest who was sent by the Bishop of Liverpool to visit our Convent [in Blackpool] was Mgr Cookson and he was much prejudiced by what he had heard of Mother Foundress.—He asked me what my opinion of her was. I replied "You have come Reverend Father to hear all the faults that I can bear witness to her having committed and I do not doubt that like every one else she has committed faults in the responsible office that she has held for so many years and which she would be the first to acknowledge. But I never saw her commit a fault that was wilful in fact after having lived with her as my Superior for twenty years I can say that I never saw anything which was not holy and edifying in her conduct and if you were appointed after her death to ask what we could testify about her holiness I should say I never saw anything that would prevent the process of her Beatification being commenced."[5]

---

[3] D63:85.
[4] D63:32.
[5] 78:68.

Buckle equates holiness with perfection: Cornelia was holy because "I never saw her commit a fault that was wilful." Her further claim—that Cornelia was not only holy but a suitable candidate for beatification—is striking, because, as Catherine Gompertz observes in a letter of 1932, Buckle was writing when the canonisation of contemporaries was not perceived as a likely possibility:

> Nobody in those days thought of Canonisation as a proximate or even a possible proposition. Is it not only recently, practically since St Thérèse, that so many canonisations have taken place of people who died but recently?[6]

Buckle's conviction that Cornelia was holy did not prevent her from criticising the founder, or expressing reservations about her conduct and decisions. She explicitly queries the wisdom of Cornelia's judgment and actions on two occasions: when she refused to see Pierce in Derby, and when she opposed Wiseman in the St Leonards property dispute. But whilst she disapproves of Cornelia's behaviour, she does not doubt her motivation:

> ... although there were many things in her conduct I did not intirely approve of and in which I thought her mistaken She was so upright and conscientious in all she said or did that I was convinced of her sanctity and that even if she was not acting as I thought was right she was doing what in her own Judgment was her duty and very often acted at a great sacrifice of her own feelings so that very likely in the inscrutable wisdom of God she received a reward for actions that were blamed in the world and even by the good and the holy.[7]

Buckle's willingness to be openly critical, to dissent, to have a different view of events and actions from that taken by the founder, seems to add force and conviction to her reiterated claims for Cornelia's goodness and holiness. The specific criticism made here, about Cornelia's independent spirit, reveals the ultramontane nature of Buckle's views, as does much else in the recollections and biography. Her theology, and more explicitly her

---

[6] The quotations from Catherine Gompertz' letters in this chapter are all taken from a correspondence with Mary Amadeus Atchison during the late 1920s and early 1930s. Atchison was at that time Superior General. The autograph letters are in the Oxford archives.

[7] D78:43. Spelling as in the original.

spirituality of religious life, were based on an unwavering conviction that obedience to the hierarchical Church was the sure and only way to salvation. Thus, obedience was the virtue that she valued and emphasized in Cornelia's life.

Buckle's view of holiness—the suggestion that it was "a higher level," a fixed state of perfection attained through suffering and sacrifice—is glimpsed again in the conventional tone of her comments on Cornelia in the first volume of the biography. The stereotypically hagiographical references to Cornelia's physical appearance are of a piece with this model of holiness:

> We may suppose she was raised by her sacrifice to a higher level and had not the common temptations to impatience or passionate feelings which those who are on their <u>way</u> to perfection have generally to fight against .... Those who saw her for the first time were impressed with her very extraordinary powers of mind—and also with that indescribable appearance of sanctity which especially towards the close of her life seemed to radiate from her eyes and her smile.[8]

Buckle was a prolific writer and translator; among her extant writings are some chapters of personal recollections, which are particularly significant because in them she allows herself to comment on Cornelia rather more freely than she does in the biography. The first chapter of the recollections, which contained "what I remembered of my life before I entered Religion,"[9] would have made fascinating reading, but has not survived.

Buckle speaks of her own "excellent education,"[10] and of having translated a good deal of Jesuit source material for Cornelia;[11] the Society necrologist confirms that "she was highly gifted and a great linguist ... with rare mental powers."[12] But her prose style is effusively Victorian and repetitive, and her spelling, punctuation and grammar leave something to

---

[8] D63:23-24.

[9] D78:2.

[10] D63:5.

[11] D78:61-62

[12] After each sister's death a necrology—an account and assessment of her life—is written and circulated among all houses of the Society. The necrologies have not been systematically collated, so no reference number can be given. A complete set of necrologies exists in the Society archives.

be desired.[13] By her own acknowledgement, Buckle was "pious" and suffered from "scruples";[14] she suggests that she became the privileged recipient of Cornelia's confidences while the founder was helping her to combat her scrupulosity.[15]

Buckle was probably not sufficiently disciplined to write a systematic biography; but there can be no question that she had in abundance the enthusiasm and affection for the founder that were needed to amass the available materials. The letters she copied and the anecdotes she recorded have been used by each succeeding biographer.

"Policy of Silence" 1879-1905

Angelica Croft had acknowledged in her letter to John Connelly that no biography of Cornelia could be published until after Pierce's death. Pierce died in 1883; Buckle completed her biography in 1886; but no attempt was made at publication. A correspondence in the late 1920s and early 1930s between Catherine Gompertz, author of the first printed life of Cornelia, and the then Superior General, Mary Amadeus Atchison, speaks of "the 'policy of silence' from 1879-1905" and discusses the possible reasons for it.

One reason was that initially Pierce was still alive, and Cornelia's story could not be told without reference to his. But the decision to keep silent was not primarily a matter of respect for Pierce's feelings or of his need for privacy. The Society had its own reasons for avoiding further connections with Pierce. His activities in the 1840s and 1850s had been publicly scandalous. His abandonment of the Roman Catholic priesthood, his widely publicised case against Cornelia for the restitution of conjugal rights, and his vitriolic pamphlets against the Roman Catholic Church in general and convents in particular, had been damaging to the public image of the Church in England and of its newly restored hierarchy. Association with Pierce in such a climate affected the reputation, not only of Cornelia, but of the Society she had founded. The clergy, especially, viewed it with suspicion.

---

[13] In general, Buckle's idiosyncratic spelling and punctuation have been retained in quotations from her work.
[14] D78:59, 9-10.
[15] D63:22.

In the years following Cornelia's death a particular concern of the Society was that its Rule had still not received approbation. And Pierce was part of that situation too: in Rome in 1848 he had claimed to be the Society's founder and submitted constitutions of his own for approval. The spurious document remained on file at Propaganda Fide, causing endless confusion. According to Gompertz, when, after thirty years, the Society was still without constitutions approved by Rome, "many of the Clergy thought the Society was on the verge of dissolution. Between 1879 and 1887 Novices were warned before profession that the Society might be dissolved." In such a vulnerable position, and anxious that nothing should impede the speedy ratification of its Rule, the Society wanted to do nothing that might rouse Pierce again: "It was always possible that he might renew his attacks .... It was therefore thought best to keep as quiet as possible about CC even within the Society."

Though the Gompertz-Atchison correspondence does not suggest this, another reason for silence about Cornelia's life may have been the effect that a biography would have on the Peacock-Connelly family and particularly on Cornelia's own children. However, a history of the family (*The Groome Family and Connections: A Pedigree*) which was published in 1907 by Harry Connelly Groome, a grandson of Pierce's brother, contained an outline of Pierce and Cornelia's marriage and their subsequent dramatic life stories. So, after 1907, this could no longer account for the failure to publish a biography.

In fact, it is clear that Angelica Croft and her advisers were not only anxious about connections with Pierce: they were concerned that association with Cornelia herself might prove detrimental to the Society's growth and reputation. Gompertz, who had "often discussed this [policy of silence] with any persons who, I thought, could explain it," notes in a letter of 4 September 1929 that Cornelia was unpopular with three groups of people: some members of the Society, some clergy and "many people in England." Within the Society, the disaffection in Preston and in the United States (as well as that among the lay sisters which Gompertz mentions later in the letter) was "personally associated with CC. It probably appeared to those in authority that internal wounds would best be healed by a complete change of personnel and a new start." The St Leonards property dispute "was directly associated with her name, and ... involved real hostility on the part of the Clergy." Finally,

Gompertz says, Cornelia "was looked upon as 'an unnatural Mother' and a disobedient and disloyal wife" by "many people in England."

These were substantial reasons for delaying a biography of Cornelia. To them must be added the suggestion that Croft's own attitude to Cornelia was questionable. Croft had suffered from ill health even as a young woman, and had had at least one serious breakdown before she became Superior General. About her psychological state at the time of Cornelia's death Gompertz offers the testimony of Philomena Poquet:

> Mother Philomena says that Mother Angelica at the time of CC's death was in a very delicate state of health on account of her "critical" age and was probably slightly unbalanced at the time.[16]

Gompertz comments:

> Mother Angelica certainly did not see "eye to eye" with CC towards the end of CC's life. Probably malcontents turned towards MA—as they are supposed to turn towards the Prince of Wales when they fall out with the King.

Gompertz seems at pains to put as positive a gloss on Croft's attitudes and actions as she can:

> Everything points to the supposition that MA was an eminently good and high principled religious, and that she conscientiously thought it her duty, in the interest of the Society, to try to obscure CC for a time at least.

Yet both in this letter, and in another of 19 October 1932, Gompertz repeats claims that Croft deliberately suppressed or destroyed material relating to Cornelia. In the 1932 letter she writes: "It is quite possible that things <u>were</u> written [about Cornelia], and that M M Angelica destroyed them. I think you know her attitude in the matter." Francis Bellasis, author of a manuscript life of Cornelia, had testified to Croft's "attitude in the matter." According to Gompertz (1929):

> M M Francis (B) told me many times that Mother Angelica ordered her to destroy all Mother Maria Joseph [Buckle]'s manuscripts for the life of CC

---

[16] This appears to be a euphemistic reference to the menopause: Croft was 40 years old at the time.

and that she disobeyed conscientiously and hid them away after having consulted an SJ.

In 1932 she adds a second claim by Bellasis, "that a row of manuscript books in CC's room after her death were found standing as before, but with all their contents torn out ...."

There is some paradox here. Why did the woman who had told John Connelly in 1879 that they were "trying to collect materials from all parts to help us in writing the details of our beloved Mother's most beautiful and remarkable life" eventually come to order the destruction of the very life of Cornelia that she herself had authorised? Was it a matter of personal instability? Or did loyalty to the growing Society seem to demand the suppression of Cornelia's story? Or is it possible that there was, in fact, no "policy of silence" at all?

When Bisgood's biography was published in the early 1960s, Marie Madeleine Amy argued robustly, in correspondence with James Walsh SJ, that the notion of a policy of silence was overstated. Amy was responsible for collecting and collating much of the historical material for the cause of Cornelia's canonisation, however. She weakened her case by commenting that the discussion of such a policy might hinder the cause, and that the issue should not be overemphasized for this reason.

Amy wrote to Walsh (who was the vice-postulator of the cause),[17] on 27 January 1963, commenting on his use of the phrase "conspiracy of silence" in his proposed introduction to Bisgood's biography:

> "Conspiracy of silence." Father, I feel you must know what my reaction would be to this. It is one of the topics on which we argued when we first met back in 1959 and I have in no way changed my opinion on the matter. I think the question has been exaggerated and gives a very false impression. Furthermore, I cannot see that stressing it will help, in any way, Mother Foundress' Cause.

---

[17] The first investigations into a putative saint's sanctity are carried out in the diocese in which he or she died. If there are no living witnesses who can testify, a historical commission is set up and a diocesan postulator, a promoter of the cause, is appointed. This was James Walsh's position from 1958. After the diocesan stage was completed, and the cause was sent to Rome, Paul Molinari SJ became the postulator, and Walsh was designated vice-postulator. For the sake of clarity he is referred to as 'vice-postulator' throughout. The process of canonisation is detailed in chapter six.

Walsh, clearly not of one mind with Amy, replied two days later:

> We shall certainly have to settle to everyone's satisfaction … the question of
> this silence. There are many indications that it must have existed. We shall
> need to produce <u>evidence</u> to counteract these indications, certainly to cover
> the time of Mother Angelica Croft's term of office. The silence during that
> time does seem to have been the official policy.

Gompertz appears to agree with Walsh. The evidence she presents for
the existence of a deliberate silence is drawn from personal conversations
with members of the Society who had known both Cornelia and Angelica
Croft; and it seems to reveal that, at the very least, Croft's attitude to the
founder was ambivalent.

Mary Francis Bellasis: *The Life of Cornelia Connelly, Foundress of the Society of the Holy Child Jesus*, 1919

According to her own account, Francis Bellasis first met Cornelia in 1854,
as a child of twelve in company with her father, Serjeant Edward Bellasis, a
parliamentary lawyer and Oxford convert. Edward Bellasis was a great
supporter and personal friend of Cornelia, who referred to him as "Brother
Bellasis."[18]

Francis Bellasis entered the Society eighteen years before Cornelia died,
and she was in close and constant contact with the founder, especially in the
closing years of Cornelia's life when she had responsibility for the novices.
Her personal regard for Cornelia cannot be doubted: it was she who
preserved the manuscript of Buckle's biography during the period when
Cornelian materials were seemingly destroyed. Gompertz (4 September
1929) states unequivocally:

> It was her influence and the production of these MSS. when M M Francis
> [Tolhurst] became Superior General in 1904 which reawakened the
> knowledge and veneration for CC.

Internal evidence suggests that Bellasis had begun her biography at least
by 1911; the completed manuscript is dated 18 April 1919, by which time

---

[18] D76:67.

Bellasis was 77 years old. The unpublished biography survives in two large bound volumes of typescript, corrected and annotated by Bellasis herself and by others, possibly including Catherine Gompertz. The "Author's Preface— (Rough Sketch)," inserted at the front of the first volume, states:

> I was asked to write the Life of Mother Cornelia Connelly for one reason and one reason only—that I had known her personally and intimately, and alone survived of those who were in a position to turn that privilege to account, by inditing a record of her life from information derived at first hand .... Her [the author's] own object throughout, to which everything else has been subordinated, has been to place on record events of Mother Connelly's life, and the characteristics of her personality as they came under her own personal observation and impressed themselves on her memory.

Bellasis' biography, written with the encouragement and approval of the superior general, Mary Francis Tolhurst, was intended for publication; and she submitted it to Herbert Thurston SJ, section by section as it was completed, for comment and criticism. Thirty-six letters from Thurston to Bellasis are extant, all positive and encouraging. His criticisms are largely stylistic: he wanted Bellasis to be aware that she was writing for an audience wider than other members of the Society and consequently suggested she avoid such terminology as "our Mother." But, typically, in the last of the letters he wrote, "I have now read it right through and very deliberately ... I do think you give an excellent presentment of her holiness and brave character." That this was more than merely generous encouragement to an old lady is shown by an undated extract from a letter that Thurston wrote to Tolhurst, the superior general:

> It must be recognised, of course, that the Life is not a masterpiece of biography. It is very simple, without any particular charm of style, without much attempt to grapple with the wider issues. And yet I think every reader will see it to be what it is, the tribute of a devout earnest and loving disciple to a much venerated teacher. For this reason I recommend its publication practically intact.

"The tribute of a devout earnest and loving disciple to a much venerated teacher" suggests at once the nature of the biographer-subject relationship in this biography. When Thurston's judgment is coupled with Bellasis' awareness of herself as the sole survivor, the only one who had known Cornelia intimately and was still capable of "turn[ing] that privilege to account," the agenda becomes clear. Bellasis is intent on recording information about Cornelia that would otherwise be lost, and her stance is one of devout and earnest veneration. Present-day writers on the genre of biography note the pitfalls both of the idealization of the subject and of the confusion between biography and autobiography. Bellasis, with her heightened awareness of herself as the last of the line, perhaps even more than Buckle, has written a biography which is "the act of [a] daughter ... an act of retrieval that is experienced as rescue."[19] Our reading of Bellasis can only be enhanced by this knowledge: we read the text for what it is, a loving (spiritual) daughter's testimony to the (founding) mother.

When Bellasis' biography was included in the documentation collected for the cause of Cornelia's canonisation, those who collated the material for the historical commissioners read into Thurston's support a defence of Bellasis' approach. He was, they write, "a notable authority on the physical phenomena of mysticism, scholarly and sceptical; and he would scarcely have endorsed the work had it been hagiographically objectionable."[20] The problem for a reader today is not that the biography is "hagiographically objectionable," but that it is, consciously and deliberately, hagiographical.

Bellasis is very much Cornelia's second biographer. She had access to Buckle's text and drew on it extensively, especially for the earlier years of Cornelia's life. (Neither biographer seems to have learnt about Cornelia's life in America from Cornelia herself; both depend heavily on the correspondence and papers supplied by John Connelly, which Buckle meticulously transcribed.) But Bellasis did not follow Buckle blindly; the surviving Buckle manuscript is annotated in Bellasis' hand from time to time. "Not correct," we find at one point, or "No—His brother's child," and so on. Furthermore, Buckle was not her only source. By 1907 Mary Theophila Laprimaudaye had completed the Annals of the Society for the years 1846-1879.[21] Whilst these do not purport to be a biography of

---

[19] Bell Gale Chevigny, quoted in Sklar, "Coming to Terms with Florence Kelley," 48.

[20] D72:ii.

[21] The Annals of the Society consist of a continuous narrative of events, recorded year by year. Today, Annals are written contemporaneously, but in the early 1900s Theophila Laprimaudaye's task was to create Annals retrospectively for the first years of the Society's existence.

Cornelia, they supply another perspective on her life from the time she founded the Society. And, of course, for the last twenty years or so of Cornelia's life, Bellasis could depend upon her own personal knowledge.

In recommending publication of Bellasis' manuscript, Herbert Thurston suggested "if the idea were not very distasteful to Mother M Francis, that some other competent hand should supplement, or rewrite, the chapter on education." It would appear that this suggestion was acted upon because in a letter to M St John McMaster of 28 November 1919, Bellasis writes:

> I like the chapters xxviii and xxix on education … very much. The last paragraph in chapter xviii [xxviii] beginning "The Book of Studies" [Fr Brown SJ] wrote in a letter to me, telling me how much he liked all he had seen. I told him I should insert it.

The *Positio* argues that what distinguishes Bellasis' text from Buckle's is that Bellasis saw Cornelia "as a pilgrim."[22] I suggest that Bellasis—in spite of her persistently convent-tinged vocabulary—had a greater sense of Cornelia as woman than Buckle had. For Buckle, Cornelia was first and foremost the foundress. Bellasis, by contrast, could write:

> Hidden in the depths of Mother Connelly's heart, far below the strain and burden of her outward life as the head of a growing Religious order, was the constant solicitude about her children. How often the young life around her must have recalled unbidden memories of the beautiful children to whom she was once the centre of love and joy and home.[23]

Bellasis' manuscript was well received within the Society, so why was it not published? The historical commissioners explain that "Mother Mary Catherine Gompertz, who had been her assistant, came to the conclusion that it was not suitable for publication and she spoke to the then Reverend Mother General, M M Francis Tolhurst, in this sense."[24] Reading the text today, even if one presupposes the reader's shared enthusiasm for Cornelia, it is clear that the judgment of Gompertz was sound. Bellasis has written

---

[22] *Positio*, 1128.
[23] D75:651.
[24] D72:iii.

with affection and has provided much firsthand detail that would otherwise have been lost. But she has not produced a biography which could survive a disinterested reading.

Cardinal Gasquet

When it became clear that Bellasis' manuscript could not be published, Francis Tolhurst approached Aidan Gasquet, a monk of Downside and Cardinal Protector of the Society,[25] who was at that time resident in Rome, and asked him if he would undertake the writing of a biography. Gasquet's mother had been at school at St Leonards and, as a small child, he had himself met Cornelia.

His surviving letters make it plain that he understood his task, not as original research, but as a thorough editing and rewriting of Bellasis' text. He wrote to Tolhurst from Rome (22 October 1919): "It needs a great deal of cutting about and leaving out." And again (19 December 1919): "I calculate that it is about 230,000 words, about 3 x what it should be .... Is the writer still alive? If so, she might be hurt by such a treatment of her work. What about this?" On 5 February 1920 he wrote to Wilfrid Meynell at Burns and Oates: "I have been at work at odd moments on a Life of Mother Connelly and have done much, for the material was already collected by the nuns."

Ultimately his efforts were not acceptable to the Society. In modern parlance he had done a cut-and-paste job, when the nuns had been hoping for a work of some literary merit. In a letter to Agnes Domitilla Dobson, of 19 March 1953, Gompertz explains why Gasquet's work was deemed unsatisfactory, and how Tolhurst carried out the delicate task of informing the cardinal that his manuscript had been rejected:

> Reverend Mother Mary Francis [Tolhurst] told me that she had confided the Life to Cardinal Gasquet; and as soon as he had completed it she sent it to me. I told her that it would not do at all. He had simply cut up M M Francis' Life and put bits together very unskilfully. He had added nothing original; and had disimproved rather than improved M M Francis' attempt.

---

[25] Gasquet was "involved in international diplomacy between England and the Holy See, in Anglo-Vatican historical research, and in the reorganization of the Beda and *Venerabile* colleges in Rome .... He remained, however, an active and much-esteemed Cardinal Protector of the SHCJ until his death in 1929." (*Positio*, 1436)

> Eventually M M Francis [Tolhurst] asked the Cardinal to call on her at Cavendish Square, which he did. She took me into the parlour with her and then I was witness to the most astonishing scene. M M Francis was telling a Prince of the Church that his work was not what was wanted; and she did it with such perfect humility, straightforwardness, truth and courtesy that he could not be offended. He accepted his practical dismissal in the same spirit, and they parted in perfect friendliness, she telling him that she was going to give the task to me.

So friendly was the parting that Gasquet wrote a preface to Gompertz' life when it was finally published in 1922. In it he summarises his understanding of Cornelia's holiness, identifying her submission to God's will, her self-possession, her calmness and her willingness to embrace suffering as its characteristics. But this account of what was to be valued in Cornelia's holiness may say more about Gasquet and his time than it does about Cornelia:

> I … express my own deep appreciation of the high personal qualities, the manifest holiness and the indefatigable labours for God of this courageous woman … the expressions I have used are not in any way exaggerated … I feel sure that few women could ever have worked under more complete submission to God's Providence than Mother Connelly displayed during the whole course of her life. Acting on this principle she was always able to show to the outside world, and even to those intimate with her, that complete self-possession, cheerfulness and calmness for which she was remarkable.[26]

> Mother Connelly was indeed a wonderful woman and a true saint, closely united to God, ready and even anxious to suffer for Him, and wholly resigned to His Will.[27]

Mary Catherine Gompertz: *The Life of Cornelia Connelly*, 1922

The Life of Cornelia Connelly 1909-1879, Foundress of the Society of the Holy Child Jesus, by A Member of the Society, with a Preface by Cardinal Gasquet, published by Longmans, Green and Co., received good reviews; though a number of people seem to have presumed that Francis Bellasis was the

---

[26] Cardinal Gasquet, Preface to Mary Catherine Gompertz, *The Life of Cornelia Connelly, 1809-1879* (London: Longman, Green & Co., 1922), ix.

[27] Gasquet, Preface to Gompertz, *The Life of Cornelia Connelly,* xiii.

author. Fr O'Hare SJ, for instance, wrote to the Mother General on 19 October 1922: "Ever since I knew M M Francis Bellasis in Oxford, I have looked forward anxiously to the completion of her work on the story of your venerable Foundress—and now I have had a rare treat. The book is of thrilling interest."

The author was, however, Catherine Gompertz. Unlike Buckle and Bellasis, Gompertz had not known Cornelia personally, and so was obliged to rely heavily on the material that they had collected. In a letter of 4 September 1929 to Atchison, Gompertz acknowledges her dependence on Buckle: "In order, however, to avoid forever quoting Mother Maria Joseph, I sometimes mentioned her by name, sometimes spoke of her as 'one of the Religious,' 'an eye witness,' 'a sister,' etc." As for Bellasis' text, a slim red notebook in Gompertz' handwriting, which has been preserved in the Oxford archives, reveals how systematically she used it, both in its original form and as modified by Gasquet.

In the notebook, Gompertz made a list of her criticisms of the Cardinal's Life, with paginated examples, and drew up charts, with page references, in which she placed her own text alongside those of Bellasis and Gasquet. Her changes, therefore, were both deliberate and significant. The notebook also contains revealing jottings to herself, such as (page 14) "General Criticisms to bear in mind. Don't be too down on Pierce at first. Don't talk too much about beauty." And again (page 21) "Mention Preston amalgamation. Don't talk too much about her beauty."

Gompertz had assisted the ageing Bellasis in her task, and now she had superseded her. A sense of the tension that must have arisen between the two women can be glimpsed in the comment of Gompertz to Atchison (4 September 1929): "Personally, I would not attach absolute credit to either M M Francis Bellasis or M M Veronica [Clack] in their reminiscences. I have found both inaccurate sometimes." And Bellasis' pained reaction to the published life is all too apparent in an undated note in her handwriting:

> N.B. I have been told that it is my duty to leave the following statement in writing, regarding this, my original m/s of the Life of our Mother Foundress, Cornelia Connelly—That I can vouch for the truth of all it contains; that I know of nothing that is false, or exaggerated in it. I cannot make the same statement of the published "Revised Life" by Longmans, Green & Co, 1922. Signed Mth Mary Francis (Bellasis) SHCJ.

That Gompertz seems to have been required to work on her biography in some secrecy must have compounded this situation. In a letter to Atchison of 19 October 1932, Gompertz outlined her difficulties:

> When I was told to write the Life I was forbidden to let anyone know I was doing it, except the General Council and my Superior. Everybody knew I was engaged on some work, but some people thought it was the Annals, and others that it was a book on psychology. Until it actually appeared, the Society believed that Cardinal Gasquet was writing the Life. This prevented me from questioning Mother M Francis B about anything; though I believe her ideas on Mother Foundress had rather crystallized into the forms in which she had written them down, and over which she had naturally been brooding for years.

Gompertz was conscious of the possibility that the cause of Cornelia's canonisation might be introduced; and it was with this end in view that the Society had looked for publication. The purpose of the biography was to demonstrate Cornelia's sanctity, and Gompertz wanted her text to be able to stand up to "the closest investigation." As she explained to Atchison on 4 September 1929:

> I always had before my mind the thought that Mother Foundress might some day be canonised, and that the book would then stand as the basis. For that reason I was most scrupulously careful not to invent anything, and to write as surmise what appeared likely, but was not certainly known. However, knowing nothing myself [i.e., not having known Cornelia personally], I was obliged to rely on the material collected by Mth M Francis (B) and Mth Maria Joseph. Evidently some of this material is incorrect in detail.

Gompertz saw her lack of personal knowledge and her dependence on secondary sources as a disadvantage. But she had a clear authorial stance, which is apparent from the very first paragraphs of her biography. Her intention was to demonstrate Cornelia's sanctity to the general public and, possibly, to the Church authorities, should the cause for her canonisation be introduced. In paragraph two of the first chapter, Gompertz reveals her concept of sanctity:

The secret of sanctity and of happiness is to yield ourselves up into the Hands of God, trusting His Power and His Love, without understanding.[28]

Gompertz was a woman of her time, and she inevitably speaks of spirituality in a dualistic way, dichotomizing the natural and the supernatural.[29] This, together with her sense that there is an essential link between suffering and sanctity,[30] leads her to see the "natural" as the enemy of spiritual growth. Her language is unequivocal. When Cornelia is left at Grand Coteau after Pierce has departed for Europe with their young son, for instance, she writes:

> Her chief enemies were her thoughts and affections, which would, in spite of herself, follow her husband and her little son across the ocean; or dwell on memories of what had passed away. While determined to overcome these obstacles to perfection …. She knows that her old self must die, and she condemns it to death without mercy. All must be for God, nothing for the indulgence of imagination or memory. The time for consolation is not now. Her God is He Who came to bring not peace but the sword, and she ruthlessly seizes the sword with her own hands to cut away every useless gratification.[31]

And this is no isolated example. Gompertz emphasizes the suffering in Cornelia's life, and holds up her silence and self-control in the face of it for admiration. Typically, she writes:

> Once again in this separation [from the children] the clash of natural and spiritual claims had become acute for the mother, and once again she had silently conquered.[32]

For Gompertz, this conquest was part of Cornelia's attainment of perfection; and there is some indication that Gompertz understood

---

[28] Gompertz, *The Life of Cornelia Connelly*, 1.

[29] For example, Gompertz, *The Life of Cornelia Connelly*, 42: "It was from her own experience that Cornelia Connelly taught her nuns in after years that God cannot begin to unite a soul to Himself until He has by sorrow closed the door to all merely natural happiness."

[30] For example, Gompertz, *The Life of Cornelia Connelly*, 24: "As she was destined to do a great work for God and to attain to high sanctity in its fulfilment, her purification came with a more searching and terrible intensity than in ordinary cases."

[31] Gompertz, *The Life of Cornelia Connelly*, 47.

[32] Gompertz, *The Life of Cornelia Connelly*, 102. For other examples see 92, 159, 160, 174, 182, 186, 229, 233, 447, 449.

perfection to be a fixed state attainable by those specially graced. Discussing Cornelia's early notebooks, for instance, she comments that they have "a fixity of purpose which intensifies but does not change."[33]

Yet, in common with all Cornelia's biographers, Gompertz marries any claim that Cornelia achieved perfection with an acknowledgement of her faults, her weaknesses, her mistakes and her errors of judgment.[34] She even seems to recognise the limitations of a definition of holiness in terms of personal perfection when she comments that, for Cornelia, "sanctity meant the fulfilling of God's will, not mere individual perfection."[35] Similarly, in spite of her tendency to polarise the natural and the supernatural, we find her linking together Cornelia's "spirit of obedience and her native common sense," and her "faith and common sense." If suffering is a component of holiness, so too is human happiness, energy and gaiety: "To the end she kept the cheerfulness, and even at times the gaiety which had always formed such an attractive feature of her sanctity."[36]

Yet, when Gompertz introduces Cornelia for the first time, she implicitly associates her with the martyr saints, using emotive language that clearly signals the view of Cornelia she is going to present:

> The life of Cornelia Connelly is a record of intense and continuous sufferings of heart and mind, borne not merely with resignation to God's Will, but with an unalterable serenity and joy of spirit at which friends and enemies alike marvelled. Physical torture even pagans have braved for love or duty, but it has been left to the saints to show an equal courage in the greater sufferings of the soul. Divine Love is the secret of their power. Cornelia Connelly had tasted the happiness of perfect human love. She was loved more devotedly and in more varieties of relationship than falls to the lot of most women. But when God took possession first of her intellect and then of her heart, her love for Him became an impelling force which stopped at no sacrifice and ever goaded her on to greater activity in His service.[37]

Today we would question these claims: did Cornelia endure suffering with "unalterable" serenity? Did she experience "perfect human love"? But the

---

[33] Gompertz, *The Life of Cornelia Connelly*, 48.

[34] Gompertz, *The Life of Cornelia Connelly*, 152-153, 216, 246-247, 248, 409.

[35] Gompertz, *The Life of Cornelia Connelly*, 248.

[36] Gompertz, *The Life of Cornelia Connelly*, 468. See also 296, 308, 314, 330.

[37] Gompertz, *The Life of Cornelia Connelly*, 2.

paragraph is extremely revealing of its author's spirituality, of her concept of holiness, and especially of her approach to her subject—her conscious presentation of Cornelia as a suitable candidate for canonisation.

Cornelia's cause was not, in the event, introduced as the Society had hoped. Agostino della Virgine, the Trinitarian Father who was consulted, gave as his opinion that there could be no possibility of a process of canonisation being introduced because, as he saw it at that time, the only witness to Cornelia's sanctity was Buckle, through the information she provided in her manuscript life. (By the 1960s much more material had been amassed: eventually 55 volumes of Cornelia's notebooks and letters and 85 volumes of additional documentation were presented to the Historical Section of the Congregation for Rites.)

Nevertheless, the object of this first published life was to outline Cornelia's story as clearly as possible; and the hope was that accurate information would thus be easily available to any postulator. But the facts of Cornelia's life are dramatic, shocking, even scandalous. And there were evidently some, even as late as 1922, who found those facts (especially concerning the Society's own divisions and disloyalties) distasteful, and who doubted the wisdom of making them public. Some notes written by Mother St John McMaster make a robust defence of Gompertz' biography. After citing Cardinal Gasquet, Bishop Amigo, Father Cuthbert and Father Galton SJ as being among those who had urged the Society to "be perfectly frank," she continues:

> The older nuns know that the facts are correct. Did people say to the Evangelists that they were disloyal to the College of Apostles when they wrote, "And the disciples all leaving him fled" or for making St Peter's denial public? We do not want to say, here again, that the truth has been shirked for the sake of making the Life more palatable.[38]

Gompertz' style is more polished than either Buckle's or Bellasis' and, after eighty years, her book is still readable. But the Cornelia she presents is almost exclusively Cornelia the religious, Cornelia the foundress. Gompertz writes from within the convent culture, presuming an audience which

---

[38] Autograph text, Oxford archives.

shares her values. Typical of her style, her attitude, her opinions and her theology is a passage about the moment in 1847 when Cornelia refused to see Pierce in the convent at Derby. Her assumptions about the possibility of achieving perfection, and her presupposition that self-reproach is a sure path to sanctification, are evident:

> But God does not punish without merciful intent a momentary lapse of judgement by a lifelong anguish. Rather we may take it that in the process of her sanctification the poignant pain of self-reproach had its destined work to do, as well as the heavy exterior trials she was called upon to bear. Hers was a strong nature, capable of immense endurance, and needing, perhaps, the subtle refining of interior humiliation to bring it to its perfection.[39]

In spite of her stated intention of introducing Cornelia to a wider audience, it is difficult to avoid the sense that Gompertz is, in fact, writing for other members of the Society. She reinforces the values with which they were familiar, and emphasizes those aspects of Cornelia's story which would reassure women who might be tempted to fret under the constraints of convent life. On occasion, the voice of Gompertz addressing her sisterly readers almost drowns out Cornelia:

> But there is one force that holds the mind steady through all the stress and strain of life, a fact worth noting in this age of neurasthenia and emotional instability: when a soul has made her home in the Heart of God earthly things retain their power to wound, but not to disintegrate, enfeeble or overwhelm.[40]

In more general ways, too, Gompertz interprets Cornelia's experience through the pattern of life in the Society in the 1920s. It is easy to imagine her contemporaries, bound by their own understanding of the vow of obedience and by their personal experiences within religious life, being inspired by a passage such as this:

> It is of interest to note that after her conversion all the important events of Cornelia Connelly's life were guided by God through the instrumentality of others. The light never came in the first instance to herself. Moreover, the

---

[39] Gompertz, *The Life of Cornelia Connelly*, 153.
[40] Gompertz, *The Life of Cornelia Connelly*, 410.

direction she received was in almost every case contrary to her own inclinations. Thus humility and mortification were preserved in her while at the same time a strong assurance was furnished that she was following the Will of God in her undertakings.[41]

For over thirty years the biography by Gompertz remained the only published life of Cornelia in English, and consequently it was deeply formative for whole generations in the Society. Gompertz' view of Cornelia and of her holiness became the received view. A second edition, abridged and revised, appeared in 1924, and a third in 1930. The centenary of the founding of the Society was celebrated in 1946, and consequently a fourth edition of Gompertz' biography, "revised and in part rewritten" appeared in 1950. But this was the work of Marie Thérèse Bisgood, and is discussed below.

Juliana Wadham: *The Case of Cornelia Connelly*, 1956

The Case of Cornelia Connelly, published in 1956, seems to have reached a less specialised readership than its predecessors, perhaps because the author was herself a laywoman. And it seems to have caused something of a stir. Certainly a correspondence ensued between Raymond Mortimer, who had reviewed the book in *The Sunday Times,* and T. McGarvey, a priest from Warrington, about whether Wadham had or had not revealed "lurid details" about Cornelia's life which, until the publication of the book, the Church had "hushed up." Wadham's "details" are, in fact, no more "lurid" than those supplied by Gompertz. The stir is perhaps, therefore, attributable to Wadham's choice of title: *The Case of Cornelia Connelly* has a racy ring, suggesting that the text might be more revelatory than it actually proved to be.

Wadham, a past pupil of the Society's schools at St Leonards and Mayfield, was a married woman in her twenties and expecting her fourth child when she embarked on her biography. She did not know what she thought about Cornelia; nothing had been written for thirty years; and, she felt that the nuns' opinions of Cornelia and their attitudes towards her were unclear too. Wadham believed that she had the full support of the Society in

---

[41] Gompertz, *The Life of Cornelia Connelly*, 47.

researching and publishing her text. In the 1950s the Cornelian materials had not been catalogued in any way, and Wadham says that at the generalate of the Society in Rome she was offered a suitcase full of original letters and documents to peruse and draw on as she wished.[42] The first of the acknowledgements in the book reads:

> I would like, above all, to thank the nuns of the Society of the Holy Child Jesus who have made this book possible. Although they had no influence upon my desire to write it, and it in no way reflects their opinion, this life of Cornelia Connelly could not have been written without their consent. They have put no restrictions in the way of my research, have made no attempt to impose their views and have been most generous in their help over original documents and letters.

An extant series of letters between Wadham and various members of the Society (particularly Marie Thérèse Bisgood, Philip Koe and Clara Eales) confirms that they and others were consulted during the preparation and revision of the book and that the manuscript was submitted to Rev. Leonard Whatmore, one of the historical consultors for Cornelia's cause appointed by the diocese of Southwark. There is, however, some hint in the correspondence that the nuns, whilst they answered all her queries as fully as they could, may have had reservations about the book.[43] Bisgood, for instance, wrote to Clara Eales (4 March 1955):

> I have just heard from Jill Wadham announcing that she has practically finished her book on Rev. Mother Foundress! Not having heard for so long one thought she had given up the idea, but no. She asks one or two questions …

Wadham undertook original research and came to her own conclusions, but she was obviously sensitive to the effect of her book on the congregation. A letter from Wadham to the Superior General (Genevieve France) of 20 October 1955 gives a flavour of her attitudes both to issues in

---

[42] Information provided in a personal conversation, 3 November 1998.

[43] Mary St Mark Dallas, the superior at Cavendish Square, consulted Cardinal Bernard William Griffin about the advisability of allowing a lay person to embark upon a biography, and in effect asked his permission for this development (Letter in the Westminster diocesan archives).

Cornelia's life and to the sensibilities of the Society. The letter contains a series of numbered queries and observations, including:

> (4) I have tried all the time to be as accurate as possible and I think you may be a bit surprised at some of the conclusions I have been led to but these seem, from the facts, to be unavoidable. For instance, it was Pierce alone and entirely who started the idea of Catholicism, not Cornelia. And it was Cornelia, not Asperti, who refused to see Pierce on his second arrival at the Derby convent …

> (5) Rupert House. This is a point which I have worked over again and again …. It is with great reluctance that I have been forced to the conclusion that over the matter of Emily Bowles Cornelia did not act quite as one would wish. I hope you will not think I have made too much of this …. If there are any documents or papers that you can find in Rome to contradict my conclusions in Chapter 12 I shall be only too relieved.

Whatever the state of relations between Wadham and the Society, James Walsh SJ, who had been appointed vice-postulator of Cornelia's cause in the Southwark diocese in January 1958, made a blistering attack on her biography in two articles in *The Month*. These were subsequently reprinted as a pamphlet, *The Vocation of Cornelia Connelly*. His attack is of particular interest here because its primary concern was Wadham's attitude to Cornelia's holiness. An explanatory note on the first page of the pamphlet reads:

> The author of this pamphlet (reprinted from *The Month*) is the Diocesan Postulator for the Cause of the Beatification of Mother Connelly. He believes that *The Case of Cornelia Connelly* may well be an obstacle to the spread of devotion to the Servant of God—a belief borne out by personal experience whilst promoting the Cause in recent journeys in the USA. Hence he has considered himself obliged to subject this book to a searching criticism, from the point of view of Mother Connelly's reputation for holiness. He has no desire to impugn the book's substantial merits in other directions, and least of all, its author's personal integrity.[44]

In her preface, Wadham acknowledges her interest in Cornelia's saintliness: "In Cornelia Connelly I thought I had found the perfect

---

[44] James Walsh SJ, *The Vocation of Cornelia Connelly* (London: *The Month*, 1959), unnumbered front page.

opportunity to study a saint at close quarters."[45] And—though Walsh's pamphlet queries this—she seems to accept that Cornelia was, in fact, a saint: "It is impossible, I think, to escape from the fact that, whatever her faults, and like all saints she had them, Cornelia was a woman of outstanding spiritual graces and capacities."[46] The assumptions about holiness and saintliness that underpin Wadham's discussion of Cornelia's spiritual growth are stated clearly: "Sanctity is a supernatural state. It has little natural appeal ... [It is the concern] of those who desire perfection and the realisation of God's love for them."[47]

And in a final paragraph (in which she also claims that her approach to the biographical material is unbiased, impartial, objective, factual—a claim modern students of biography will automatically find suspect) she outlines the issues that concerned her as she wrote the life:

> It is difficult for us, as it must have been for her, to decide how near Cornelia came to realising God's will for her .... But however one decides in her regard, from the facts—and throughout I have tried to let them speak for themselves and, in situations where it is impossible to reconcile two opposing opinions, or to decide upon which is the most likely, to give them both as accurately as I can—one thing must, I think, be clear. This is no case of hysterical piety or hypercritical attainment. It is an exploration of how human personality can survive such cruel pressures of circumstance to become, if not a saint in the sense of canonisation, then a saint in the sense of complete identification with the will of God. That, more than the trial which is the climax to the first half of her life, provides THE CASE OF CORNELIA CONNELLY.[48]

If Wadham makes a claim for objectivity, Walsh's pamphlet demonstrates his emotional engagement with Cornelia, and his determination to defend her against criticism of any kind. (In an appreciation circulated among SHCJ after Walsh's death, Elizabeth Mary Strub describes him as a "sometimes overenthusiastic defender" of Cornelia.)

---

[45] Juliana Wadham, *The Case of Cornelia Connelly* (London: Collins, 1956), 15.

[46] Wadham, *The Case of Cornelia Connelly*, 16.

[47] Wadham, *The Case of Cornelia Connelly*, 17.

[48] Wadham, *The Case of Cornelia Connelly*, 17.

Walsh takes issue with Wadham's theology, castigating what we might call her "low" view of holiness, and implying that it is basically heretical:

> At the root of Mrs Wadham's defective analysis of Cornelia's holiness [is] an unconsciously Pelagian outlook, in which it is taken for granted that sanctity is capable of being explained exhaustively in terms of modern psychology.[49]

His own approach to the theology of holiness is, by contrast, "high"—and firmly linked to the value placed on a life of suffering:

> That holiness is revealed in its perfect lineaments in the person of Christ our Lord, and in the saints in their possession of the spirit of Christ, in that keeping of the word which is to "receive Him" and to live His life; that holiness is to be nailed with Christ to His Cross so that it is not the servant living but Christ living in the servant—it is this supernatural fact that Mrs Wadham fails so often to allow for and account for.[50]

Our primary concern here is with Wadham's views rather than Walsh's. Nevertheless, his pamphlet highlights Wadham's focus on Cornelia's struggle, the cost in human terms of her desire to be faithful to the perceived will of God. Wadham explores Cornelia's limitations and weaknesses in a way that is not consistent with Walsh's notion of saintliness: "sanctity which reproduces in an extraordinary manner the holiness which Christ our Lord, in His human life on earth, revealed ...."[51] It is this definition of holiness that obliges Walsh to defend Cornelia against any suggestion of imperfection, whilst Wadham's definition leaves her free to acknowledge Cornelia's human dilemmas.

The Case of Cornelia Connelly differs from the earlier biographies primarily because Wadham adopts a more openly questioning and critical stance towards Cornelia than her predecessors did (though Buckle, Bellasis and Gompertz all acknowledge Cornelia's mistakes, errors of judgement and weaknesses). In conversation in November 1998 Wadham suggested that Cornelia was litigious and, on occasion, duplicitous; and she expressed her difficulties with any woman who "abandoned her children."

---

[49] Walsh, *The Vocation of Cornelia Connelly*, 9.
[50] Walsh, *The Vocation of Cornelia Connelly*, 9.
[51] Walsh, *The Vocation of Cornelia Connelly*, 5.

For all this, and in spite of being addressed to a more general readership, the book seems to have been written without any questioning of the assumptions of convent culture. Whilst one might expect a pregnant author in her twenties to be drawn to the personal, and tragic, aspects of Cornelia's life—the breakup of her marriage and her loss of contact with her children—Wadham, like her predecessors, ultimately wrote a life of the founder of the Society rather than the woman. Though the circumstances of her own life have some painful parallels with Cornelia's (she too has lost children), in 1998 she seemed to make no connections between Cornelia and herself. Cornelia belonged to the nuns; Cornelia the wife and mother was submerged.

Marie Thérèse Bisgood: *Cornelia Connelly: A Study in Fidelity*, 1963

Letters in the Oxford archives reveal that Bisgood was responsible for the 1950 revision of Gompertz' Life, and that it was this project that subsequently led her to write an entirely new biography. In 1946, the celebration of the centenary of the Society's foundation had revived interest in Cornelia's story, and it seemed opportune to revise the biography rather than just reprint it. Gompertz felt unequal to the task. Genevieve France, the superior general, wrote to Mary Paul O'Connor, the English provincial (5 December 1948):

> I quite understand M M Catherine's attitude. Her heart was not in it from the first; as M M Thérèse suggests, she is probably too old. And one does lose energy for attack as one gets older! It would be waste of time to ask her under the circumstances, because she would not do it well. I think M M Thérèse would do it well. As to the extent of the revision necessary you and she together will have to judge.

On 7 January 1949 France wrote to Bisgood, informing her that "speed is of the essence." And she certainly seems to have worked at speed. The dust jacket of the new edition claimed that the book "has been completely revised and rewritten," and yet Bisgood evidently completed the task of updating in a couple of months. On 9 March 1949 Mary Callista McLaughlin wrote to her:

> You must be greatly relieved to have finished the revision of the book—at least of the text. Doubtless you will have hours of work completing all the etceteras.

So the fourth edition of Gompertz' biography appeared. But already, in 1949, France queried the wisdom of merely revising, and proposed that a new biography be undertaken. To Bisgood she wrote (7 January 1949):

> Is the opinion—among those competent to form one—that the whole book should be remodelled, reinterpreted—in fact, rewritten in the modern spirit? Why not do a new book straightaway? ... If any really valid and cogent reasons have since arisen to prove that it would be better to rewrite and modernise the Life I should like to hear them. It would seem to me at present that what is required is a <u>new</u> Life.

Ultimately Bisgood undertook the task of writing the new biography, which appeared as *Cornelia Connelly: A Study in Fidelity* in 1963. I would question the aptness of this title for Bisgood's book, since fidelity does not appear to be a central thread within the text; and a letter of Bisgood's to T. F. Burns at Burns and Oates (18 July 1962) makes clear that this was only one of a number of titles which she was willing to consider:

> A point we did not discuss was the title. "Cornelia Connelly" was that of the previous edition [*sic*]. Do you think it ought to be at least modified, by a subtitle or something? I had thought of "A Study in Fidelity" or "Fortitude" or something like that.

Bisgood, and James Walsh in his introduction to her work, root this biography in the documentation being collected at the time of writing for Cornelia's cause. Walsh writes, "This biography is based on the exhaustive research of the historical commission and its assistants"; and Bisgood states in the Foreword, "the material used has been taken entirely from the documentation collected and classified in the archives of the Cause of Cornelia Connelly in the Old Palace, Mayfield, Sussex." Extant letters show that Bisgood (who was living at St Leonards) was in constant communication with Madeleine Amy and Evangelist Stewart, who were involved in the archival work of collecting and collating.

Yet, in spite of Walsh's claim that it would "correct many mistakes and fill in the lacunae of the previous biographies," telling Cornelia's story "accurately, lucidly and fully, for the first time," this biography is surprisingly similar to its predecessors. It even repeats the claim that Cornelia led Pierce to Catholicism, rather than he her—an inaccuracy that Wadham had corrected seven years earlier.

Bisgood was elderly, 72 years of age, when the biography was published. She seems to have been an extremely reserved person, not particularly in tune with the developments in the contemporary Church when Vatican II was in progress. (In fact, the Society necrologist observes that "She would have been quite at home in an 18th-century salon.") It is hard to escape the suggestion that her biography emphasizes those aspects of Cornelia's personality and spirituality which resembled her own. Over and over again she stresses Cornelia's calmness in the face of every adversity, and praises her lack of emotional response. Bisgood was scholarly, and wrote well about the founder of the congregation, but she seems to have had no grasp of the wider issues with which Cornelia the woman must have struggled.

It is possible, however, that Bisgood's view of Cornelia was distorted in the printed text. I have been informed by several members of the Society that a substantial section on Cornelia's spirituality was cut by the publishers, and that Bisgood's text is thereby impoverished. A letter from Bisgood to Madeleine Amy dated merely "Corpus Christi" appears to confirm this:

> What do you think of Burns and Oates' reader? ... The chief point of course is the omission of those last two chapters. I never meant to lengthen it like that; it was Fr Walsh who made me. But now I suppose it means getting leave to omit them, either from Rev Mother General or the Promotor Fidei, who has read and approved it as it stands. I don't mind putting the Epilogue into the text, except for the bother, but I disagree that the material about CC is already contained in the book, especially if all the cuts are made that the Reader wants. It looks to me as if it will be rather like Hamlet without the Prince of Denmark by the time we've finished ...

This is evidence, at the very least, that she wrote more than was published. But, as far as I can ascertain, the deleted chapters are no longer extant. The remaining text is solidly pre-Vatican II in attitude and theology.

Bisgood's biography, like its predecessors, reveals a dependence on Buckle's initial choice of anecdotes, events and emphases—and a marked tendency to replicate her conventionally hagiographical approach. Like the others, it concentrates on demonstrating Cornelia's virtues and justifying or explaining away her human failings and limitations. And it illustrates her holiness by stressing individual virtues (notably calmness in the face of adversity) and by suggesting that Cornelia had in some way reached a state of perfection. It was not until the material supporting the cause for Cornelia's canonisation was presented in the 1980s that this basic approach was substantially challenged.

The Institute of SHCJ Studies and Ursula Blake

The history of the biographies of Cornelia is, at least from the 1950s onwards, inextricably linked with the process for the cause of Cornelia's canonisation, which was formally introduced in 1953. Three SHCJ, Madeleine Amy, Clara Eales and Evangelist Stewart, researched exhaustively the extant documentation about Cornelia's life, and prepared it for presentation to the diocesan commission in Southwark. James Walsh SJ had been vice-postulator since 1958, and Paul Molinari SJ became postulator in 1960 after the diocesan process was completed and the cause was submitted to the Sacred Congregation in Rome.

In 1966 Walsh proposed that an Institute for the Historical Studies of the Society of the Holy Child Jesus and its Spirituality be established; for the next ten years the SHCJ members of the Institute engaged in scholarly research and reflection on many aspects of Cornelia's life and spirituality. Caritas McCarthy was appointed director of the Institute, but its most significant and influential member was Ursula Blake.

Blake was a scholar by inclination and a linguist by training, having read French and Italian at Oxford. She had been headmistress at St Leonards for sixteen years, when, in the mid-1950s, she became a student at the newly opened Regina Mundi Institute in Rome, writing a master's thesis on christology. Subsequently she edited *The Pylon*, a Society journal in which Cornelian topics were frequently aired. In 1969 she became the first woman president of Regina Mundi and negotiated its recognition as a pontifical institute and its affiliation to the Gregorian University. In 1972 Blake was asked to undertake the writing of the *Positio*, the formal investigation into Cornelia's heroic sanctity that was required by the Sacred Congregation if her cause was to proceed. In this task she was assisted by other SHCJ, notably Annette Dawson; but it was her own scholarship and perception that shaped the text.

She worked on the *Positio* under the direction and guidance of Fabijan Veraja, at that time Aiutante di Studio of the Historical Section of the Congregation—though Walsh and Molinari also contributed insights. By 1984, only the *Informatio*—the introductory section of the *Positio*—remained to be written. But Blake's health was deteriorating, and she returned to England after thirty years in Rome. Walsh therefore committed himself to the writing of the *Informatio*, but he never actually began the work. Elizabeth Mary Strub explains:

> He … made gestures towards getting into position to write it, but by this time he was pretty ill in a chronic way. My instinct tells me that he rationalised putting it off on the grounds that all causes were being held up by the patterns of beatification and canonisation introduced by John Paul II, telling himself there was time enough, but that in fact he lacked the energy and clarity of mind to make what he thought of as a grand summing up of all he knew of Cornelia's holiness. He died without beginning the *Informatio*.[52]

Instead, it was Strub herself who wrote the *Informatio*.

Elizabeth Mary Strub: The *Informatio*, 1987

The Congregation for the Causes of Saints equates holiness with heroic virtue, and requires that the life of each prospective saint be presented in such a way as to demonstrate that he or she has practised the theological and moral virtues to a heroic degree. As she arranged the material for the *Informatio*, Strub recognised the limitations of this approach. She was constrained by ecclesiastical requirements and obliged to present Cornelia's life under the headings of her heroic virtues, but she contrived to widen the portrait that she drew.

Contrary to the Congregation's guidelines, Strub took as her starting point, not the virtues that had to be proved, but the life that Cornelia lived: "categories … Cornelia dictates to me, not what I dictate to her."[53] So she was free to explore Cornelia's life more fully (her experiences of marriage and motherhood as well as her achievements as a religious founder) and to

---

[52] Elizabeth Mary Strub, "James Walsh, Cornelia Connelly and the Society of the Holy Child Jesus," *Letters and Notices*, 87 (Christmas 1986), 194.
[53] Strub, quoted in Woodward, *Making Saints*, 274.

stress the virtues that she believed Cornelia particularly embodied. The *Informatio* departs from the notion of holiness as a state of perfection, and provides some sense that Cornelia continued throughout her life to grow and develop in what the Sacred Congregation calls holiness but Strub prefers to call the love of God.

Strub takes an explicitly Ignatian approach to Cornelia's spirituality. Along with the others engaged in Cornelian research at this period, she came strongly under the influence of Walsh and Molinari. From them the SHCJ scholars learned of developments in Ignatian studies, and of what amounted to a rediscovery of the Exercises in an individually guided form.[54] As they experienced and came to value these new approaches in their own lives, they inevitably noticed and emphasized the Ignatian influences, patterns and attitudes in Cornelia's spirituality too. (Strub has since written an account of Cornelia's dependence on Ignatius and the Exercises.)[55] This personal interest of the biographer has possibly led to some distortion: Strub's Cornelia responds to Christ through the framework of the Exercises, and her Ignatian roots are exhaustively explored; but the influence of Francis de Sales and Francis of Assisi on her spirituality, whilst acknowledged, is less fully researched.

Strub was unquestionably both original and creative in her approach to the ecclesiastical requirements for the *Informatio*. Woodward praises her work, calling it "a spirited departure" from the norm.[56] Nevertheless he makes a serious criticism of her presentation:

> [A]s a whole [it] still remains something less than a full-scale study in spiritual development because no account is provided of the moral faults or other weaknesses of character others saw in her.[57]

This is a major flaw if the *Informatio* is being examined as biography. But, as a study of holiness, Woodward believes that Strub's approach is

---

[54] After Vatican II, the Jesuits, like all other religious congregations, re-examined the original inspiration of their founder—Ignatius of Loyola. One result of this renewal was the retrieval and promotion of the individually guided (rather than preached) approach to making Ignatius' Spiritual Exercises.

[55] Elizabeth Mary Strub, *Ignatius, the Spiritual Exercises and Cornelia: A Retreat By All Means* (San Diego: Society of the Holy Child Jesus, 1996).

[56] Woodward, *Making Saints*, 274.

[57] Woodward, *Making Saints*, 278.

theologically important. Whilst she has respected the Congregation's requirement to demonstrate Cornelia's heroic virtue, her interest has not been primarily in the virtues themselves but in Cornelia's developing relationship with God:

> It is difficult not to conclude, therefore, that the harmony one finds in her life, the uniqueness and integrity of her virtues, the calm in the eye of so many storms, is not the mastery of moral skills but the gift of God's love. In short, the theological message appears to be that saints are not holy because they are virtuous, but virtuous because they are holy.[58]

Radegunde Flaxman: *A Woman Styled Bold*, 1991

A Woman Styled Bold, published in 1991, is more scholarly and more substantial than any of the earlier biographies. It is grounded in the materials collected for the cause of Cornelia's canonisation and draws upon two major thematic studies of Cornelia: John Marmion's doctoral thesis of 1984, *Cornelia Connelly's Work in Education, 1848-1879*, and Caritas McCarthy's *The Spirituality of Cornelia Connelly: In God, For God, With God*, published in 1986.[59] In this biography the details of Cornelia's story are fleshed out, and a wealth of relevant explanatory background material is provided. We learn a great deal about the places in which Cornelia lived; the people she came to know—even the more minor characters in her story; the legal procedures in which she was caught up; the educational situation which confronted her in England; and the anti-Catholicism and attitudes to converts which prevailed there.

Any biographer is faced with decisions about how to present coherently a constant stream of events and situations which are occurring simultaneously. And Cornelia's life is extraordinarily complex; sometimes there is virtually no material to draw on (hardly anything is known, for instance, about the first twenty years of Cornelia's life, and even later there

---

[58] Woodward, *Making Saints*, 279.

[59] Since the publication of Flaxman's biography there has been further research into Cornelian materials, notably by Susan O'Brien who is exploring the history of women religious in Britain, and by members of the Society in the in-house journals *Source* and *History*.

are tantalising lacunae); at other times there is an *embarras de richesses* in which we know day by day, almost hour by hour, what was happening.

The gaps in Cornelia's story push Flaxman—whose intellectual rigour and integrity cannot be questioned—into the language of speculation and hypothesis. The text is littered with phrases denoting conjecture: "at a guess," "there is a strong likelihood," "something can be surmised," "it can be fairly safely assumed," "developments suggest that," "he would surely have been," "one deduces," "one suspects."[60] Where others might have glossed over a lack of evidence, Flaxman calls attention to it:

> There is no record of what precisely had happened nor of what he now told her, but there is enough evidence to advance a theory.[61]

> The details of the crisis as it developed are now beyond retrieve [*sic*]. Missing pieces of evidence force conjecture. But the main lines of what happened are clear, and because they scarred for ever the hearts and lives of both Connellys and of their children, have their place here.[62]

The limited access to concrete information about the inner lives and personal views of both Cornelia and her husband has two effects on Flaxman's biography. Firstly, she prefers to focus more on external verifiable events than on interior growth and change; and secondly, what speculation there is about the inner world of the main characters is necessarily coloured by the author's own attitudes, assumptions and opinions—and Flaxman's authorial opinion is often strongly worded. For instance, when Pierce left Cornelia behind at Grand Coteau, going to Europe with their son Mercer in the hope of gaining papal sanction for his ordination, Flaxman's judgement is clear:

> No word of Cornelia's survives from this patch of time, not even any protest she made about Merty's removal to England .... Practical wisdom perhaps

---

[60] Radegunde Flaxman, *A Woman Styled Bold: The Life of Cornelia Connelly 1809-1879* (London: Darton, Longman and Todd, 1991), 177, 113, 171, 12, 125, 35, 48, 131. Other examples may be found on 10, 12, 41, 55, 63, 71, 98, 100, 125, 148, 165, 182, 193.

[61] Flaxman, *A Woman Styled Bold*, 98.

[62] Flaxman, *A Woman Styled Bold*, 125.

convinced Cornelia she must agree with the pig-headed Pierce .... But often agreement does not describe the heart's inclinations.[63]

Flaxman's dislike and disapproval of Pierce permeates the whole text. She presents him as a lonely and depressive figure, but her approach to him is consistently unsympathetic. Her attitude is revealed across the biography in epithets, asides, and heavily critical comments:

> If this was indeed heroism for the sake of truth it was also an ill-judged and precipitate action. ...
>
> His action characteristically lacked judgment and disregarded consequences for others. ...
>
> Pierce appears here as an irresponsible trouble-maker. ...
>
> With bare-faced snobbery Pierce told his brother. ...
>
> With snobbish pseudo-humility Pierce informed his brother. ...
>
> Pierce appears as pathetically needy of approval and astonishingly forgetful. ...
>
> It would appear that for her husband the situation was more humiliating than his self-importance could easily bear.[64]

The presentation of Pierce as monstrous, even demonic, is not peculiar to Flaxman, but characteristic of the biographies in general. Yet the acerbity of Flaxman's tone is so evident that when she speaks of Cornelia's "love-hate for her husband"[65] one wonders whether the biographer is confusing her own feelings with those of her subject.

Like her predecessors, Flaxman is concerned to defend Cornelia and to present her in the best possible light. Dealing with those aspects of Cornelia's life which have aroused the most criticism in the past, Flaxman is both explanatory and defensive; occasionally she chooses to minimise an incident. That their contemporaries would have been approving rather than critical of the arrangements which the Connellys made for their children, for instance, is heavily underscored,[66] and the suggestion that Cornelia ever "gave up" her

---

[63] Flaxman, *A Woman Styled Bold*, 82.

[64] Flaxman, *A Woman Styled Bold*, 26, 88, 90, 90, 108, 38, 63. See also 16, 41, 82, 89, 100, 131, 135, 136, 142.

[65] Flaxman, *A Woman Styled Bold*, 135.

[66] Flaxman, *A Woman Styled Bold*, 91-92.

children is presented as untrue. Rather, Cornelia was "devoted to her children," who were initially removed from her care by Wiseman and then "stolen" by the "traitorous"[67] Pierce. Flaxman states unequivocally:

> Although later Cornelia refers to having "given up" her husband for the work of God, she never spoke of having given up her children. On the contrary, when in regard to them fearful injustice and suffering overtook her, she maintained the opposite, passionately.[68]

About other incidents and indictments, however, Flaxman's defence of Cornelia seems less well grounded. A waspish letter of Cornelia's, quoted against her by Pierce, is explained away as "the quick judgment of a lonely woman … probably fearful of what lay before her."[69] Her letters to her young son at Stonyhurst, which reveal a lack of any intuitive sympathy with his situation, are only mildly criticized: "For the twentieth century they smack altogether too much of advice, virtue and piety."[70]

On one occasion Flaxman goes so far as to gloss over a difficult situation in which Cornelia's wisdom, judgement and even integrity might be called into question. As the principal of the teacher training college at St Leonards, Cornelia agreed to a dubious arrangement for a former student of the Liverpool college: she admitted her to St Leonards even though she had already failed her exams in Liverpool. And, for reasons that are not clear, she enrolled the student under her mother's maiden name. Though Flaxman records "how Cornelia felt and acted," this is one incident which she chooses not to record in detail: "The voluminous … twists of this affair have to be left aside."[71] This glossing over is marked because it is uncharacteristic.

Flaxman is not unwilling to acknowledge Cornelia's faults, but she is also defensive about them. Typically she offers a positive spin even as she names the limitation or cause of grievance:

> The love of God moved her to action but it had to be routed through her own imperfect but compelling personality. Given her giftedness and energy

---

[67] Flaxman, *A Woman Styled Bold*, 134, 131.

[68] Flaxman, *A Woman Styled Bold*, 93.

[69] Flaxman, *A Woman Styled Bold*, 197.

[70] Flaxman, *A Woman Styled Bold*, 155-156.

[71] Flaxman, *A Woman Styled Bold*, 251.

it is almost inevitable that accumulated experience made her sometimes too sure and too arbitrary. …

Any ecclesiastic at that date could have mistaken Cornelia's undeniable independence of mind for irreverence, pride or disobedience.[72]

Independence of mind and of spirit are characteristics which Flaxman clearly admires in Cornelia, and she sees them as central, not only to Cornelia's personal development, but also to her relationship with God. Thus, for Flaxman, Cornelia's independence is an integral part of her holiness.[73] She presents Cornelia as a psychologically strong, straightforward and practical woman who was passionate, self-possessed and, above all, compelling (an adjective she uses on a number of occasions).[74] She explores Cornelia's understanding of obedience and of her relationship with the hierarchical church, and her faith and desire for union with God. But the aspect of Cornelia's spirituality which she emphasizes most strongly, at every stage of her life, is her understanding of accepted suffering. At the very beginning of her Catholic life, Cornelia attended the Mass at which Anthony Blanc was consecrated bishop of New Orleans. Flaxman writes: "The homilist's theme (the adopted theme of her own life) was the place of accepted suffering in the life of the Christian."[75]

Flaxman says, summarising the standpoint of the elderly Cornelia— who had experienced dissent among members of the congregation and the bishop's setting aside of the Constitutions that she had written:

> Cornelia had long ago chosen for herself to be poor with Christ poor in the many meanings of that word. Humiliation had often come her way and especially since the cabal, and was always to be accepted as suffering for and with Christ …. As the years passed it was the things she suffered … that taught her more and more deeply how obedience with Christ could be life-giving.[76]

---

[72] Flaxman, *A Woman Styled Bold*, 204-205, 294. See also 122, 221, 263, 272, 293, 294, 296, 298, 341.

[73] Flaxman, *A Woman Styled Bold*, 37. For further exploration of the theme of independence see 33, 108, 111, 122, 170, 205.

[74] Flaxman, *A Woman Styled Bold*, 49, 67, 93, 103, 131, 200, 272, 294.

[75] Flaxman, *A Woman Styled Bold*, 36.

[76] Flaxman, *A Woman Styled Bold*, 310-311. For further exploration of accepted suffering see 39, 71, 79, 127, 195, 312, 315, 344.

It is from comments such as this that Flaxman's views on Cornelia's sanctity have to be inferred: sanctity is not a concept which is discussed explicitly in this biography. And yet, by implication, Flaxman makes some major claims about Cornelia's personal holiness. On a number of occasions she associates Cornelia with major biblical figures and great saints: with Moses and Samuel, King David, the prophet Habakkuk, St Paul and St Francis of Assisi.[77] And, once, she speculates about "whether Cornelia Connelly was a mystic":

> She was reticent about the ways of God upon herself but one may adduce at least that she had sometimes been given direct and profound knowledge of God, so joyfully sure was her conviction of merciful, saving love always at work—even when only darkness and pain surrounded her …. If we attribute this kind of gift from God to her we can believe that her prayer, "Possess me, rule me, inflame me," was granted, and we can better understand how she can tread her path so unswervingly, and speak with such authority as the years went by of the intense consolation with which it filled those who went the same way … [78]

Flaxman had more material to conjure with than her predecessors did, and she handles it skilfully; she is careful never to say more about Cornelia's inner life or her sanctity than the written sources can support. But if we are looking to her for a fresh approach to the biographical task we will be disappointed. The basic format of her book is similar to that adopted by the earlier biographers; it seems largely uninfluenced by current thinking on the genre, and reflects the structure that Virginia Woolf so much deplored: "the old chapter headings—life at college, marriage, career." Further, the biography reflects Flaxman's "*pietas* towards her foundress," and consequently she finds it "difficult to adopt a fundamentally critical approach to her subject."[79] Reviewing Flaxman's biography in *The Guardian* on 9 May 1991, Peter Stanford found it "thoughtful" and "resolutely impious." But ultimately he considered it a "conventional account of an unconventional life."

---

[77] Flaxman, *A Woman Styled Bold*, 70, 103, 108, 200.

[78] Flaxman, *A Woman Styled Bold*, 199-200.

[79] V. Alan McClelland, review of *A Woman Styled Bold* in *Heythrop Journal*, 34 (January 1993), 342.

The framework is basically chronological, an exploration of Cornelia's life from birth to death; Flaxman does not adopt the thematic approach favoured by Edel. ("The task and duty of biographical narrative is to sort out themes and patterns, not dates and mundane calendar events which sort themselves.")[80] Somewhat surprisingly, the structure Flaxman adopts separates Cornelia the wife and mother from Cornelia the foundress. The text is divided into two quite distinct sections—Part One, 1809-1851 (what might be called the Family Years), and Part Two, 1849-1879 (the St Leonards Years); Part Two is even furnished with its own preface. And yet Cornelia the person cannot be so easily divided up; Flaxman not infrequently makes connections across her caesura. She points out, for instance, how motherly Cornelia's approach to education always was,[81] or how the competence, single-mindedness and courage which could be discerned in her as a young woman were strengthened over the years "by responsibility and hard circumstance."[82]

Flaxman's scholarship and erudition offer new insights into the Cornelian biographical material, notably through her thorough research into the background of Cornelia's life, and through her unflinching presentation of the views of Cornelia's adversaries. Cornelia emerges from her account as an intensely private person, much criticized, enduring many misunderstandings, and not easy to know.

Cornelia's Canaries

The exploration in this chapter of the differing and developing presentations of Cornelia suggests that one reason for the differences that have been identified is the personal stance and interests of each biographer. If, to use Virginia Woolf's term, the biographers are Cornelia's canaries, some information about their contexts may help us to understand the differences in the tunes they sing about their subject.

---

[80] Edel, *Writing Lives*, 30.

[81] Flaxman, *A Woman Styled Bold*, 238-239.

[82] Flaxman, *A Woman Styled Bold*, 294.

Maria Joseph Buckle (1822-1902)

Elizabeth Buckle (Maria Joseph) was born in Gloucestershire, the oldest of five children of wealthy evangelical Anglicans. Her father, who had fought at Waterloo, numbered Oliver Cromwell among his ancestors; and her mother claimed descent from a Doge of Venice.[83] Buckle converted to Catholicism, along with her whole family, after her father, an Oxford MA, had been influenced by Newman's conversion. Buckle wrote that Cornelia "became very much attached to both my parents .... She said they reminded her of the holy Patriarchs."[84] Certainly Buckle's father, "a successful business executive,"[85] provided Cornelia with financial assistance. He advanced Maria Joseph's inheritance of £1800 towards the purchase of Layton Hill, and, at Charles Towneley's invitation, became one of the lay trustees of St Leonards.

Buckle's mother attended a number of retreats organised by Cornelia, first at Derby and later at St Leonards; from the evidence of her execrable poetry she was conventionally pious.[86] One of Buckle's sisters became a member of the Visitandine community at Westbury-on-Trym.

Buckle was intelligent and had been carefully educated (though her spelling is sometimes a little uncertain). Her own self-critical summary is that "the faults of my character were increased by a Protestant education, too much indulgence and an over eagerness that has always been an obstacle to my perfection."[87] Within the Society she taught in the schools

---

[83] Manuscript account of Buckle's early life, "The Story of a Vocation" by Mary Xavier Gwynn (Oxford archives).

[84] D78:8.

[85] *Positio*, 1119.

[86] A box of her papers and poems is preserved in the Oxford archives.

[87] D78:63.

and the noviciate, had responsibility for the postulants, and "gave private Retreats to ladies who came for that purpose to the Convent."[88] Her knowledge of classical languages was particularly valued by Cornelia, whose own Latin was limited.[89] For a short time Buckle taught Greek to the older pupils at St Leonards, "so that they could begin to read St John's gospel in the original."[90] She translated the Jesuit Constitutions and the Decrees of their General Congregations from Latin texts provided by Peter Gallwey SJ, as well as the *Ratio Studiorum* and "Father Aquaviva's *Hints for Superiors.*"[91] She also "translated nearly half the Breviary but left off when I heard it was being translated by Lord Bute."[92]

The Society necrologist claims, rather romantically, that:

> Her first wish was to join the English Nuns at Bruges. She was, however, prevented from going abroad by very severe storms & this delay was the means of bringing her to our dear Society.

According to Buckle's own account, she had intended to join the Society of the Sacred Heart, but was encouraged by James Clough SJ, during a retreat at Derby, to join Cornelia's congregation instead.

So, she first met Cornelia in April 1848 and from then on lived with her continuously in community at Derby and St Leonards until 1869. After 1869 Buckle moved to Blackpool, and later to Neuilly. She remained in correspondence with Cornelia, and spent some weeks with her in Neuilly in 1877. In 1879, at Cornelia's request, she returned to St Leonards to be with the founder during her final illness. She spent the rest of her life at Neuilly, dying in 1902 aged 82.

---

[88] D78:61.
[89] D64:153.
[90] *Positio*, 1344 (Chapter XV, note 11).
[91] D78:61, 62.
[92] D78:38.

Mary Francis Bellasis (1842-1923)

A good deal is known about the life of Mary Francis Bellasis (seen here on the left, with her sister Aloysius) prior to her entering the Society, because she was the third daughter of Mr Serjeant Bellasis, a parliamentary lawyer and prominent nineteenth-century convert to Catholicism. His biography, *Memorials of Mr Serjeant Bellasis 1800-1873*, was written by his son Edward and published by Burns, Oates and Washbourne in 1893; it ran to at least three editions.

Serjeant Bellasis and his wife, Eliza Jane Garnett, had thirteen children—four sons and nine daughters—of whom ten survived to adulthood. If this makes Bellasis a Victorian patriarch, he was a liberal, intelligent and loving patriarch. From the evidence both of his biography and of the extant letters between the Serjeant and his children, relationships within the Bellasis family were notably happy, and were marked by mutual respect and intellectual freedom. The *Memorials* quote the Serjeant's own account of his conversion to Catholicism, and it is clear that even in this crucial matter he avoided bringing any pressure to bear on the choices of his wife and children:

> I did not at first put our children under regular instruction, but the elder ones, Margaret, Katherine, and Mary [Cornelia's biographer] went sometimes with me to Catholic churches, and indeed, so did my dear wife, but the children, who knew a good deal, tended more and more to the Catholic religion, till my wife, seeing their disposition, said to me, "I see their hearts are with you, and if you wish to put them under instruction I shall make no opposition." Accordingly on the 3rd of April, [1851] I took my three elder girls to Hill Street, and introduced them to Father Brownbill, and they went regularly to see him every other day until Maundy Thursday,

the 17th, when they were all received into the Church, and made their first
Communion at Farm Street on Easter Sunday.[93]

Bellasis and his wife "had many careful conversations upon various
matters (difficulties at the time) in the Catholic system. These
conversations [he] put to paper in the form of dialogues between
'Philotheus and Eugenia' ...."[94] Mary took responsibility for editing a
selection of these dialogues before she was twenty years old—an interesting
fact in view of her future work as a biographer. The selection appeared in
print as *Philotheus and Eugenia: Dialogues between two Anglicans on Anglican
Difficulties* in 1861—the year that Mary became a novice.

Serjeant Bellasis became a personal friend and adviser to Cornelia. His
daughter's biography of Cornelia provides details of the relationship:

> From his first introduction until his death—a period of eighteen years, he
> was a true and faithful friend and benefactor, ever ready to aid her at any
> personal cost or inconvenience. Let her express a mere wish to see him, he
> thought nothing of spending a night with his Briefs in order to find himself
> free the following morning to run down to St Leonards. She would ... call
> him "Brother Bellasis" .... [F]ive of his daughters [were] placed in the
> school, and he would say, that if he had fifty he would send them all to St
> Leonards![95]

Mary Bellasis was nine when she was received into the Church, at
Easter 1851. Evidently at this time she was being educated at home. Like all
her sisters except the eldest, Margaret, she later attended school at St
Leonards, although her name does not appear in the register until January
1857, when she was almost fifteen. She entered the Society in 1861 taking,
at Bishop Grant's request, the rather ornate religious name Mary Francis of
the Blessed Sacrament. A letter from her father to A. F. Bellasis, written in
November 1861, describes his reaction:

> I first heard of her wishes two years and a half ago, and then told her that it
> was my duty to test her vocation, and that she must come home [from

---

[93] Quoted in Edward Bellasis, *Memorials of Mr Sarjeant Bellasis* (London: Burns, Oates and Washbourne, 1923
[1893]), 96.
[94] Bellasis, *Memorials*, 63.
[95] D74:413.

school], visit with her father's friends, associate with her sisters, go into society with them, and see what kind of a home she had, before I would even consider the subject. She did this, went to balls and parties like the rest, visited among our friends, accompanied us into Switzerland last year, and was as bright and merry as the best of them, and during two years the subject was never mentioned. At the end of that time … I talked to her, and found her heart set upon it, and so, after taking the best and most skilful advice I could get, I consented, and she has been now four months in the convent, and her letters are full of the "intense happiness" she feels. Happily it is an Order which is not shut up, but occupied in teaching and in visiting the poor, so that we can see her and hear of her as often as we like.[96]

Her father's biography provides ample evidence that Francis Bellasis was the child of a happy and prosperous family in which affections were easily expressed, ideas were exchanged, and spirituality was accepted as part of daily life. Even before their conversion to Catholicism, her parents attended the daily service at "a small chapel in Margaret Street."[97] She was a member of the Society for eighteen years before Cornelia's death and, living at St Leonards and Mayfield, came to know her superior well.

The necrologist describes Bellasis as "gifted with strong intellectual powers, and great force of character"; and Cornelia quickly entrusted her with responsibility. Five years after her final profession she was appointed novice mistress, a post she was still holding at the time of Cornelia's death. She continued to be valued by Cornelia's successor, Angelica Croft. According to the necrologist:

> In 1886 Mother [Mary Francis] was sent to Rome by Reverend Mother Angelica in company with Mother Maria Rita Bethell to present a petition for the approbation of our Rule, and for over a year she worked with the Jesuit Father Cardella in making the necessary adjustments to Mother Foundress' original draft. She was thus instrumental in procuring the five years' approbation granted in 1887 by the Holy Father Leo XIII, and less immediately in that granted by the same Pontiff in 1892, in perpetuum.

Bellasis served for many years on the general council of the Society and continued to be a local superior until she was over seventy, by which time she was also engaged in writing the biography. She is, in fact, Cornelia's

---

[96] Quoted in Bellasis, *Memorials*, 150.

[97] Bellasis, *Memorials*, 39.

oldest biographer, 77 years old when her text was completed. Her necrology records:

> Her declining years were spent at Harrogate, where her venerable figure, slowly making its way to the Chapel, was a source of inspiration to the Community and Children alike .... Her happy and peaceful death took place on June 8th 1927, and her two Oratorian brothers attended the last Rites.

Mary Catherine Gompertz (1880-1963)

Little is recorded of the childhood of Elsie Gompertz, except that she was born and grew up in British India. When she was 13 she was sent to school at St Leonards; she then spent a year at the Holy Child finishing school at Neuilly, before entering the Society and taking the name Catherine. So, from 13 onwards, school rather than home became the major formative influence in her life; in the limited school holidays, the lengthy sea voyage to India was not feasible.[98]

The *Positio* describes Gompertz as "something of an infant prodigy," and suggests that "she was the first woman religious in Britain to obtain a university degree."[99] The necrologist makes the more modest claim that "she was the first member of the SHCJ to get her degree." She studied at Bedford College, London University, together with Mary St Raphael Paley, the first

---

[98] A memoir exists of Mary Agnese Ross, a near-contemporary of Gompertz both at school and in the Society. Ross was also born in India, but was sent back to Britain at the age of four; the memoir states that she met her parents only four times before she entered the Society.

[99] *Positio*, 1437, note 69.

principal of the training college in Cavendish Square. For about twenty years Gompertz was vice-principal of the college and lecturer in psychology.

Whilst at Cavendish Square, she played a significant part in the establishment of the Association of Convent Schools. (This was a body formed by the major teaching congregations in Britain to promote and support a professional approach both to the education of the religious themselves and to the management of their schools.) During this time she wrote the biography of Cornelia, and also a life of Mary Christina Patmore SHCJ, *A Daughter of Coventry Patmore,* which was published in 1924 by Longman, Green & Co.

All this activity suggests a woman with a vigorous mind and a considerable capacity for hard work, an impression which is borne out by her later life. After the Second World War, when she was in her late sixties and living in Oxford, she acted as administrator of the Religious Diploma for Sacred Studies for Great Britain—a correspondence course established by Mgr John Barton to provide women religious with opportunities to study theology, scripture and church history. Her necrology speaks of Gompertz' "unremitting efforts in procuring and allocating tutors, arranging for examinations and summer courses and in carrying on the ever-increasing secretarial labours."

Gompertz died at Mayfield in 1963, aged 82.

Juliana Wadham (b. 1926)

Juliana Wadham's *The Case of Cornelia Connelly*, published by Collins in 1956, is the only full-length biographical study of Cornelia not written by a member of the Society. Wadham is further distinguished from Cornelia's other biographers by being a wife and mother, and also by her age: she was only 30 when the biography was published.

Wadham (born Jill Macdonald-Walker) shares a number of characteristics with Gompertz. Her childhood was spent partly in India, partly in South America, before she returned to be educated in England.

Her family had Holy Child connections and their daughter was initially sent to school at Mayfield. After the outbreak of the Second World War she transferred to the St Leonards school, which had been evacuated to Hedsor Park in Buckinghamshire. Like Gompertz, she was academically gifted, winning a state scholarship to read history at Oxford at the age of seventeen.

At Oxford she met and married Rowan Wadham, a descendant of the founder of Wadham College. (Among the acknowledgements which preface her life of Cornelia is one to "my husband without whose unfailing and invigorating discouragement this book would never have been written.") After Oxford she was employed as a publisher's reader, but she quickly found herself with a growing family. Her fourth child, with whom she was pregnant during her work on the biography, was named Cornelia, and the book is dedicated to her—"to Another Cornelia." That she was able to research and write a full length biographical study whilst caring for a number of small children is explained by references in her letters to both a nanny and a cook.

Wadham now lives in East Anglia, and is currently writing the story of her husband's illustrious ancestor.

Marie Thérèse Bisgood (1891-1975)

Margaret Bisgood's necrology describes her as "a spoilt child of great charm." She was never robust; as a child she was considered delicate, and the closing years of her life were marred by a "slow but relentless breakdown" that left her feeling lonely and isolated in herself, and wanting to withdraw from those around her.

The second of four sisters, born in Richmond, Surrey, she was educated by the Notre Dame sisters at their boarding school in Clapham. She followed her older sister to Oxford, where she took a degree in modern languages in 1913. At Oxford she lived in the students' residence run by the Holy Child sisters at Cherwell Edge, and she subsequently entered the Society in 1914.

Bisgood held many positions of responsibility within the Society. For about fifteen years before the Second World War she was on the staff of the training college at Cavendish Square, where she was tutor, vice-principal and finally principal. In 1939 she was appointed local superior in Oxford. Thereafter, she was continuously the superior in different houses, and a member of the provincial council for over twenty five years.

Bisgood died at Mayfield in 1975, aged 84.

Elizabeth Mary Strub (b. 1930)

Strub is not, strictly speaking, a biographer of Cornelia, but she produced a substantial account of the founder's life in a section of the *Informatio* which was submitted to the Sacred Congregation for the Causes of Saints in 1987 in support of Cornelia's canonisation process. It is included in this study of the biographies because it marks a significant shift in Cornelian studies, and a watershed in the approach to the biographical material.

Strub is a Californian, born in San Francisco, and she is both the first US American and the first theologically educated writer to produce a biography of Cornelia. She had studied at the Regina Mundi Institute in Rome and at St Louis University. According to her own account, she "was rusticated" from Regina Mundi "for radical ideas."[100]

---

[100] E-mail, 11 August 2001.

Strub entered the Society in 1951. At that time the Holy Child houses in the United States were administered as a single province, although later they were subdivided into three provinces, with the Rosemont and New York provinces being created by the 1958 general chapter, and the Western province by the 1964 chapter. In 1965 Strub was given responsibility for formation in the newly established Western province. The doctoral programme in scripture which she began in St Louis in 1969 had to be abandoned when she was called to Rome to become a member of the Society's general council in 1970. She served as a councillor for six years, and then, from 1976 to 1986, she was superior general. It was in the year that she left office, and while she was still in Rome, that she wrote the *Informatio.*

Having returned to the United States, she gained a masters degree at Weston School of Theology in 1989. Her thesis, subsequently developed and enlarged, explored the influence of St Ignatius and, more specifically, the Spiritual Exercises, on the spirituality of Cornelia. It was published by the Society in 1996 as *Ignatius, The Spiritual Exercises and Cornelia: A Retreat By All Means.* Since 1989 Strub has lived and worked in Chile.

Radegunde Flaxman (b. 1917)

Flaxman's life of Cornelia, *A Woman Styled Bold*, was published by Darton, Longman and Todd in 1991. Flaxman was a convert to Catholicism, who had been received into the Church in 1950. She obtained a degree in English at Royal Holloway College, University of London, taught in Birmingham schools during the blitz, and explored a theatrical career in stage management and acting. She spent eighteen months as a novice at Stanbrook Abbey, and taught briefly at St Leonards, before entering the Society in 1955. She was an influential teacher at

Layton Hill, the convent grammar school in Blackpool, in the years leading up to Vatican II (1958-1963). She then began a master's thesis on Cornelia's educational philosophy, because it was intended that she should become principal of a teacher training college which the Society planned to establish. In 1966, when the Society withdrew from the project, she was appointed principal at Cavendish Square. After that college closed in 1969, Flaxman, who was already a member of the newly established Institute of Holy Child Studies, was given responsibility for initial formation in the European province. In 1976 she was elected to the general council of the Society, and continued to live in Rome until 2002, when she moved to Mayfield. She spent ten years researching and writing Cornelia's biography after she came out of office in 1980.

Flaxman believes that all the experiences of her life were formative of the biographer she became, and of the particular insights she had into Cornelia's life:

> With hindsight I see the whole of my life as a Catholic (to which I was able to bring a little of both education and creativity) as a gradual understanding of who Cornelia was and of God's merciful purposes at work in her—convert, lover of the Church … and of its liturgy; … and educator …. Directing novices deepened my understanding of what to be "like the Holy Child Jesus" meant for the following of Christ. Becoming a member of the [general] council flung me into the maelstrom of the whole Society, thinking of all that was contained in CC's great desire "that we may all be one." … To be asked … after that to write a biography was a very great challenge. And insights that come with old age show me how much I missed of who this woman was.[101]

A Way Forward

In a book of this length, there is not enough space for detailed discussion of all the biographies of Cornelia, as well as for a re-examination of the source material in the light of current biographical practice. Consequently, I shall now be concentrating on three pivotal biographies: the first, by Maria Joseph Buckle, which had a seminal influence on all that was written later;

---

[101] Flaxman, e-mail, September 2001.

Marie Thérèse Bisgood's, which emerged from pre-Vatican II convent culture and sought to reinforce it—a typical use of biography within women's religious congregations; and Elizabeth Mary Strub's *Informatio*, which tentatively experiments with a different approach to the biographical task.

Chapter Four

THROUGH BUCKLE'S EYES: THE MAKING OF A MYTH

In autobiography, the present life experiences and preoccupations of the writer influence what is remembered and emphasized from the past:

> A successful autobiographer must be an artist in the reconstruction of memory. The circumstances, events, thoughts, and feelings that made up the writer's past are filtered through the lens of present needs, attitudes and expectations. From the perspective of the present, certain episodes or relationships assert themselves as primary or crucial, while others disappear, "forgotten" as irrelevant to the shaping of a life into a story.[1]

No autobiography of Cornelia Connelly exists but, within six weeks of Cornelia's death, Maria Joseph Buckle began to collate material for a biography in accordance with the wishes of the second superior general, Angelica Croft.

Buckle's intentions were not autobiographical. However, as she shaped the material she collected about Cornelia, she was recording and interpreting events and experiences which she had lived through herself, which had shaped her own life, and about which she had her own opinions. Following the principles suggested by Atkinson, it would seem important, therefore, to establish what in Buckle's situation at the time of writing may have influenced her "remembering" of Cornelia's personality, reactions and choices—her shaping of the biographical material.

The years preceding Cornelia's death had been painful ones for the founder and for the whole Society. The extensive revision of the Constitutions which Cornelia carried out in 1869 under the direction of Anselmo Knapen OFM, the *consultore* appointed by Propaganda Fide, had not been well received in the Society. Buckle speaks of disunion, and "a

---

[1] Clarissa W. Atkinson, "'Your Servant, My Mother': The Figure of St Monica in the Ideology of Christian Motherhood," in *Immaculate and Powerful: The Female in Sacred Image and Social Reality*, edited by C. W. Atkinson and others (Boston: Beacon, 1995), 140.

strong feeling of aversion created to Mother Connelly."[2] In Preston the dissent almost led to schism. At the first general chapter of the Society, in August 1874, James Danell, second bishop of Southwark, responded to these constitutional disputes by imposing upon the Society a new rule which he had written himself. Buckle tells us that for those members of the Society "who knew [Cornelia] less long and loved her less well," the result of the bishop's "censures on her conduct … was want of confidence—and it must be said opposition to her views and wishes." By contrast "the oldest professed," (of whom Buckle was one) "redoubled their loyal expressions of affection."[3] Though Cornelia strove to retain something of the spirit of the original rule, the situation had not been resolved at the time of her death. Thus Buckle's biography is material collated by a loyal and affectionate member of the Society in a context of what she, at least, perceived to be opposition towards the foundress.

Another complicating fact is the importance that Buckle placed on obedience to ecclesiastical superiors, and her claim that "every line has been written in obedience to Superiors"—especially since Angelica Croft, the main superior to whom she owed obedience, was ambivalent about preserving Cornelia's memory.[4] It seems possible that Buckle was torn between loyalty to Cornelia and loyalty to Croft. Her references to the second superior general in the course of the biography certainly hint at such a tension. She comments on Croft's first profession of vows in the Society in 1859, for instance:

> On the 13th of January the Sacristy Journal tells us that Sister Angelica now (Mother General) [*sic*] … who was destined to take so important a part in the formation of our Institute was received into its bosom as a professed member …. [She] will we trust carry out the plans and designs of the first Mother General as far as they are the "Will of God."[5]

Extant correspondence suggests that Croft's attitude to the founder (and consequently to the biography) became less positive as time went by.

---

[2] D66:188.
[3] D67:54.
[4] D63:32.
[5] D66:1-2.

And Buckle, whose "striking ... child-like obedience to all in authority" was commented upon by the Society necrologist, struggled to remain loyal both to the founder and to the changing attitude of the current superior general.

Against this background, Buckle had a twofold agenda in writing the biography: to re-establish, or at least to reinforce, Cornelia's reputation for holiness; and to root in the authentic spirit of the founder the growth and change that was then taking place in the Society. The second part of this agenda was as explicit as the first. Buckle writes, for instance:

> I say this because some mistakes have arisen ... and I state what I know to be the case that she [Cornelia] never wished or encouraged it but desired everyone to have moderation in all things.[6]

And in another place:

> [Cornelia's] wonderful vocation ... called her ... to give a tincture of her own practically energetic and longing spirit first to her own Houses and then to the other Catholic Educational houses in our country. But this is a task that her children will only be able to fulfil by being imbued with the true spirit of the hidden life she so much loved and by learning from her to copy the Childhood of the Divine Child Jesus.[7]

However, Buckle states that her primary intention was to write as objectively as she could about Cornelia: "To place the story of her life as impartially as we are able before our readers."[8] Today objectivity is considered a dubious concept; we no longer accept that Buckle could present an impartial picture. Rather, her own perspective, which necessarily influenced what she wrote, has become a significant dimension of the biography, something of interest in its own right. We receive from Buckle a Cornelia viewed from a particular perspective—that of Buckle's own attitudes, values and unexamined assumptions, which reflect her context at the time of writing. We need to understand Buckle's perspective in order to assess her biography of Cornelia.

[6] D78:42.
[7] D63:11.
[8] D63:32.

Buckle's Background, Views and Assumptions

Buckle was the well-educated daughter of wealthy parents who had converted to Catholicism. In April 1848, Buckle attended a retreat with her mother, given by James Clough SJ at Derby; immediately afterwards she sought admission to Cornelia's community. The Jesuit retreat director influenced her decision, and her spirituality remained consciously Ignatian throughout her life.[9] But, in a typically nineteenth-century way, she combined with this a strong desire for perpetual adoration and for the recitation of the divine office in choir in the houses of the Society. She had a devotion to the Blessed Sacrament and felt called to found a Congregation of Oblates of the Eucharistic Heart of Jesus among the senior pupils at St Leonards (though this never materialised).

Buckle was asked to prepare the biography because, at the time of Cornelia's death, she was perceived in the Society as intelligent, educated and devout; she admired Cornelia; and she had spent many years living in close proximity to the founder. "She was my novice mistress in 1848 and my Superior till 1869 when I went to Blackpool and for twenty years I had the opportunity of seeing her daily in the intimacy of community life."[10] But another aspect of Buckle's personality was also relevant to the biographical task: she was extremely, even excessively, scrupulous. She describes the crippling nature of her scruples:

> At last I got into such a state of uncertainty that I really did not know what I had done and accused myself of everything I could possibly have committed to be on the safe side.[11]

This inherent tendency resulted in an eagerness to record every detail connected with Cornelia. This proved a valuable asset to her as a collator of the primary Cornelian sources, though she was not above censoring or suppressing material which did not seem to her sufficiently wholesome.

Buckle's scrupulosity perhaps accounts for the great store she set by obedience to all ecclesiastical superiors and reverence for them. She

---

[9] The extensive notes that Buckle wrote whilst making the Exercises in full with Fr Holden SJ in Blackpool in the 1870s are preserved in the Oxford archives.
[10] D78:43.
[11] D78:9.

claimed to be absolutely loyal to Cornelia: "I … never opposed any thing she ordered and took her part most loyally against those who rose against her authority."[12] She adopted a similar attitude to chaplains, retreat givers, confessors, and especially to bishops. Consequently the not infrequent occasions when she had to record Cornelia's conflicts with bishops and other clergy were problematic for her. The text reveals Buckle's inability to be critical of the hierarchy, and her struggle to find ways of upholding both Cornelia and her clerical adversaries:

> It is one of those inexplicable cases where holy persons with the best intentions oppose each other, and all we have to do in a work like the present is to shew how this fresh affliction was felt by Mother Connelly. …
>
> If a cloud passed between him [Wiseman] and our Foundress, it was one of those misunderstandings between good and holy souls permitted for some unseen end and to prove that even in the most exalted enterprises and with the purest intentions differences may arise. …
>
> That his Lordship [Danell] acted throughout from the best motives and on what he was led to believe most trustworthy information, only proves that the crosses of holy persons come from the holy and that the affliction is never more poignant than when the afflicting party does what seems to be most right and just and when those who are thus afflicted are misunderstood by their nearest and best friends.[13]

By and large, the prejudices and unexamined assumptions revealed in Buckle's writings are those that would be expected from a woman of her background, class and upbringing. She was convinced of the absolute superiority of the British system of government, of the aristocracy, and of all things English; she questioned neither the class system nor the sexual stereotyping of women. But such assumptions created problems for her with regard to certain aspects of Cornelia's life and character (her American nationality, her powers of reasoning and judgment). Could an independent, strong-minded American woman be made to fit Buckle's preconceived notions of English propriety, let alone appear demonstrably holy?

Independence and strength of mind were not praiseworthy attributes for women in Buckle's scheme. She could not deny Cornelia's strength, but

---

[12] D78:45.
[13] D65:108; D66:148; D67:31.

she went to some lengths to assert that it did not prevent her from being a model of stereotypically feminine virtue. Buckle's comments reveal more about her own lack of sympathy with the contemporary demand for women's emancipation than they do about Cornelia:

> Such was Mother Connelly as gentle as she was strong .... There was not the slightest trace of the masculine woman or what is commonly now termed the "strongminded female" in derision of the self assertion and want of modesty sometimes displayed by modern ladies—Still less was there anything of the blue stocking or the pedantic woman who has in contempt the pursuits and occupations of her sex—No—Mother Connelly was thoroughly domestic in the world and we can bear witness to her rare talent in all ornamental and useful needlework.[14]

In describing Cornelia, Buckle deliberately underplayed her Americanness and stressed her appreciation of English ways, her assimilation of the values of "the land of her adoption":

> Her accent was slightly American but not to hinder the sweetness of her speech. ...

> Though Mother Connelly felt the sacrifice of her beloved country her mind was too well balanced not to value the advantages of a Mother House in England and she always mentioned it as one of the great mercies of God to our Society that though its Foundress was American the religious body was essentially English in its origins. ...

> Mother Connelly though American by birth and education, adopted the sentiments and customs of the Mother Country, and desired that all her children should share in the spirit of distinguished submission that can only be found in a monarchy and, in her admiration of the time honoured institutions of Great Britain .... So although Mother Connelly was brought up in a Republican country she was sufficiently large hearted to enter warmly into all the advantages of an ancient monarchy. No English woman could more devoutly admire the excellences of British rule. She always spoke of the English law as a perfect system of political government if well carried out. She rejoiced in the respectful veneration of rank and noble birth saying always how much America had lost when those ancient landmarks were removed.[15]

---

[14] D67:148-149.
[15] D78:3; D65:7; D63:14-16.

It is not easy to hear Cornelia's voice in all this, to disentangle Cornelia from Buckle. Buckle was unquestionably a British imperialist. Nevertheless, since the mid-nineteenth century was a high point in the power and influence of the British empire, it is possible that Cornelia also shared the general conviction that British rule could bring Christianity and civilisation to the darker corners of the earth. However, Cornelia's assimilation was never complete: the "Foundress was American." Whilst Buckle herself could not resist making references to influential, affluent, titled pupils, and to visits by foreign royalty to St Leonards, she had to acknowledge that Cornelia "had an especial dislike for courting the rich and powerful."[16] The passages quoted above reveal much about Buckle's attitudes and assumptions but probably less about Cornelia. They suggest that, while despising snobbery, Cornelia was not anti-British, but rather acknowledged the merits of British rule and the British system of government "if well carried out."

No biographer can be free from assumptions, prejudices or social conditioning. My purpose here is accordingly not to undermine Buckle's credentials as biographer, but to bring to the fore some of the less conscious, less deliberate attitudes that underpin this first (and extremely influential) presentation of Cornelia.[17] Society's assumptions about women and the Church's attitude to the hierarchy are embedded in Buckle's text; to question or challenge them was inconceivable to her.

But, in other ways, Buckle's biographical stance was more self-conscious. In spite of her desire to present an impartial picture of Cornelia, she knew that she was not impartial. She was a disciple, "a close, attentive witness" with a "special, intimate perspective,"[18] one of "the oldest professed [who] redoubled their loyal expressions of affection"; and she was consciously writing an apologia for a well-loved leader. She was not, however, sycophantic, and was not afraid to express criticism and reservations regarding Cornelia. So I shall begin by examining Buckle's biographical method, analyzing the claims she made for herself as biographer, the limitations that she was aware of, and the sources that she drew on.

---

[16] D66:34.

[17] Buckle's influence on later biographers is discussed below.

[18] Language used by Atkinson to describe St Augustine's presentation of his mother, St Monica, "'Your Servant, My Mother'," 141.

Buckle's Biographical Method

It has been suggested that every biographer seeks a key that will give meaning and cohesion to the subject's life.[19] If Buckle found a key, it was perhaps Cornelia's conviction that God's will "is made known to us by circumstances."[20] Buckle set herself to explore, to the best of her ability, all the circumstances of Cornelia's life and her responses to God in them.

Buckle had certainly known Cornelia well: she had lived in community with her from 1848 to 1869, spent some weeks with her in Neuilly in 1877, and returned to St Leonards to be with her during her final illness in 1879. Buckle spent seven years collating material for the biography and commenting on it, producing a work of eight manuscript volumes.

She wrote in obedience to her superiors; but she also claimed that she was particularly fitted for the task, having known Cornelia intimately for 31 years:

> Although others of the early members of the Society were admitted to her more intimate confidence and might be able to give more details of her interior life and inmost feelings, I may say for myself that for all the 31 years that I was with her in the Society I had almost daily intercourse with our revered Foundress and could form my judgement of her not only from her dealings with myself but from the way that she treated the rest of the community both separately and collectively ... [21]

This assertion of competence contains a hint of self-justification, an awareness of the competing claims of those who had been "admitted to [Cornelia's] more intimate confidence." Buckle expressed the same concern after attempting to outline Cornelia's spirituality. Again, she sought refuge in obedience, and in confidence in God:

> I think this is pretty nearly all I can glean of Mother Connelly's spirit from the remains that are left to me to collect from—I know that the sketch is incomplete and those who enjoyed more of her confidence than I did might perhaps have traced the features better, but as obedience has given the task to me, I think that Our Lord will help me in saying the truth about our

---

[19] An idea explored by the biographer Ray Monk in a lecture at Southampton University, November 1996.
[20] D78:5.
[21] D63:79.

venerated Foundress and that where I am unable to speak worthily of my self His grace will make me say or inspire others to add what ought to be said on this subject.[22]

Perhaps to reinforce her credentials as biographer, Buckle claimed her own privileged status with regard to Cornelia. The scrupulosity and the desolation that she had experienced as a novice had led to particular intimacy, she says:

> She was always ready to help and console me in my difficulties and from the peculiar circumstances of my vocation she told me many things that perhaps had it not been with a view to my own soul, would never have been spoken to any creature on earth.[23]

Similarly, Buckle reminds the reader that she had been present when Cornelia paid her last visit to France, and so "I was able to take notes in my memory of the last days of our beloved Foundress' life."[24] Recalled to St Leonards, she could "bear full witness" to Cornelia's final illness, remembering "all my intercourse with her at this time which perhaps was the most intimate of my whole life."[25]

However, the text reveals that Buckle did not rely solely upon her own experience and her own memories, but drew extensively on notes written by other members of the Society. Sometimes these were pre-existing documents, like the sacristy journals at St Leonards and Neuilly, and the diaries kept by Ignatia Bridges, Cornelia's private secretary. Bridges was so closely associated with the founder that the pupils at St Leonards dubbed her "Reverend Mother's shadow."[26] Other material was solicited by Buckle and written explicitly for inclusion in the biography. The account of the first days in Derby by Aloysia Walker, and a historical overview of Mayfield "written for insertion in these pages,"[27] fall into this category. Sometimes the hoped-for information proved elusive, but its very absence demonstrates Buckle's method:

---

[22] D63:72-73.
[23] D63:22.
[24] D67:42.
[25] D67:28.
[26] D73:244, Francis Bellasis' life of Cornelia.
[27] D66:64.

> The papers at Mayfield which were written for insertion here and which Mother Agatha compiled from notes taken at the time are not at my disposal, but I will insert an extract from her letter accompanying them—I had written to her to send me full details of the American Foundation ... [28]

Over and over again Buckle acknowledges her dependence upon such sources, and she complains when they prove inadequate and she is faced with lacunae:

> As the dates of these important events are not mentioned or the Sisters named I cannot give them. ...

> And now there is unfortunately a very imperfect chronicle to go by ... and I must go on as best I can with my own recollections to fill up the blanks in the Annals of the Mother House. ...

> It is exceedingly difficult to write anything of this early settlement at Derby—The notes of M M Ignatia are a blank and the book kept of passing events has had all the Derby part of it taken out. The only thing I can do is to piece together what I can find hoping that later on more materials will throw light on this important period.[29]

This last quotation is particularly interesting, because Buckle had entered the Society at Derby and knew something of the Derby community at first hand. However, elsewhere she admits: "the scruples I have mentioned ... made me too troubled about myself to take much notice of my surroundings."[30]

In the early stages of the biography, Buckle clearly had the full support of the superior general, Angelica Croft. Croft herself wrote to John Connelly, Pierce's brother, giving him details of Cornelia's final illness and death and responding gratefully to his offer of information about Cornelia's family life.[31] After a long first chapter, in which she detailed her own reflections and recollections and assessment of Cornelia, Buckle assiduously copied out all the material received from John Connelly, as well as all the letters from Cornelia to her family and to members of the Society

---

[28] D66:48.
[29] D65:116; D65:181; D65:37-38.
[30] D78:24.
[31] D76:26.

which came into her possession. Cornelia had shared very little about her own life, and the Society was heavily dependent upon the Peacock/Connelly family for information regarding her early years. Whilst regretting the loss to the Society, Buckle perceived Cornelia's silence as a virtue:

> In the love of the hidden life in scrupulously concealing her self her sufferings her early talents her history—in all these points we behold the religious of the Holy Child Jesus—Witness the dearth of information about her early life and her family among those who intimately conversed with her and who could have treasured any anecdote ... [32]

To die to the details of one's life was a spiritual discipline that Cornelia had advocated. Buckle wrote:

> Mother Connelly used to recommend this spiritual exercise of death and resurrection to us—and she very early practised it her self—No one could live more like a dead person to her former life—for she positively left us no details about it. [33]

Buckle's ignorance of what now appear to be particularly significant moments in Cornelia's life is proof of Cornelia's reticence. For instance, Buckle was obliged to add a rider to her text when she "afterwards heard that it was on the feast of St Edward the Confessor Oct 13 1840 Mr Connelly and herself were walking home from Mass that he told her then his prospect of being a priest for the first time and for her to be a nun." [34] This may appear to be a detail, but a synchronicity of dates—the first house of the Society being established on 13 October 1846—gave the information heightened significance.

Buckle's uncertainty about the details of John Henry's death is even more telling. Buckle was simultaneously ignorant and knowledgeable about this event: she made some incorrect assumptions about how the child's accident happened (assumptions that fitted her world, not his), and yet she had total clarity about the significance of the event for Cornelia:

[32] D63:47a.
[33] D64:88.
[34] D64:44.

> This terrible event was the beginning of Mother Connelly's vocation ....
> She described this child as extremely lovely with light hair and fair
> complexion but dark eyes, the delight of her heart just able to run alone—
> she had not lost sight of him but for a few moments when a cry of agony
> was heard—the little fellow had climbed up to the kitchen boiler and fallen
> in. ...

> It is said that in one day we sometimes live long lives and that after a great
> trial the soul comes forth with the experience of years—We may be sure of
> two things—first Mother Connelly must have felt this trial as Père Abbadie
> says "as a mother and as a Christian mother" and secondly that like St Jane
> Frances Chantal she was enabled to correspond to the great grace that
> followed the great sacrifice.[35]

We may infer that Cornelia shared the significance of John Henry's death in
her own spiritual development with the early members of the Society, but
was unwilling to revisit the details of the accident.

In both of these instances, Buckle added further information to her text
when she acquired it. Her purpose was not to produce a polished
biography, but to accumulate as much material about Cornelia as she
possibly could. And yet there were occasions when she deliberately
suppressed or censored information that she had to hand. This is
particularly apparent in the case of Pierce's letters and pamphlets. Of one of
his letters to Mercer, she writes: "His own letter to his son is in terms too
gross to be repeated here—He talks as if he were out of his right
mind...."[36] Of his petition to the House of Commons, she says: "The
contents are not fit for perusal."[37] (In fairness it must be added that she was
supported in this opinion by the House of Commons itself, which banned
the publication of the petition.)

Buckle's hostility to Pierce, though defensible in the light of his vitriolic
letters and pamphlets, did not originate with Cornelia (whose extant
writings contain no attacks upon her husband). But it was highly influential.
The material Buckle collected, and the gloss she put upon it, quickly

---

[35] D64:35-36. Buckle later corrects the information about John Henry's death. Then further information has been
added in another hand. (Flaxman's claim [73] that "the early biographers ... had them [details of John Henry's
death] from Cornelia's own account" is not supported by the Buckle text, which states that the early Society
learned the details from John Connelly.)

[36] D63:182.

[37] D63:183.

crystallized into a myth of Cornelia's life for members of the Society. All the available information about Cornelia was contained in the biography, and consequently it shaped people's perception of the founder. Subsequent biographies, especially those written before Vatican II, were unashamedly derivative from Buckle, often copying whole passages more or less verbatim or retaining such strong verbal echoes that they could not possibly have been written independently of the Buckle text. To offer an example almost at random, here is an extract from Buckle's account of the conflict over Wiseman's desire for a marine residence at St Leonards:

> The Cardinal became seriously displeased, and from being the Father and indulgent protector of the inmates of the Convent he even talked of suppressing the Community and dispersing the members among other convents .... It is one of those inexplicable cases where holy persons with the best intentions oppose each other … [38]

Francis Bellasis, writing between 1911 and 1919, uses virtually identical language:

> It is one of those inexplicable facts, proved by history and experience, that holy souls often oppose each other …. The Cardinal became seriously displeased, and from being the Father and indulgent protector of the Community, he became its hostile critic, and even talked of suppressing the Society.[39]

Bellasis certainly studied Buckle's text assiduously and drew on it extensively; the manuscript of Buckle's material that was submitted to the Historical Commission for the Causes of Saints had been annotated and corrected by Bellasis in a number of places. But Bellasis, like Buckle, had personal knowledge of Cornelia and had also carried out independent research. Against Buckle's account of the finding of Mr Jones' will, for instance, she writes: "This is one of two accounts given of the recovery of the will. The one inserted in the 'Life' is that given by Mother Theresa (the one who found it). Mth Mary Francis."[40]

---

[38] D65:106-107.
[39] D74:309-312.
[40] D65:81. Punctuation as in original.

Usually Bellasis' corrections and emendations involve factual inaccuracies or the addition of information unknown to Buckle, but occasionally she challenges Buckle's interpretation—the myth of Cornelia which Buckle, consciously or unconsciously, was responsible for creating. Buckle, defending Cornelia over the dismissal of Emily Bowles, writes:

> Mother Connelly acted throughout in this matter on the high convictions of duty and on what she thought would be best for the Society, she who had given up her children and her husband, and who had acted with such fortitude under the trial of the law suit was not likely to be moved from what she thought best for the Society by the persuasion of others outside the community who must know less of the interior necessities of those she governed than herself.[41]

But Bellasis is not swept along by the rhetoric here. Instead, the strength of her own conviction is apparent when she crosses out the phrase "given up" and writes above it "been deprived." In a marginal note she adds:

> ... 'given up' this expression is not correct, she never gave up her children, they were taken away from her care and responsibility by Mr Connelly at the time of his defection. MMF.[42]

In spite of Bellasis' efforts, the tradition that Cornelia gave up her children was apparently already too well established to be changed; the Society has certainly been defending her against this charge ever since.[43]

Buckle's biographical writing shaped the myth of Cornelia, but that was not her conscious aim. Her stated intention was more limited, more mundane and less ambitious:

> This introductory chapter is to show how much she deserved a better biographer than myself. I shall now ... patiently collect all that I can find from all the sources at my command to compose a biography of our much loved Foundress—It is however only a beginning and must be helped by others who will aid me in the task of collecting materials and when I shall

---

[41] D65:129.

[42] Punctuation as in original.

[43] Cornelia's relationship with her children, and her response to their loss, is discussed in chapter eight.

have given in my share of what I can write myself or collect from others I shall [rest] contented at having done my little best in holy obedience … [44]

Introducing Buckle's text, the compilers of the material for Cornelia's beatification stress her intimate knowledge of the founder, arguing that "the author's undoubted knowledge of her subject and a certain spiritual perception combine to render [this work] important contemporary evidence of *fama sanctitatis*," [45] and that to have lived "under the same roof as her subject" was an "advantage so desirable for a biographer." [46] The counter-argument is that Buckle lacked distance in her portrayal of Cornelia. On occasion, she confused her own reactions to events and circumstances with Cornelia's. Writing in a pre-Freudian world, Buckle had fixed, rather than developmental, concepts of virtues, of perfection and of sanctity, and she framed Cornelia's life to fit her preconceived categories. The notion of elucidating Cornelia's personality for the reader was entirely foreign to her. Support for these claims can be found both in Buckle's admiration for Cornelia, and in the criticisms she makes of her.

Buckle's Admiration of Cornelia

Buckle's intention was to demonstrate Cornelia's sanctity. An almost universal characteristic of women saints, in the lives that Buckle had read, was that they were beautiful. Cornelia, Buckle said, was beautiful. But this is more than hagiographical convention: there is disinterested evidence that Cornelia was a woman of striking appearance. The *Morning Herald* was totally unsympathetic to Cornelia, but it acknowledged her beauty. Explaining in 1853 (when Cornelia was forty-four) why she was "detained" at St Leonards, it commented:

> It is not, at all events solely, for her beauty, which we learn was once singularly great, for that is now necessarily on the wane; though we are told she still retains sufficient to render her a grace and an attraction to the show-establishment over which she is nominally placed. [47]

---

[44] D63:85.

[45] "Reputation for holiness." A candidate's *fama sanctitatis* has to be established before canonisation.

[46] D63:ii.

[47] CC43:24. The attack on Cornelia in the *Morning Herald* is discussed in chapter eight.

So it is not surprising that Buckle drew attention to Cornelia's looks. What is noteworthy is that her observations about them were invariably overlaid with stereotypically hagiographical inference. Buckle was imitating the language and style of the saints' lives which she had read, consciously implying that Cornelia was a suitable candidate for sainthood:

> Those who saw her for the first time were impressed with her very extraordinary powers of mind—and also with that indescribable appearance of sanctity which especially towards the close of her life seemed to radiate from her eyes and in her smile of benevolence. ...
>
> Beauty perhaps was the first external attraction possessed by Mother Connelly in common with many others, but the features of our Foundress had a wonderful power of expressing her feelings and a remarkable air of calmness as a general rule pervaded her countenance—I have known her for 31 years and have seen her deeply afflicted and tried in every way but I may say I never saw her forget that calm dignity and placid demeanour so much admired in one in authority.[48]

In the same fulsome way Buckle commented upon Cornelia's intellect, her clarity of mind, her capacity to influence others, her talent for administration and her artistic ability:

> Although there was nothing masculine in her manners or ways, her judgment was as clear and her powers of reasoning as sound as is possible to exist with the gentler virtues and docility of the truly female character. ...
>
> Mother Connelly's mind was endowed with natural clearness of perception ... on any subject of deliberation she was accustomed to draw out the pro's and cons with the greatest clearness and then to form her line of conduct from reason not feeling as too many of our sex are apt to do. ...
>
> ... she had the most remarkable gift of influencing the minds and hearts of others ... no one could go away from her without feeling how much she excelled in the qualities of mind and of heart and also they could not leave her without being impressed by her sanctity. ...
>
> And now the talent Mother Connelly possessed for organisation was fully developed and it was beautiful to see her interest in the subjects studied while she was determined to arrange matters so that the Students might ... be led to God as well as prepared for the Scholarships. ...

---

[48] D63:24; D63:22-23.

> Mother Connelly as we have seen was a talented Artist herself and her mind naturally aspired after the true the beautiful and the good.[49]

Clarity of mind, talent for administration, and artistic ability are not virtues, nor in themselves proofs of Cornelia's sanctity. But Buckle discussed them in language which suggests that they are. The implication is that Cornelia had developed her natural talents to the full, and used them unstintingly for the greater glory of God.

Buckle wanted to demonstrate Cornelia's sanctity. Even at Derby, she says, Cornelia "was very far advanced in perfection and quite understood practically the science of the Saints."[50] Through events and everyday incidents in Cornelia's life Buckle illustrated her kindness, patience and forbearance,[51] her spirit of joy,[52] her calm dignity and courage in the face of criticism,[53] and her humility.[54]

Buckle was not entirely consistent in her presentation of Cornelia, as we will see when we turn to her criticisms. But underlying everything she wrote about Cornelia's virtue and holiness was the idealized image of a person who had achieved perfection—a person who no longer made mistakes, and whose human emotions had been totally mastered and controlled. Buckle's world had not been influenced by developmental psychology, and she saw such perfection as a state which some favoured individuals, with the grace of God, could achieve.

Cornelia had acknowledged her own youthful faults (fits of passion, untidiness) but, Buckle claimed, she had "perfectly conquered" them and "gained a perfect control over herself."[55] Buckle wished to present a portrait of Cornelia as living, aside from these peccadilloes, in an unvarying state of perfection:

> ... so completely had she given up all to God that there was afterwards no change in this respect in her soul—Outwardly calm and inwardly self-

---

[49] D63:77; D65:154; D65:134; D65:141.
[50] D78:7.
[51] D78:10; D78:63.
[52] D63:51, 65:198.
[53] D78:70; D78:73.
[54] D78:75; D63:27.
[55] D64:38.

possessed she seemed raised to her level of spirituality and though she developed and proceeded on her way—there was no change of her position as it were before God until the end of her life. ...

She was raised by her sacrifice to a higher level and had not the common temptations to impatience or passionate feelings which those on the way to perfection have generally to fight against. ...

These little notes ... point out clearly the beauty of her soul before God, and how the type of her peculiar character of sanctity was formed from the first ... [56]

Buckle believed not only that Cornelia was holy, but also that she was a suitable candidate for canonisation—an assertion that she claims to have made during Cornelia's lifetime. Questioned in Blackpool by Mgr Cookson, who "was much prejudiced about what he had heard of Mother Foundress," she had responded: "I never saw anything that would prevent the process of her canonisation being commenced." [57] It does not seem unreasonable to infer that Buckle had an eye to Cornelia's possible beatification, and moulded Cornelia's life in the biography to fit her own preconceptions about sainthood. In fact, Buckle herself made the connection between her readings of the lives of saints and her recording of Cornelia's life when, speaking of Cornelia's fractured relationship with Wiseman, she wrote:

I have read in the lives of the Saints that it is considered a mark of holiness to be persecuted by good and holy people who certainly would never oppose what they knew to be good or holy ... [58]

Cornelia's life was being "remembered" by Buckle in the context of hagiography. The events and attitudes in which Buckle perceived evidence of holiness were influenced by her reading of saints' lives, and by contemporary assumptions about sanctity.

An illustration of this is Buckle's use of the language of martyrdom. An article on the *Connelly* v. *Connelly* trial (reprinted from *The Tablet* in a Philadelphia paper, *The Catholic Herald,* on 25 April 1850, before the trial

---

[56] D64:60; D63:23; D64:34.
[57] D78:68.
[58] D78:43.

was finished) shows that such language was the common coin of religious writing and thinking at the time. The suggestion that persecution by Protestants in a Protestant country was a contemporary form of martyrdom was quite explicit. Buckle quotes at length:

> It is pleasing to know that throughout this protracted trial so lacerating to the feelings of a refined and delicate woman she has conducted herself with the firmness and heroism of a martyr .... Well! We cannot believe that Almighty God will fail to protect one whom he is putting to such heroic trials—training for saintliness by a persecution so dreadful, that it is not very easy to find a parallel to it in the lives even of the holiest Saints and Martyrs. Her reward, if she remains constant, is so certain that we can hardly bring ourselves even to pity her.[59]

However, Buckle was not primarily concerned to present Cornelia as the martyr-victim in the public arena. Instead, she stresses "the true spirit of the hidden life she so much loved,"[60] and presents Cornelia's sufferings, especially those brought about by the loss of her children, as an interior, hidden martyrdom:

> It must have been a martyrdom for her to act as she did. ...
>
> All these afflictions seem singly enough to break the heart of a wife and mother, and to overwhelm the spirit of any religious Foundress—but when united—what can we say but that Mother Connelly was a martyr in heart and that the exterior sufferings she endured were sufficient to make a saint of no ordinary degree of heroic constancy. ...
>
> While this exterior life of religious peace and active labour was being zealously carried out by Mother Connelly and her Community—her own heart was undergoing a martyrdom unparalleled in the lives of any holy person we have known.[61]

This emphasis on the interiority of suffering, and of religious experience generally, seems to have accorded with Cornelia's own preference. Cornelia's writings stress that it was in and through everyday circumstances, the ordinary events of community life, that members of the

---

[59] D63:180-181.
[60] D63:11.
[61] D78: 43-44; D63:31-32; D65:103.

Society were to deepen their relationships with God and grow towards holiness. Several times Buckle adverts to Cornelia's devotion to St Gertrude, and the reason for it:

> ... and she used to tell us that the Life and Revelations of St Gertrude were most in accordance with the spirit she wished to see us imbibe because she was formed on the Liturgical year of the Church, and was eminently a saint of the common life—living with her Sisters in the daily performance of the duties of religious life rather than carried away by an extraordinary vocation into some wonderful exhibition of the power of God's grace to heights which it would seem impossible to attain.[62]

Here, as elsewhere, it seems possible to hear the authentic, realistic, practical voice of Cornelia herself. But even where Buckle's text is most "impeded by poetical effusions"[63] and by unexamined assumptions, there can be no doubt that she loved and admired the founder, and intended to provide evidence of her sanctity. Buckle's honesty and integrity, however, as well as her desire for completeness, obliged her to include criticisms of Cornelia in her text. Some of these criticisms have been retained in the myth, but others seem to have been downplayed by later writers.

Buckle's Criticism of Cornelia

It was not difficult for Buckle to acknowledge that Cornelia had been criticized by priests and lay people who had not known her personally but had formed their opinions on the basis of what they had read in the press or learned through hearsay and gossip. Given the opposition to Cornelia within the Society at the time Buckle was writing, this was a nettle that it was crucial for her to grasp.

Buckle names the criticisms—that Cornelia was severe, proud, heartless, unfeeling, independent; and she offers two different responses—firstly that Cornelia had been misunderstood, and secondly that she had endured criticism with praiseworthy fortitude and forbearance.

Much of the criticism concerned the breakdown of the Connellys' marriage and the court case:

---

[62] D63:71-72.

[63] D63:ii. Introduction to Buckle's material written by the compilers of the documents for Cornelia's beatification.

Many thought she was a proud and heartless woman who did not know the affliction of her soul, nor how much it cost her thus to stand alone. The very publicity of the trial was an unspeakable pain to her a delicate and high bred female—and when we consider that her spiritual life was formed of the Hidden mysteries of the Holy Childhood of Our Lord, and how much she shrunk from speaking of any of the graces or consolations God afforded to her spirit—then we can understand what an agony it must have been to have had her name mentioned in the public papers and the case discussed by strangers—to have priests Bishops against her and her own children rising up and refusing to have any communication with their mother. ...

I have heard it said by those who did not know her well that her heart was rather hard and that she did not feel like others or know what others felt. This was one of the hard bits she used to bear in silence; but God only knows how much she had to suffer ... [64]

However, it was not only Cornelia the wife and mother who was criticized, but Cornelia the founder. Increasingly, and most noticeably in the 1870s, during the years of uncertainty and crisis about the Constitutions, priests and bishops opposed her and encouraged dissent within the Society. Buckle speaks of "priests very much prejudiced against her,"[65] and praises Cornelia's "calm dignity" in the face of opposition:

Mother Foundress visited Blackpool every year and I was much struck by the calm dignity with which she encountered all the opposition she met with and the many humiliations she had to undergo—Indeed things came to such a climax that people spoke publicly in the parlour and other places of the speedy dissolution of the Society.[66]

Even this priestly criticism Buckle was able to counter. Cornelia might have been accused of being too independent of priests, but the truth, Buckle argues, was that she always acted in humility and obedience:

We may also notice how humbly she speaks of acting under the direction of her spiritual Father ... and yet Mother Connelly was represented (afterwards by her enemies) as acting too independently of direction in her

[64] D63:30; D 65:26 (the testimony of Aloysia Walker).
[65] D78:70.
[66] D78:73.

religious life—Whatever her conduct <u>may have been</u>, it was altered by circumstances, her principles of obedience were the same ... [67]

In two significant areas, however—Cornelia's relationships with bishops (especially Wiseman and Danell) and her response to internal Society politics—Buckle had her own criticisms of Cornelia, which she did not hesitate to air in a straightforward manner in spite of her insistence elsewhere on Cornelia's perfection. Her ability and readiness to do so contrast with the tendency of later biographers to downplay divisions.

About the bishops Buckle had issues of her own: she found it extremely difficult to criticize them. She needed to believe that the Society would have been safe in their hands, and that they would always have taken the best decisions if they had been fully cognisant of the facts:

> She acted in this as I have said in obedience to the Cardinal but had she explained matters to him when he had received a false impression from Miss Bowles I always thought things would have ended differently and Mr Connelly would not have apostasized or the children left the true religion with their father .... Then again in the dispute of the Convent with the Cardinal about the Church at St Leonards I was always sorry Mother Foundress did not put herself intirely [*sic*] with intire [*sic*] confidence in the hands of the Cardinal and let him act as he pleased—He would have been a great Protector of our Order ... [68]

These are serious criticisms of Cornelia's judgement. By temperament Buckle was inclined to submit in obedience to hierarchical authority, and she regretted Cornelia's more independent spirit. This independence led Buckle to make her one serious theological criticism of Cornelia and, coincidentally, to reveal how far her "remembering" of Cornelia was bound up with her own life story and self perception:

> I always thought too that from being a Convert and an American convert there were protestant ideas mingled with her Catholic convictions and a certain independence and want of those Catholic traditions which the Holy Father has since condemned under the name of "Americanism"—Having said this I will only add that the conviction of these mistakes being made in

---

[67] D65:6.

[68] D78:43-44. The first part of this quotation refers to Emily Bowles' reaction to Pierce's visiting the convent at Derby without the bishop's permission.

the Society was my great cross and I suffered in my own way nearly as much as Mother Foundress, because I loved and respected her as a Saint, I loved the Society and was ready to die for holy Religion and it was the deepest grief to me to see things which I thought were not perfectly right.[69]

However, Buckle's major criticisms of Cornelia, her personal differences with her, concerned internal Society politics. Susan O'Brien calls attention to the fact that many women's congregations at this period faced not only "gender-defined confrontations between men and women" but "disputes among sisters." Usually, she suggests, such conflicts focused on the question of who was to wield ultimate power and control:

> For the new English foundations conflicts over the control and direction of embryonic communities, some of which occurred between senior members of the congregations and others between the foundress and a priest or bishop, could be serious.[70]

O'Brien then cites, by way of example, Cornelia's conflict with Emily Bowles, "her first coadjutor and friend," as Buckle describes her.[71]

"The gifted and zealous Miss Bowles,"[72] a convert to Catholicism, had been invited by Wiseman to join Cornelia in establishing the first house of the Society at Derby (from the beginning, she was his choice, not Cornelia's). Ten years later, without consulting Cornelia, Bowles committed the Society to a mortgage that it had no means of repaying, and subsequently left the Society. Her acrimonious departure and its aftermath created problems for Cornelia and the Society for years to come. Unlike Cornelia, Bowles was English and had many influential contacts, including both Wiseman and Newman. Some of her defamatory letters about Cornelia are extant, as is evidence of her involvement in dinner-party gossip.

Buckle, however, did not see the events in black and white; she did not choose to write the story in unequivocal terms, with all the right on

---

[69] D78:45. This and the previous quotation are taken not from the biographical material but from Buckle's personal recollections where, arguably, she felt able to express herself more freely.

[70] Susan O'Brien, "Religious Life for Women," in McClelland, *From Without the Flaminian Gate*, 118-119.

[71] D63:34.

[72] D63:34.

Cornelia's side and all the wrong on Bowles', as might have been expected of one bent on establishing the credentials of a saint. She had lived with both women and had reason to admire, and to criticize, both. She presents the whole affair in terms of a struggle for ascendancy between two powerful and gifted women:

> We have to record in truth that from the first she [Bowles] did not agree with Mother Connelly's plans and it was only too evident that sooner or later there would be a separation.[73]

She seems genuinely to regret that there could not be room for both Cornelia and Bowles within the Society:

> Miss Bowles, ... after involving the Society in heavy expenses at Rupert House, left us with feelings of bitterness and animosity against Mother Connelly—which it was painful for those who knew and valued both of them to witness.[74]

Buckle admired Bowles' intellect and education: "she was very clever," "a highly gifted individual."[75] But she also criticized Bowles' lack of obedience, the virtue Buckle particularly valued: "I was struck by her over activity and constantly reasoning upon matters where it would have been more perfect to obey."[76]

In Buckle's view, Bowles' position in the Society differed from that of other members because she was Cornelia's "first coadjutor and friend." Bowles had potential for leadership, and Buckle acknowledges the possibility that Bowles, "so well calculated to be the successor of Mother Connelly,"[77] might one day have become superior general.

Her departure was, therefore, a matter for regret, not for relief. She later desired to be readmitted to the Society, but this was not possible, Buckle says, because the tension and acrimony between herself and Cornelia would undoubtedly have resurfaced. Buckle's summary of the affair, whilst not

[73] D65:49.
[74] D63:34.
[75] D78:11; D65:128.
[76] D78:7.
[77] D64:165.

defending Bowles, certainly implies some criticism of Cornelia, or at least an acknowledgement of her limitations, and it seems important enough to quote at length:

> During the next year Miss Bowles left the Society. Serious differences had arisen between herself and Mother Connelly, or rather we may say the different views they entertained on the subject of the Institute and the means most conducive to carrying out the work for the greater glory of God became every year more evident. Miss Bowles therefore applied for a dispensation from her two vows of poverty and obedience and left the Society to the regret of a good many of the Sisters who admired her talents and zeal. Since that time Miss Bowles has applied to be received again and Fr Galway [*sic*] interested himself in her behalf but without success. It was better as it had been settled, as the same differences would only have begun again and Miss Bowles perhaps have had the pain of again leaving the Society.
>
> Without entering into the question we must here remark that Mother Connelly lost in this highly gifted individual one who was able to raise the fame of the Society in a literary point of view as her books which have been written since abundantly testify—We may be allowed to regret this event as a misfortune for had Miss Bowles become a well trained religious full of the spirit of the Holy Child Jesus and of submission to the rules, she might have done an immense deal towards the foundation of the Society—Unhappily for herself and for us she came to an order first beginning with unformed traditions and unwritten rules, one that was not founded by a Bishop or Priest but by a convert like herself and these circumstances may lessen any blame that would otherwise be attached to her independent spirit.[78]

Again, Buckle's reservations about Cornelia surface: she was a convert, not sufficiently subject to the authority of a bishop or priest, and, like Bowles, she was an independent spirit.

Bowles was not alone in resisting Cornelia. The dissension that arose in the Society about the Constitutions in the 1870s was accompanied by a ground swell of opposition to the founder. Buckle calls it "the crowning affliction [of] our beloved foundress," and says that "none but those who witnessed the struggle can realise the pain" that it caused her. But she is nevertheless forthright in naming both Cornelia's part in what went wrong and the extent of the animosity that her actions provoked. The emotive nature of the events is reflected both in Buckle's expressed intention—"we

---

[78] D65:127-128.

shall endeavour to keep as far as possible to the limits of truth and moderation"—and in her "allowance for mistakes and even faults on both sides."[79]

In 1869, immediately before Vatican I, Thomas Grant, the bishop of Southwark, had advised Cornelia to present her Constitutions in Rome and have them examined and edited by a *consultore* appointed by Propaganda Fide:

> The General Council in Rome was expected to be opened on the Feast of the Immaculate Conception [1869] when as the Bishop informed us in a conference he gave to the nuns at St Leonards, one of the most important questions would be the confirmation and recognition of the modern active orders, all of which date their existence since the last council of Trent. Most of the Foundresses or Generals then belonging to this category visited Rome before the commencement of the Council to have their rules examined by the Consultores appointed by the holy see—the Bishop therefore also advised Mother Connelly to visit Rome at this important time ... [80]

Under Anselmo Knapen's supervision, Cornelia undertook a much more extensive revision of the Constitutions than she, or anyone else, had anticipated. She spent the winter at Hyères, sending the revised text to England and America by post for the approval of members of the Society. The response was quite different from the one that she expected; and though Buckle places the responsibility for what ensued firmly with Cornelia herself, she first offers the only defence of Cornelia that makes sense to her: that she had acted in obedience to her ecclesiastical superiors:

> She went [to Rome] first in obedience to her Bishop and then intending to put all her plans unreservedly in the hands of the ecclesiastical superior who would be given as consultore and intending to put down her own judgment whenever it was contrary to the dictates of obedience—This should be remembered in order to understand what we have hereafter to relate.[81]

Given Buckle's constant emphasis on the importance of obedience, it is ironic that obedience, and not independence of spirit, brought about the most serious crisis in the Society during the founder's lifetime. Buckle might have

[79] D63:34.
[80] D66:181.
[81] D66:181-182.

been expected to decry the membership's want of obedience in what followed. But she does not, because the responsibility for the crisis was Cornelia's:

> Here we may remark that Mother Connelly quite miscalculated the effect the new rule would have on members of the Institute ~~and~~ had she taken the rule herself and read it publicly in each house, her influence would perhaps have obtained what the mere perusal of it at a distance failed to effect—The house sisters were deeply wounded at the change in their regard and several thought of leaving the Society and though I do not think any house sister left on this account there was a strong feeling of aversion created to Mother Connelly .... In America the rule was received with strong disapproval though it was only in Preston that measures were taken to appeal to the Holy See on the question.[82]

Buckle concludes that the root of the problem was a failure of judgement on Cornelia's part, a failure which she proceeded to compound. She had presumed that the Society would accept the revised rule in simple and unquestioning obedience; faced with a totally different response, she failed to manage the dissent in any effective way, retreating into silence and the acceptance of suffering.

Buckle states that the dissent was widespread:

> She who a few years previously had enjoyed the profound veneration and devoted love of her whole Society, with two or three exceptions was now left nearly alone, with hardly any of the Professed of the Society to take her part .... But now nearly all the Superiors became incensed at the measures our Foundress had taken.[83]

Bellasis annotates this passage: "Not correct, exaggerated. The discontent was confined to the Superiors in the North, Mother Lucy and Mother Alphonsa." And in this instance, perhaps because the Society found it difficult to acknowledge dissent and disloyalty in its own ranks, it was Bellasis' version of events and not Buckle's which became the dominant myth, the master narrative. But Buckle substantiates her claim, naming some of those who opposed Cornelia:

---

[82] D66:187-188.
[83] D63:34.

> That great dissatisfaction was felt at all the convents is certain—Some objected to the Franciscan affiliation—some to the change in the vows—and Sr Francis Kerby who left soon afterwards took upon herself to write her objections to Rev Mother Foundress—M Christina and M Francis Xavier Cusack also wrote their objections and Fr Cobb, the Jesuit Confessor at Preston, also ~~wrote~~ sent his strong disapprobation of the alterations in the rule by a message through M M Christina when she wrote from Preston. Mother Connelly wrote a circular letter on the vows to all the houses, and sent the substance of Kate Kerby's letter to Cardinal Barnabò who replied to the appeal by dispensing Sr Francis Kerby from her vows which dispensation was sent to St Leonards.[84]

Later Buckle adds:

> The effect of this last and perhaps the heaviest cross was as far as we could perceive most sad in [Cornelia's] regard as it tended to estrange from her so many of those who had in former years been her most devoted children.[85]

Buckle regretted this estrangement, but she did not suggest that it was groundless: rather, her assessment of the Constitutional crises contains explicit criticism of Cornelia.

Cornelia was not conventional. For all Buckle's efforts at a hagiographic stance, there were events in Cornelia's life and aspects of her personality which could not be squeezed into a pre-constructed mould, and Buckle's honesty obliges her to acknowledge the fact. Even in describing Cornelia's final illness she cannot avoid including an implicit criticism of what seemed to her Cornelia's personal limitations:

> If she ever had too great an assumption of authority and too independent a spirit—all this had gone away … the interior work of Grace had been transforming and spiritualising what was so noble and admirable though perhaps excessive in her natural character.[86]

Similarly, tucked into a "poetic effusion" (as the compilers of Cornelia's beatification documents put it), is the suggestion that she was sometimes subject to "failings and shortsightedness":

---

[84] D66:194.
[85] D67:54.
[86] D67:28.

> [From heaven] may she look down upon us her children and inspire those in authority to carry out her views, not as they were when she was encompassed with difficulties and subject to the failings and shortsightedness incident to our poor human nature, but as she sees her designs now in the eternal decrees … [87]

Buckle was more willing than the later biographers to explore Cornelia's limitations and to criticize her actions and decisions. When Francis Tolhurst succeeded Angelica Croft as superior general in 1905, the mood in the Society changed. Bellasis' emendations (for instance that Cornelia "never gave up her children, they were taken away from her care," and that Buckle had "exaggerated" the opposition to Cornelia within the Society) reflect the new, more protective, approach. In view of this development, Buckle's text assumes an added importance in providing a less constrained version of events, at least as regards Cornelia the founder. But whether Buckle's breadth of vision extended to Cornelia the wife and mother is another question.

Cornelia as Wife

Buckle's knowledge of Cornelia's life before the foundation of the Society was limited, even scrappy, and some of the statements she made were inaccurate. So, Buckle is not to be relied upon as an interpreter of Cornelia the wife. She was, however, a student of Cornelia's spirituality. The editors of the material presented to the historical commission note the reliability of her "testimony to [Cornelia's] interior life." [88] Therefore it is not insignificant that Buckle claimed to see a consistency between what Cornelia had written in her spiritual notebooks at Grand Coteau, and what she herself knew from first hand experience of the older Cornelia:

> These little notes which have come accidentally into our hands are the more valuable as they were not intended for others to see and they point out clearly the beauty of her soul before God, and how the type of her peculiar character of sanctity was formed from the first even to the little axioms, maxims and

---

[87] D63:76.
[88] D63:ii.

reflections that she writes down for herself. We shall see that "Actions not words" and "God alone" are as it were the key to her interior life.[89]

This observation aside, Buckle's major contribution to our understanding of Cornelia as a wife would seem to be her totally unsympathetic, even hostile, depiction of Pierce. Cornelia herself was hurt by Pierce and angry with him for breaking his promises to her, but no extant writing of hers reveals the hostility found in Buckle. Cornelia expressed only sadness and a loving concern—typical of the nineteenth century—for her husband's eternal salvation. Even Buckle acknowledges that not all the early members of the Society would have concurred in the effective character-assassination of Pierce which the pages of the biography contain. Teresa Hanson, in particular, who had known the Connellys in Rome, was a staunch defender of Pierce and maintained contact with him and the children after the separation:

> Mother Teresa knew all as she was intimately acquainted with the family of the Connellys and she had a great opinion of Mr Connelly's talent, fervour and good dispositions till the fatal separation. It seems that he had brought a present from the Pope Pius the IX to give to his Wife, but the chaplain Dr Asperti would not permit him to see Mother Connelly alone—This gave him deadly offence as he had constantly seen her in private at the Trinità Convent in Rome and Miss Bowles most injudiciously interfered and wrote to the Cardinal that things were going on in the Convent contrary to religious propriety—This made him Dr Wiseman [*sic*] act in the way which led to the apostasy and law suit—Mother Teresa laid all the blame on Miss Bowles who misrepresented the whole affair.
>
> Mother Teresa acted throughout as the affectionate friend of all parties and by the permission of Bp Grant who was afterwards Our Superior she saw Mr Connelly several times before he left England and tried to conciliate him. By the same permission and by the advice of Our holy Bishop she cultivated the friendship of Frank and Adeline sending them little presents.[90]

These comments on the opinion and actions of Teresa Hanson demonstrate that a different interpretation of the events was possible, and that a different myth about Pierce could have been established. But in her

[89] D64:34.
[90] D78:25, 26.

conventional nineteenth-century piety, Buckle judged Pierce's apostasy and his attacks on the Church harshly. The subsequent biographers accepted her demonization of Pierce because it reinforced their defence of Cornelia, and so the myth became unchallengeable.

I do not use the word "demonization" lightly: it is an accurate reflection of Buckle's attitude. "He talks as if he were out of his right mind and says he will pray for Mother Connelly 'as one given up to the devil'—The possession if any was certainly on his own side," she wrote.[91] Her language about Pierce is often extreme, more reminiscent of the gothic novel than of hagiographic literature:

> Then her unhappy husband took upon himself the course which perhaps is unexampled in the history of the Church—From his affection and devotion expressed in all his letters to his wife—his Angel as he called her he changed into the most cruel of adversaries … with a malice which seemed almost like possession. …

> Here we see the refined man of genius, the speculation for building churches and working on the interest of the planters—certainly no very supernatural way to spread the Gospel in Natchez!—He alludes to the admiration his wife received and though she appears to have suffered little by the flattery—her husband's head seems quite turned!! And step by step we shall see the descent downwards.[92]

Buckle calls Pierce Cornelia's "unworthy husband,"[93] and castigates "the vain complacency he takes in the notice of great people"[94] and "an absolute adoration of rank,"[95] though these were temptations to which she herself was not immune. Similarly, although she too was a convert to Catholicism, she comments disparagingly on Pierce's status as a convert. At the time of his acceptance for the priesthood he was "a convert of eight years standing" and Buckle highlights, inaccurately, his lack of preparation for ordination:

---

[91] D63:182.
[92] D63:168-169; D63:104-105.
[93] D63:29.
[94] D63:102.
[95] D63:131.

> We must be convinced that Pierce Connelly was not acting in the way best fitted to prepare for the step he took of ordination in next May in the Catholic Church—We hear of no previous study—only a great deal of travellings and worldliness....[96]

As Buckle copied out his letters, nothing that Pierce wrote met with her approval, and after each letter or two she allowed herself a paragraph of editorial comment, the asperity of which jumps off the page:

> From all this we see ... the vain complacency he takes in the notice of great people thus sowing the seeds of after evils—and also we remark passionate affection to his family—not being able to live without wife or children—no great marks of a vocation to the priesthood—Altogether we may suppose Mr Connelly to have been a very fascinating companion but not gifted with those qualities of heart or head that would justify expectations of his persevering in a heroic sacrifice. ...

> He has hardly mentioned holy things when he says something about "distinguished persons and their opinions" as though this miserable world and not the concern of his vocation to the priesthood was uppermost in his thoughts—These letters are valuable as showing the man—and how he at times mistrusts his strength in making the sacrifice and how glad he is to have it delayed—May God forgive and pity him! ...

> This letter shows the same uncertainty of purpose, and if we may say so, the same hollowness of arguments to excuse his worldliness—Altogether the misgivings he gives way to are the signs of a weak more than a wicked character so we may hope that want of intellectual clearness rather than malice united to the madness of overwrought feelings and misplaced jealousy may have been the cause of the terrible course he afterwards pursued.[97]

These editorial comments were influential in establishing the Society myth of the monstrous Pierce, a man more or less beyond redemption. No attempt is made by Buckle, or by the later biographers, to square this presentation with Cornelia's deep and passionate love for him, because a simple rather than a complex picture seemed more satisfactory: the worse Pierce was, the better Cornelia appeared.

[96] D63:131.
[97] D63:102; D63:144; D63:150-151.

Cornelia as Mother

Buckle had rather more knowledge of Cornelia the mother than of Cornelia the wife (she had met Adeline and Frank, and remembered Mercer's death), and she clearly felt more comfortable in exploring this area. Whilst Cornelia's sexual passion for Pierce was unmentionable—perhaps unthinkable—Buckle readily affirms her passionate motherly feelings. Buckle's theology allowed her to believe that Cornelia's home life had been set aside because of "a higher duty" but she acknowledges the cost to Cornelia, whose "heart broke in the struggle":

> Altogether the letters of Mother Connelly and her little girl [Adeline] speak of deep love between them and the passionate affection of Mother Connelly's southern nature centred in her home with all a woman's most devoted feelings, till a higher duty called her upwards and then as we shall see the coldness of hard hearted strangers thought the Mother's affections diminished, when her heart broke in the struggle and was only supported by extraordinary help from heaven to fulfil her hard task to the end.[98]

Perhaps because Victorian sensibilities were so outraged by the idea of a woman separated from her family, Buckle makes the same defence of Cornelia in several places, affirming her love for her children and her suffering when she lost them. "I can bear witness to the suffering of Mother Connelly and to her great affection for her children. It must have been a martyrdom for her to act as she did."[99]

According to Buckle, Cornelia was torn, not only by physical separation from her children, but by a concern for their immortal souls. The urgency and depth of this anxiety is foreign to present-day thinking, but it was keenly felt nonetheless:

> To lose their [the children's] friendship was not sufficient trial for Mother Connelly; as she said to me once, "If their souls were safe I would willingly give them up." But these children so dearly loved lost their faith also, and their father never in this life gave signs of repentance.[100]

---

[98] D65:37.
[99] D78:43.
[100] D63:31.

Buckle presents this concern for the children as part of Cornelia's spirituality; the language she uses, deliberately reminiscent of Scripture, links Cornelia's sufferings to those of Our Lady: "It is a sad and a kind of melancholy foreboding of the future evils that came on her children and pierced her own poor Mother's heart through and through."[101]

This comment concerned a response that Cornelia made to a letter from Mercer, who was at school at Stonyhurst. Buckle copied out the letters that Mercer had saved, which were subsequently returned to the Society. To a modern reader they appear to be a totally unsatisfactory response to the boy's situation, full of piety and exhortations to remember his meditation, and lacking both sympathy and insight. Buckle, however, judges them differently. For her they were proof of Cornelia's unwavering and consistent application of the values of religious life, and Buckle's tone is one of praise:

> These letters speak for themselves—They shew the same character and spirit as her later letters will do and prove the truth of what her husband had said of her, that in everything she was a professed nun long before she wore the dress—We have her ~~peculiar~~ strong and practical views of spirituality and we see the severe interior mortification she always exacted of her self and her children.[102]

To exact "severe interior mortification" from an adolescent boy would not today seem praiseworthy. Cornelia's letters, and Buckle's editorial comments, confirm the different, and now quite alien, spiritual context in which they lived.

However, Cornelia's response to Mercer's death is wholly comprehensible to the modern reader. Buckle writes:

> This additional blow was felt most profoundly by his poor Mother—For a few days she seemed quite overpowered with affliction and unable to do anything but pray to God in secret. The affliction was the more terrible as he had apostasized together with his unhappy Father. Mother Connelly never had the satisfaction of hearing any thing consoling of his last moments.[103]

---

[101] D65:37.
[102] D65:13.
[103] D65:113.

The depth of Cornelia's grief at the loss of her eldest child is immediately apparent. Yet Buckle herself seemed unattuned to it, and unsympathetically pragmatic in her judgement of Mercer. Immediately after the paragraph above, she continues:

> He was the same light and unstable character as his Father, and deeply as the blow was felt by Mother Connelly there is no knowing what additional trouble he might not have caused his poor mother in future times. Still the sorrow was inexpressible, and can only be known by a Mother's heart. Soon however Mother Connelly resumed her composure … [104]

Alongside her physical motherhood, Buckle explores and affirms the motherly nature of Cornelia's relationship with members of the Society. My own reading of Cornelia's writings suggest a more nuanced understanding of motherliness in this context.[105] But for Buckle it appears to have been a straightforward transposition of family values: Cornelia was ten or fifteen years older than even the oldest of the professed; she was the superior; and she assumed the role of mother for the members of the Society. Buckle comments on this on a number of occasions: "We told her … all that one might say in confidence to a Mother"; "She quieted me in a very motherly way"; "Postulants used to find her as sympathetic and affectionate in their early difficulties as the most tender of Mothers."[106] Buckle particularly noticed the mother-daughter relationship between Cornelia and Teresa Hanson, commenting that "a more than motherly love was the bond of their union."[107] In her personal recollections she expanded on the background to their relationship:

> Then was formed the friendship which ended in her vocation. Indeed Mother Foundress used to say when Mother Teresa was professed in 1848 after a year's noviceship that she considered she really entered the Society at Rome or rather she heard all the plans of Mother Foundress who accepted

---

[104] D65:113-114.
[105] For a full discussion of "motherliness" in the Society see chapter eight.
[106] D78:7-8; D78:10; D63:39.
[107] D64:155.

her as one of her own children at the Trinità—she was really her Mother as sponsor and godmother at her Confirmation.[108]

There is just the slightest suggestion of unacknowledged jealousy or irritation in Buckle's tone (perhaps a hint of what, appropriating Buckle's family analogy, might be called sibling rivalry for the mother's attention and approval) when she comments further:

> Mother Teresa was always suffering though one of the most active members of the Society and trusted most fully by Mother Foundress whose ideas she never heard but to admire and was in everything not only her affectionate child but her devoted adorer—if such an expression is not too strong but she never thought Mother Foundress could do anything that was not admirable—In this she was the direct opposite to Miss Bowles whose opinions were generally in opposition to those of Mother Foundress.[109]

Whatever impact Cornelia's motherliness had on relationships between members of the community, Buckle recognised its importance for Cornelia herself; in fact, she saw mothering, both of her biological children and of members of the Society, as central to Cornelia's spirituality and holiness.

What Was Buckle's Cornelia Like?

Buckle filled eight manuscript volumes with details of Cornelia's life and she established the dominant myth of Cornelia. Until the original documentation was collated in the 1960s, Cornelia could only be approached from Buckle's perspective: Buckle's interpretation of the events of her life was the basis for all future reflection, whether by subsequent biographers or by general readers. Even where later biographers disagreed with Buckle, that was always what they were doing: disagreeing with Buckle rather than putting forward their own different and independent arguments. Only she had the opportunity to present the material uninfluenced by a previous commentator. But even she was not totally free; her interpretation of Cornelia was influenced both by her conscious intentions (to present Cornelia as saint and to root developments in the

---

[108] D78:12.
[109] D78:17.

Society in the spirit of the founder) and by her unexamined assumptions (about the nature of society and of the Church).

Further, Buckle herself claims that her presentation of Cornelia was hampered by the founder's preference for privacy and cultivation of it. So much about her was unknown, even to those who had lived in close proximity to her:

> She never used to encourage much thought or much talk about self either in spiritual or temporal concerns—with a true humility when she had any thing to say to the nuns she would find some passage from a favourite Author which she would apply to the occasion, that she might not have the glory of the good thoughts and also that her advice might come with the authority of the great masters of the spiritual life from whom she gained her knowledge of the things of God.[110]

And yet this privacy, this interiority, and the determination to live totally in the present which went with them, were at the same time an important element in Cornelia's spiritual makeup, and one which Buckle emphasizes repeatedly:

> She was not one of those for ever asking <u>why</u> and certainly the lesson of her life is unmistakable—<u>Live for the present</u>—Actions not words—God alone—She would have thought it waste of time and waste of grace to brood over possibilities of past events—and in one word would chide such reflections by calling them self occupation—or the littleness of self love. ...

> This abandonment of self into the Divine Hands and of simply doing each moment what appears to be the most perfect, without any return on self was the special devotion of Mother Connelly. ...

> Exteriorly full of action the centre of great works and constantly weighed down by temporal cares—within her own interior she was leading another life—one hidden with Christ in God .... Her abandonment of self and her secrecy about her interior trials never allowed us to see the beautiful edifice she was raising in the temple of her heart.[111]

So, the reticence and privacy would appear to be an authentic part of any picture of Cornelia. But, according to Buckle, they were balanced by a warmth and generosity towards others and a capacity to enjoy life:

---

[110] D66:156-157.
[111] D65:194; D63:50; D66:157-158.

In her direction of others Mother Connelly by precept and example waged war against the littleness of self occupation—twining as she called it round self like a woodbine on a wall or a convolvulus round a stick—However when any real trial came to her knowledge which was being borne by us or by her friends or the children, her tears of sympathy were never refused and she had in a singular degree the power of giving … consolation. …

But though Mother Connelly knew how to exact self renunciation and self forgetfulness from those who were called to perfection, she was a most indulgent Superior to the young religious.[112]

The Cornelia we meet through Buckle was, above all, the revered Mother Foundress, presented by an admiring member of her congregation. Buckle knew Cornelia well, but only in this one context and from this one perspective. The portrait she offered was that of a religious superior drawn by a member of her community. It was not—and did not claim to be—a full and rounded picture of Cornelia the woman. But it did establish a master narrative, a founding myth about Cornelia which remained unquestioned for many years and is only now being re-evaluated.

---

[112] D63:37; D63:39.

Chapter Five

CONVENT CULTURE:
A STUDY IN FIDELITY

Rewriting a biography is very different from telling the story for the first time. Marie Thérèse Bisgood's *Cornelia Connelly: A Study in Fidelity* was written just over a century after the foundation of the Society of the Holy Child Jesus. Why was a new version of the story needed in the 1960s? What changes of emphasis and preoccupation are discernible in the new presentation? Was the current pattern of life within the Society reflected in this telling of the story? How was the Society responding to, and using, the life of its founder at this date?

Bisgood's biography was published in 1963 when, it might be said, the Society of the Holy Child Jesus was on the crest of a wave. Its membership was larger than it had ever been (or has been since) and the English province, in which Bisgood lived, had seen a record number of entrants in 1962.[1] In Britain the prime minister was Harold Macmillan, who had famously asserted during the 1959 election, "You've never had it so good." The Society's schools were benefiting from the 1944 education act, from the general conviction that academic qualifications would provide access to better jobs, and from increasing enrolments as those born in the immediate post-war population bulge reached secondary school age.

In this climate of optimism a new biography of Cornelia seemed timely, especially since information about her life was being retrieved as a preparatory stage in the process of her canonisation. The task of the diocesan historical commission for the cause, which was established by Cyril Cowderoy, Bishop of Southwark, in December 1953, was "to collect and evaluate all [Cornelia's] writings ... and all documentation about her to be found in ecclesiastical and secular archives."[2] From 1958, when Bisgood began work on the biography, she had access to this material; and the *Positio*

---

[1] It is perhaps worth noting that only one of the women who entered in 1962 is still a member of the Society.
[2] *Positio*, vi.

makes the unequivocal claim that the commissioners "discovered, listed and authenticated copies of every document that had any bearing on the life of the foundress or that had been written about her."[3] James Walsh's introduction to Bisgood's biography calls attention to the historical commissioners' research:

> This biography is based on the exhaustive research of the historical commission and its assistants. It does not claim to be a critical study of all the documents .... But it does correct many mistakes and fill in the lacunae of the previous biographies ... [4]

The cause of Cornelia's canonisation made progress (she was officially declared "venerable" in 1992), but in other respects the wave broke. In Britain, Macmillan resigned the premiership, with the last year of his government marred by the Profumo affair—a not insignificant milestone in public attitudes to morality, both political and sexual. In the Church, the Second Vatican Council (convened by John XXIII) was in session, and among its many consequences was radical change in the lives of women religious.

Convent Culture

There is no hint in Bisgood's text of what lay ahead (human beings are not generally prescient), but, even as she wrote, the customs of religious life that she took for granted were being questioned. The *nihil obstat* and *imprimatur* of Bisgood's biography are dated December 1961, although the book was not published until 1963. *The Nun in the World*, Cardinal Suenens' call for reform in the living patterns of woman religious, was written at much the same time. It appeared in English in 1962, and James Walsh refers to it twice in his short introduction to Bisgood's biography.

In his Foreword, Suenens expressed the hope that the forthcoming council, Vatican II, would free religious life from "the anachronisms that fetter it at present."[5] His book is based on exhortations given by Pius XII

---

[3] *Positio*, vii.

[4] James Walsh, introduction to Marie Thérèse Bisgood, *Cornelia Connelly: A Study in Fidelity* (London: Burns Oates, 1963), ix.

[5] Léon-Joseph Cardinal Suenens, *The Nun in the World* (London, Burns Oates, 1962), v.

during the 1950s, which, Suenens said, he "sought only to comment on and paraphrase." As early as 1952 Pius XII questioned the continuing appropriateness of convent customs:

> In September, 1952, the Pope … [speaking about vocations] called upon Superiors General to see that "customs, the kind of life or asceticism of religious families did not constitute a barrier or a source of failure." He was speaking, he continued, of "certain customs which, though they formerly had some meaning in a different cultural context, no longer have any and in which a young, fervent and courageous girl would find nothing but fetters inhibiting her vocation and her apostolate."[6]

Suenens, "pleading … for a pruning," spoke with "candour"[7] about the current situation in many convents, and the urgent need for reform:

> Religious too often seem to be living in a closed world … a fortress whose drawbridge is only furtively and fearfully lowered … an enclosure which, if it is not hermetically sealed, at least looks out on the world through openings more like arrow slits than bay windows . …
>
> Whence comes … the contrived and artificial nature of certain customs in religious houses—a sort of "house etiquette," a stilted, stereotyped and unnatural behaviour? It has been said of certain congregations of nuns that they are "the last strongholds of the very studied manners of the middle-class woman of the nineteenth century." …
>
> To put it briefly, the dusty old wax flowers should be replaced by living blooms … [8]

The "house etiquette" which Suenens saw as anachronistic was not superficial, however. It was rooted in a theology and formed the very fabric of women's religious life, "handed down … from generation to generation … [by] an unbroken chain of celibate mothers and daughters."[9] Within the convent enclosure, separated from "the world," women religious entered a subculture in which personal perfection was the goal, physical comfort was

---

[6] Suenens, *The Nun in the World*, 133.

[7] Suenens, *The Nun in the World*, vi.

[8] Suenens, *The Nun in the World*, 19-20.

[9] Patricia Curran, *Grace Before Meals: Food Ritual and Body Discipline in Convent Culture* (Urbana and Chicago: University of Illinois Press, 1989), vii.

suspect, penance was encouraged, and discipline, order and hierarchy were primary values.

Patricia Curran argues that the culture of convent life was influenced by Neoplatonism and Stoicism, and by heresies found in Evagrius, as well as by orthodox teaching such as Cassian's. Gradually, a culture evolved that was influenced by "subtle dualisms," "bred a contempt for material creation," cast "physical satisfaction in the role of tempter of the soul, [and moulded] celibacy and fasting into agents of control."[10] Its ascetic traditions and rituals created conflicts between nature and grace, encouraged an ambivalent attitude to the body, and stressed the value of "an ordered universe, a graced officialdom, a cohesive community."[11]

> Energies were deflected to the purification of the passions, and self-mastery overtook ministry on the road to perfection. When bodily realities define a fallen state, and intellectual contemplation defines union with God, the beatitudes of Jesus take second place to the blessedness of perpetual tranquillity. When the unenlightened masses and their carnal realities detract from the pursuit of holiness, rules of enclosure are a logical corollary. When the physicality of the incarnation and resurrection are passing stages to a more perfect incorporeality, the goods of creation lose their lustre. Pleasure no longer expands the affections with prayers of praise but constricts the heart with fear of temptation. Wine needs water, for safety's sake.[12]

By the 1950s, individual nuns interpreted this theology, spirituality and way of living to mean that "what was naturally repugnant was spiritually beneficial"[13] in their own lives. But their attitude was being called into question as Bisgood wrote. The practices challenged by Pius XII, Suenens and Vatican II were also resisted by the women entering religious orders:

> The novice of the 1950s was already different from her predecessors in manifesting the analytical and critical spirit of her contemporary culture, and such questioning of cultural values is itself a sign of their loss of power .... The custom books of the 1930s ... were not only unacceptable in 1960, their formalism and perfectionism were now amusing; the lifestyle based on

[10] Curran, *Grace Before Meals*, 105.

[11] Curran, *Grace Before Meals*, 101.

[12] Curran, *Grace Before Meals*, 104-105.

[13] Curran, *Grace Before Meals*, 144.

a mystique of self-abnegation was now unattractive and its archaic qualities were seen as an impediment to apostolic accomplishments.[14]

By the 1950s convent culture was so at variance with contemporary culture that it was in urgent need of reform. Suenens urged women religious to adopt "a modern approach" in "the modern world," whilst safeguarding "the essential and indispensable components of the religious life"[15] (though he failed to specify what these were). But Vatican II unleashed the passions and energies of women religious in a way his book did not anticipate. Nuns embraced the teachings of the Council and of liberation theologians, and engaged with the issues of their contemporaries "on the personal and political levels." "Congregations who once marked progress in the spiritual life by the presence of tranquillity and the control of the senses"[16] found themselves in turmoil.

But Bisgood had entered the Society in 1914; for nearly half a century she had absorbed and lived out the theological and cultural values of convent tradition. They had become the substance of her life—much more than a veneer that could easily be removed. The argument of this chapter is not just that Bisgood's writing reflects the values of convent culture, but that—consciously and unconsciously—she is using the story of the founder to reinforce values that were being called into question. Bisgood offers a detailed analysis of Cornelia's sanctification through suffering, and presents tranquillity, calmness and order as significant virtues in her life.

Bisgood's Background, Views and Assumptions

Marie Thérèse Bisgood (1891-1975) came from a privileged and educated background. She read modern languages at Oxford. She was, fundamentally, an Edwardian, entering the Society at the beginning of World War I, when she was 23. Her necrology speaks of her "pleasure-loving and somewhat languid personality," and her "deep faith and tenacity of purpose." The necrologist—reflecting the values of convent culture even in 1975—sees these characteristics as conflicting, and observes that "the struggle

---

[14] Curran, *Grace Before Meals*, 136.

[15] Suenens, *The Nun in the World*, vi.

[16] Curran, *Grace Before Meals*, 157.

between natural temperament and vocation was acute and lasted all her life."

Necrologies, whilst striving to be honest, tend towards a positive presentation of the individual; the subtext, the issues that are no more than hinted at, can be particularly revealing. In the following paragraph, for instance, the complexity of Bisgood's personality is delicately explored:

> Sister Marie Thérèse was an outstanding personality in the Society of her time not by an outward show of strength but by that power which is made perfect in infirmity. She had great natural gifts, "charming, witty and very intelligent" as one of her Oxford students describes her, and was loved and respected by her communities, students and a wide circle of friends. Some were in awe of her forthright judgments and the occasional caustic turn of her keen wit, but many pay tribute to her kind understanding, wise advice and spiritual influence. Unknown to all but her close friends was "a diffidence astonishing in one of such intellect and mature judgement" which caused her to cling to them for support and encouragement, sometimes a little too closely for the general good. Reserved in manner she was capable of deep affection, loving perhaps more in depth than breadth. She was a true and loyal friend.

Bisgood "was an outstanding personality in the Society," but some criticism is detectable at least in the suggestion that she clung to her friends "sometimes a little too closely for the general good." The necrologist goes on to indicate the physical and mental weakness that clouded her final years:

> In spite of the care lavished on her in the Mayfield Infirmary her last years were years of pain. Hypersensitive about the weaknesses of old age and her dependence, she gradually withdrew from those around her while suffering greatly from the consequent loneliness and isolation.

But Bisgood's academic gifts were fully used in the Society: she was given positions of responsibility both at the college in Cavendish Square, London, and at Cherwell Edge in Oxford. During the Second World War the superior general and her council were isolated in Rome, out of contact with the rest of the Society for months at a time, and more responsibility for decision making was necessarily assumed within the provinces. Bisgood had been appointed a local superior in 1939 and remained in office for twenty years. She was still a member of the provincial council in her late sixties when she began to write her biography. The necrologist speaks of her "forward-looking ideas, fearlessly expressed even when most unorthodox." As one who had held positions of authority for a significant time, however, she also had much invested in the furtherance of the Society and its founder; and, in the optimistic climate of the 1950s, she had a confidence in the Society's continuing expansion.[17]

The personality, values, attitudes, natural preferences and experiences described by the necrologist are relevant to the biography Bisgood produced. And, within the context of convent culture, they perhaps explain the willingness of such a gifted woman to be influenced beyond due measure by James Walsh, the vice-postulator of the cause. Walsh reveals his control of the biography in a letter to Leonard Whatmore, a Southwark priest who was one of the historical commissioners. Walsh assumes that he and Whatmore will determine its contents:

> Mother Marie Thérèse and myself have now decided that the interim Life should break away entirely from the 1950 abridgement of Mother Mary Catherine. I have drawn up a scheme for her to cover Cornelia's life between 1846 and 1879. I would like to know what you think in general of this scheme. The first part of the Life Mother Marie Thérèse had already written. This appeared in serial form in THE PYLON six or seven years ago. It went as far as Cornelia's arrival in Paris in the August of 1846. On the whole the first part is written in quite an impressive style ... I have suggested to her that she begins immediately with Derby, and then later on she can go back to the first part. So I will continue to make my notes on the 1950 Life as far as Derby and send them to you, as usual, for your additions and observations. Then, with regard to the rest, I think perhaps we could just set down, you and I, whatever documentation occurs to us as the most important for each chapter in the new scheme. Do you approve of this? (28 October 1959)

We must bear in mind, in all discussion of this biography, the existence and influence of Walsh as *eminence grise*. Obedience to authority, especially priestly authority, was a *sine qua non* of convent culture.

Nevertheless, the consonance between Bisgood's description of Cornelia and the necrologist's description of Bisgood is striking. When Bisgood presents Cornelia as "well-bred, well-educated, highly intelligent,

---

[17] A large noviciate wing had recently been completed at Mayfield and the entrants of 1962 included the first African SHCJ.

and one whose spiritual experiences fitted her to be the leader of others,"[18] is she merely recording the facts known about the founder, or is she finding in her subject a mirror of herself? Similarly, the necrologist's comments on Bisgood's "loneliness and isolation" recall the image Bisgood applies to Cornelia: "Cornelia's hand had been put to the plough, and the first step had been taken along the furrow which she was to drive straight and lonely to the end."[19] Bisgood had to choose an angle from which to present Cornelia, and her choice seems, understandably, to have been influenced by factors in her own life experience and personality, and particularly by her unquestioning acceptance of the values of convent culture.

Initially it would seem that a clue to Bisgood's Cornelia is offered in the subtitle of the biography, *A Study in Fidelity*. The dust jacket displays a photograph of the mature Cornelia dressed in the habit of the Society and enclosed in a circlet of ivy, symbol of fidelity. Yet an examination of the text reveals little overt discussion of fidelity as a central theme in Cornelia's life. The theme that predominates is calm detachment—a quality cultivated and prized within convents in the mid-twentieth century, and perhaps particularly attractive to the "reserved" Bisgood herself.

Bisgood makes constant reference to Cornelia's calmness and detachment:

> ... in any circumstances and into her old age her serenity remained unruffled. She ... viewed the success or failure of her schemes *sub specie aeternitatis*.[20]

> Except for the occasional cry of anguish ... or an indication of strain once or twice ... she shows herself calm, objective, interested in everybody's problems, completely in control of the situation as far as it lay within her.[21]

> She had no moods. Her temper was always equable, the tranquillity of order reigned about her .... To the outside observer she presented a bright

---

[18] Bisgood, *Cornelia Connelly*, 66.

[19] Bisgood, *Cornelia Connelly*, 11. This is not an isolated reference to loneliness. See, for instance, 134, "a lonely position to take up," and the description of Cornelia's final illness, 303-308, where her isolation from those she cared for most is stressed.

[20] Bisgood, *Cornelia Connelly*, 164.

[21] Bisgood, *Cornelia Connelly*, 281.

serenity of demeanour which never seemed to be disturbed …. She was always completely in control of any situation.[22]

On numerous other occasions she comments on Cornelia's "unalterable serenity," on her remaining "detached in spirit, patient and unalterably calm" and "impress[ing] her own calm and recollected spirit on her surroundings and train[ing] the nuns to the same control over circumstances."[23] Quoting letters written by Cornelia in moments of crisis, she describes them as written "with the usual serene impersonality," "tranquilly," "calmly."[24] Instances occur on page after page; in the course of three short paragraphs, for example, she describes Cornelia as "heartbroken but amazingly detached," "this calmly detached woman," who "kept her head and her dignity … [and] wrote calmly …."[25] Perhaps most revealing is Bisgood's assessment of Lucy Ignatia Newsham, one of the first members of the Society to die in America:

> The accounts of her sweetness and unselfishness, and the courage and calmness with which she met her death, mark her out as a true daughter of Mother Connelly's training and the ideal of a Holy Child nun.[26]

The ideal here is, of course, Bisgood's ideal. Cornelia herself, the evidence suggests, often felt anything but calm and detached. As late as 1872 (when she was 63) Cornelia accused herself, in her private spiritual notes, of,

> … thinking too much of self, weighing every little slighting word and act of others, yielding to wounded feeling and anger, compassionating myself, giving way to sadness and tears.[27]

In her writing Bisgood reduces authorial comment to a minimum, evidently subscribing to a theory of biographical objectivity, of allowing the facts of Cornelia's life to speak for themselves (though, of course, Bisgood has selected the facts). The store she sets by objectivity is revealed in her

---

[22] Bisgood, *Cornelia Connelly*, 314.

[23] Bisgood, *Cornelia Connelly*, 32, 35, 43, 119.

[24] Bisgood, *Cornelia Connelly*, 70, 97, 107. These adverbs signify authorial interpretation.

[25] Bisgood, *Cornelia Connelly*, 106-107.

[26] Bisgood, *Cornelia Connelly*, 215.

[27] CC 22:16-17.

approval of Cornelia's own views. Her description of Cornelia as "calm, objective, interested in everyone's problems" has already been noted. Similarly, she comments: "What was remarkable about Mother Connelly's search was its complete objectivity."[28]

In spite of her desire for authorial distance, Bisgood's social attitudes and her assumptions about religious life and spirituality inevitably colour the text. Her early-twentieth-century, upper-middle-class English background can be detected in the observation that: "Only the servants, with the direct intuition of simple folk, felt there was anything unusual about her [Cornelia]."[29] (This is an isolated comment, in no way typical of the general tone and style of the biography, but to a modern reader it sounds gratuitously patronising.) Her pre-Vatican II view of the Church is revealed in her resounding description of Newman's conversion as "the submission of John Henry Newman to the irrefragable claims of Rome."[30] Her understanding of religious life is similarly dated, and firmly rooted in the assumptions of convent culture. She speaks of the life of Sacred Heart nuns as a "spiritual haven,"[31] and she seems to equate religious life with perfection. Of Cornelia's experiences at Grand Coteau, she observes:

> Cornelia's friendship with Reverend Mother Cutts and the wise direction of Father Point, Rector of the College, were valuable supports in guiding her first steps along the path of perfection which opened out before her.[32]

> Cornelia was already considerably further along the road of spiritual maturity than many a professed religious.[33]

Bisgood accepts the dualism of convent culture, often opposing "duty" to "worldly position,"[34] and the natural to both the spiritual and the supernatural:

---

[28] Bisgood, *Cornelia Connelly*, 134.

[29] Bisgood, *Cornelia Connelly*, 45.

[30] Bisgood, *Cornelia Connelly*, 65.

[31] Bisgood, *Cornelia Connelly*, 49.

[32] Bisgood, *Cornelia Connelly*, 25.

[33] Bisgood, *Cornelia Connelly*, 36.

[34] Of the adolescent Cornelia (about whom she acknowledges that very few facts are known) she writes: "Already her life was shaped on principle and guided by what she saw as duty. And before long those principles were to be tested by a sharp conflict with family affections and worldly position." (5)

On the natural plane can be adduced fatigue, suspense and mental strain. But there is another factor to be considered on the supernatural level. After the fateful October 13th, 1840, Cornelia clearly entered upon that path of progressive detachment from the natural and *legitimate* joys of the world.[35]

Her constant use of the word "supernatural" has a very 1950s ring. She says, for instance, and without further explanation, that Cornelia had "a supernaturalised quality of leadership,"[36] and speaks of her "natural and spiritual ascendancy" over the rest of the community.[37] Bisgood's use of dichotomies reflects the values of convent culture, and her acceptance of what Philip Sheldrake describes as "an inherent tendency towards excessive 'refinement' conceived in hierarchical terms: the spiritual was above the material, withdrawal was superior to engagement, contemplation a better way than activity."[38]

Placing a value on ever-increasing "refinement" leads inexorably, through the desire for "detachment from the natural and *legitimate* joys of the world," to an acceptance of suffering and sacrifice, and an assumption that these are a preferred way to perfection and sanctity. Bisgood takes for granted that God puts people to the test and that sacrifice has intrinsic value:

> This was the supreme moment to which God had been leading her; she did not fail in the test.[39]

> We can only stand hesitating and reverent on the threshold of that inner sanctuary within which the sacrifice was being consummated.[40]

This highly charged language points not only to how the rhetoric of sacrifice and suffering was central in convent culture, but also to Bisgood's use of the biographical material to reinforce that rhetoric. The reader is to

[35] Bisgood, *Cornelia Connelly*, 57-58 (her italics). This is not an isolated use of the natural/supernatural dualism. See also, for instance, 50-51, 54, 78, 79.

[36] Bisgood, *Cornelia Connelly*, 78. When I entered the Society in the mid 1960s we were still being encouraged to "supernaturalise" events and to "rise above" them.

[37] Bisgood, *Cornelia Connelly*, 84.

[38] Sheldrake, *Spirituality and History*, 63.

[39] Bisgood, *Cornelia Connelly*, 31.

[40] Bisgood, *Cornelia Connelly*, 34.

learn from Cornelia's example, to desire to emulate her, "to stand hesitating and reverent."

Convent Culture: Mortification, Renunciation, Detachment, Sacrifice

The closing sentences of Bisgood's biography make a strong claim about the significance of suffering in Cornelia's life:

> Cornelia … learnt the secret of self-abnegation which led her further into abandonment to God's Will. Throughout her life, choice after bitter choice was laid before her, and she never refused to drink of the chalice her Model had drunk of. "Doing the Will of God," she said on her deathbed, "is the only happiness, and the only thing worth living for." That is the lesson of her life. "If the good God asks the sacrifice," she had cried out in the shock of that first call to renunciation at Grand Coteau, "I am ready to make it to Him and with all my heart." And four years later, after the extent of her offering had been measured and fully accepted, she noted in her little book the phrase which is an epitome of her life, "Refuse no sacrifice that would be for His greater glory."[41]

It seems fair to assume that, in this final paragraph, Bisgood is attempting to encapsulate Cornelia's spirituality—what she has been wanting the biography to communicate. The message is clear: "self-abnegation"; "abandonment to God's will"; "she never refused to drink of the chalice"; "call to renunciation"; "her offering had been measured and accepted."

This was powerful and emotive language in the convent world of the 1950s and 1960s, but attitudes to suffering were changing even as Bisgood wrote. Within religious communities, younger women were questioning and rejecting the negative concept of the self that lay behind the practice of physical penances:

> In the novititates of the 1960s … candidates no longer thought in [the same] ascetical framework. They did not understand the origins of refectory customs [public penances]; they were mystified by the anti-body attitudes they implied; they executed them out of necessity without owning them interiorly.[42]

---

[41] Bisgood, *Cornelia Connelly*, 317.
[42] Curran, *Grace Before Meals*, 82.

Something like the instinctive response of young women entering religious life also underlies Valerie Saiving's seminal article, "The Human Situation: A Feminine View", which appeared in 1960. Saiving argues that a theology and a spirituality rooted in self-abnegation and self-denial are unhealthy, and are particularly unhelpful for women, since they reinforce negative social expectations. Her article ends:

> If it is true that our society is moving from a masculine to a feminine orientation, then theology ought to reconsider its estimate of the human condition and redefine its categories of sin and redemption. For a feminine society will have its own special potentialities for good and evil, to which a theology based solely on masculine experience may well be irrelevant.[43]

Despite the fact that Bisgood and Saiving were writing contemporaneously, they were poles apart: Saiving is calling for something new, while Bisgood affirms the value of what she has known and experienced, and what has, perhaps, brought her to personal holiness. Cornelia undoubtedly developed a spirituality of suffering; her life, as Bisgood says, "is so full of harsh renunciations, tragic misunderstandings, hazardous undertakings,"[44] that these events have to be the stuff of her spiritual experience. But the emphasis on mortification, renunciation, detachment and sacrifice in this biography is not the whole picture; it is the picture as Bisgood, formed by convent culture, saw and understood it.

The passive acceptance of suffering and injustice strikes the reader today as less than holistic, less than healthy. But Bisgood and Walsh believed that it could be, not only healthy, but a path to spiritual maturity and holiness. In his introduction, Walsh defends a spirituality of "radical, often violent, renunciation of personal inclinations and aversions," and speaks of a God "who used more violent means than death to break the bond of natural love and duty which tied her to her husband and family."[45] Today we resist such a violent God, just as we resist Bisgood's testing God.

---

[43] Valerie Saiving, "The Human Situation: A Feminine View" (first published in *The Journal of Religion*, 40 [April 1960], 100-112), reprinted in *WomanSpirit Rising: A Feminist Reader in Religion*, edited by Carol P. Christ and Judith Plaskow (New York: HarperCollins, 1992 [1979]), 41.

[44] Bisgood, *Cornelia Connelly*, 135.

[45] Walsh, introduction to Bisgood, *Cornelia Connelly*, v.

Bisgood's presentation of the biographical material reveals her assumptions about suffering and abnegation, and her unquestioning acceptance of a spirituality based on detachment, self-mortification and self-denial. The Rule of the Society in the 1950s validated Bisgood's outlook: "the greatest and most effectual efforts of everyone ought to be directed towards obtaining from Our Divine Lord the grace of continual progress in self-abnegation and mortification in all things."[46] Bisgood's inclusion of this sentence in her biography reinforces its significance for members of the Society by associating it with the founder. She refers to the Rule by which she and her contemporaries were living twice in two pages, whilst describing Cornelia's life at the Trinità dei Monti, before the Society had even been thought of:

> She was not spared the trial of misunderstanding and tactless criticism …. St Ignatius' exposition of the third degree of humility she was already making her own in practice and would embody it in the Rule of her Society. …

> She already practised what in future her Rule will teach in the matter of mortification; "the greatest and most effectual efforts of everyone ought to be directed towards obtaining from Our Divine Lord the grace of continual progress in self-abnegation and mortification in all things."[47]

Another convent value that Bisgood particularly stresses is silence—especially Cornelia's silence in the face of calumnies and accusations. When people attacked Cornelia, as they frequently did, and made unjust and false charges, Bisgood says: "she schooled herself to make no defence against personal criticisms or recriminations."[48] And these were no minor matters. During the dispute about the St Leonards property, Bisgood writes:

> Mother Connelly found herself attacked on all sides. She was accused, and not only by irresponsible elements, of influencing Col Towneley to gain her own ends, of misappropriating funds, of attempting to destroy the St Leonards mission. Dr Duke in his innumerable letters did not hesitate to describe her as artful, untruthful and dictatorial, and the echoes of the

---

[46] Quoted in Bisgood, *Cornelia Connelly*, 37-38.

[47] Bisgood, *Cornelia Connelly*, 36, 37-38.

[48] Bisgood, *Cornelia Connelly*, 36.

dispute reached London, where her name was bandied about at dinner-parties as a hypocritical adventuress.[49]

Dr Duke, a leading layman in the St Leonards parish, was Cornelia's implacable enemy, and he spread his opinion of her far and wide, to everyone from cardinals in Rome to the fishboy who called at the convent. Bisgood describes Cornelia's response to this onslaught:

> In all her letters there is no faint echo of resentment about it, either then or at any other time. She was not insensible to it; on the contrary, she was often deeply wounded, but her strongest comment … after she had endured seven or eight years of it … [was] "it is rather vexing."[50]

This choice of quotation provides a clear example of Bisgood's selection of material to reinforce convent values. She could, in fact, have presented a quite different picture of Cornelia here. The letter from which the phrase "it is rather vexing" is taken, written to Colonel Towneley, from St Leonards on 21 October 1858, is preceded in the letter book by a much more impassioned reaction to Dr Duke. Cornelia did not send this first version of the letter, but it reveals, in Cornelia's response to the situation, rather more than a "faint echo of resentment":

> I feel more hurt than I can tell at the last accusations—so false, so unjust, so uncalled for! All hope of future peace is at an end—when Dr Duke dies his sons will come forward with the same spirit and this would go on age after age, to our discomfort and injury.[51]

But Bisgood's Cornelia is not passionate; she is a model of calm detachment, silent endurance and suffering. This is the aspect of her life and spirituality that Bisgood stresses in the closing pages of the biography:

> From the earliest records she made of her spiritual life—that is, in 1840—we know that she was practising that intense interior mortification known as self-control.[52]

---

[49] Bisgood, *Cornelia Connelly*, 178-179.

[50] Bisgood, *Cornelia Connelly*, 179.

[51] D4:38.

[52] Bisgood, *Cornelia Connelly*, 314.

> The hidden life for her was not merely the choice of retirement and solitude, or even the love to be unknown. It was a relentless stripping of self, a total renunciation of the ego. It was a life "hidden with Christ in God," a death to self-determination, a complete surrender to the all-embracing Will of God .... There is no sentimentality here. It was not the *charms* of childhood that Cornelia loved, but its humiliations.[53]

Such language and such spirituality are, at the very least, unfashionable today. But Bisgood is unhesitating in her conviction that detachment from human affections, the conquest of the self, mortification, self-discipline, the suppression of feelings, renunciation, surrender to the judgment of others, and the relinquishment of one's own will constitute the road to holiness. Bisgood distrusts "sentiment and feeling" and values "fixed and methodical principles, carefully worked out in accordance with the demands made ... by duties."[54] She presents incident after incident to demonstrate Cornelia's continued growth in this negative spirituality. There can be no doubt that Bisgood herself valued it highly, and stood in awe when she saw it practised by others.[55]

Bisgood's insertion into convent culture, and her personal preference, seem to have led her to emphasize a particular dimension of Cornelia's spirituality. But she offers enough concrete examples and quotations to convince the reader that suffering, and the way in which Cornelia found God in it, were so central to Cornelia's life that no biographer could ignore them. Influenced by both the spirituality of the nineteenth-century Church and the social *mores* of Victorian England, Cornelia constantly chose to trust the judgment of others rather than her own feelings, believing that submission, especially to those in legitimate authority, was submission to God, and that obedience would guarantee that she was doing God's will. As Bisgood says:

> God's will was the mainspring, one might say the ruling passion, of her life, and she sought it unwearyingly amid the labyrinths of claims and counter-claims, commands and hindrances, recriminations and calumnies, in which her life was spent.[56]

---

[53] Bisgood, *Cornelia Connelly*, 316 (her italics).

[54] Bisgood, *Cornelia Connelly*, 26.

[55] See, for instance, Bisgood, *Cornelia Connelly*, 34.

[56] Bisgood, *Cornelia Connelly*, 134.

The circumstances of Cornelia's life after she came to England were certainly hard: there was "the scandal of her husband's lawsuit" against her, the "embarrassment" she caused "to the leading members of the Hierarchy," and "one failure after another."[57] In all of this, according to Bisgood, she consciously chose silence, "unless justice for the Society and the honour of God or the Church demanded it."[58] She never defended her own reputation:

> Each of [her] trials dealt a harder blow to her reputation, brought about a deeper humbling of the spirit which was accepted without bitterness and with exterior equanimity.[59]

About loss of reputation Bisgood offers one of her rare authorial comments, revealing her own standpoint clearly:

> To have one's personal integrity so attacked, to be held up before the world as lacking in truthfulness and elementary honesty is the ultimate humiliation.[60]

Perhaps Cornelia's biggest source of suffering, as the founder of a congregation, was that the Rule of the Society remained unratified by the Church, and consequently the Society's stability and its survival were not assured. Both Bisgood and Walsh link this disappointment directly with Cornelia's spirituality of suffering. Walsh observes:

> Cornelia died as she had lived, in the shadow of the Cross. It was only in the luminous darkness of her perfect faith that she saw the survival of her work.[61]

Bisgood develops the crucifixion imagery even more fully. Noting that Cornelia died exactly thirty-three years from the day on which she left Rome to found the Society, "to begin the task appointed her by God," she continues:

---

[57] See Walsh, introduction to Bisgood, *Cornelia Connelly*, vii.

[58] Bisgood, *Cornelia Connelly*, 312.

[59] Bisgood, *Cornelia Connelly*, 310.

[60] Bisgood, *Cornelia Connelly*, 312.

[61] Walsh, introduction to Bisgood, *Cornelia Connelly*, vi.

Outwardly she had left it unfinished. But it was completed in His eyes. She had given all, done all, He asked of her. Through life she had given Him an undivided heart. Her life and the living of it was her work, brought like Christ's to triumphant achievement in failure.[62]

Though both Walsh and Bisgood make hagiographical claims ("her perfect faith," her "undivided heart"), the facts of Cornelia's story oblige Bisgood to acknowledge that the sufferings of her life were extremely costly for Cornelia, and that accepting them and learning to recognise God in them did not come easily to her. Here is a subtext that counters the claims of perfection and calm detachment.

Twice, in describing Cornelia at the Trinità dei Monti, Bisgood speaks of her "taut spirit."[63] Cornelia intended to become a member of the Society of the Sacred Heart, but at the Trinità she seems to have experienced both spiritual desolation and depression. She "felt a sense of unspeakable dread weighing upon her"; "solitude descended like a heavy burden on her spirit"; "the comforting sense of God's love and protection and guidance left her"; she was "weary, desolate."[64] Bisgood finds it difficult to acknowledge such struggle and resistance because they are at variance with her preferred model of Cornelia as living the values of convent culture with calm detachment. "Peace she possessed, if not joy," Bisgood claims, quoting a letter that Cornelia wrote at this time. The description that immediately follows presents Cornelia as anything but peaceful—though Bisgood puts as positive a gloss on the situation as she can:

> November brought the community retreat, but no respite from suffering. She was ill, her health giving way under the strain she was enduring. Death would have been a welcome release. But the indomitable will forced the exhausted body into co-operation.[65]

Bisgood draws a distinction between the "physical fatigue, suspense and mental strain" that Cornelia was experiencing on "the natural plane," and "the supernatural level" where Cornelia was caught up in what she

---

[62] Bisgood, *Cornelia Connelly*, 308.

[63] Bisgood, *Cornelia Connelly*, 42, 54.

[64] Bisgood, *Cornelia Connelly*, 54, 56.

[65] Bisgood, *Cornelia Connelly*, 56.

elsewhere calls "deep spiritual experiences,"[66] enduring "an avalanche of temptation and desolation."[67] The struggle, the pain, the darkness, the deadness, Bisgood describes in terms of spiritual "progress":

> Cornelia entered upon that path of progressive detachment from the natural and *legitimate* joys of the world, which leads through St John's "passive purgation of the senses" to the Illuminative Way. This she reached during the retreat she made in September 1841, when she received and recognised her new vocation, and offered herself to follow it faithfully to the end.[68]

This experience at the Trinità is the most fully documented instance of desolation in Cornelia's life. But there are hints elsewhere in Bisgood's biography that it was not the only occasion when Cornelia struggled with a spirituality that valued submission and duty above instinctive human responses. At Mercer's death, for instance, "she gave way to her grief, and refused to be comforted."[69] Increasingly as she grew older, Bisgood notes, physical illness accompanied every major crisis. At the time of the Kenworthy case, Cornelia "collapsed under the strain ... ill for several months with bronchitis and rheumatic gout."[70] Returning from Rome, where she had been working on the Constitutions with Anselmo Knapen, "she was on the verge of a serious breakdown in health."[71] "She was in fact for most of her religious life a very suffering woman, and in the last years, with the unbearable strain put upon her, a very sick one."[72]

For all Bisgood's emphasis on detachment and mortification there is no evidence in the biography that Cornelia saw self-denial and self-discipline as ends in themselves. Cornelia's spirit is rooted in the Incarnation and her spirituality is fundamentally one of life, not death. As Bisgood observes:

> Her life ... is so full of harsh renunciations, tragic misunderstandings, hazardous undertakings, that there would seem to be no room for laughter

---

[66] Bisgood, *Cornelia Connelly*, 79.

[67] Bisgood, *Cornelia Connelly*, 57.

[68] Bisgood, *Cornelia Connelly*, 58.

[69] Bisgood, *Cornelia Connelly*, 112.

[70] Bisgood, *Cornelia Connelly*, 245.

[71] Bisgood, *Cornelia Connelly*, 264.

[72] Bisgood, *Cornelia Connelly*, 314.

or the happy simple things. And yet, in spite of all, cheerfulness keeps breaking in.[73]

Cornelia, it seems, cannot be pigeon-holed. She suffered greatly, and she experienced God not only in the major but also in the many minor vicissitudes of her life. Bisgood calls attention to the continual criticism Cornelia endured:

> No work or action of Mother Connelly's ever seems to have been free from that corroding blight ... the wear on the nerves, the deadening drag on the spirit, of sheer spiteful tittle-tattle—she had to endure this minor cross all her life; and the wonder is that she retained her buoyancy.[74]

But she did retain her buoyancy which, if Bisgood is to be believed, was both a natural trait and a "supernatural grace bestowed upon her largely for the encouragement of others."[75] In the opening pages of the biography Bisgood describes the young Cornelia, as yet totally unformed by the events of life: "lovely and spontaneous, ... merry and very intelligent."[76] After her conversion to Catholicism, when Cornelia was living in Rome as a married woman, Bisgood speaks of her developing spirituality in open and positive terms. At this time, she says, influenced by her experience of the liturgy and by Catholic friendships, notably that with Gwendalin Talbot:

> A certain character was stamped on her spirituality that remained with her to the end, a largeness and nobility combined with a confiding simplicity in her approach to God.[77]

In Rome, Bisgood presents the Earl of Shrewsbury (Gwendaline's father) speculating that Cornelia would be just the person whom Wiseman needed to found the congregation he envisaged, "bringing into it, moreover, the broad-mindedness of a convert and the free outlook of an American," and so being "the pioneer in this adventure for the glory of God."[78]

---

[73] Bisgood, *Cornelia Connelly*, 315.
[74] Bisgood, *Cornelia Connelly*, 157.
[75] Bisgood, *Cornelia Connelly*, 79.
[76] Bisgood, *Cornelia Connelly*, 3.
[77] Bisgood, *Cornelia Connelly*, 19.
[78] Bisgood, *Cornelia Connelly*, 67.

Once the Society was established in Derby, Bisgood stresses that its spirituality was influenced and shaped by Cornelia's own. Cornelia had "sublime confidence in God" and "she communicated it to her companions."[79] Bisgood reinforces this claim by quoting the recollections of Aloysia Walker, a member of the Derby community: Cornelia "had everything to do" and "Her beautiful confidence and trust in God grew upon us so that the thought of not succeeding never entered into our minds."[80] Later, discussing Cornelia's educational philosophy, Bisgood herself makes much the same point:

> Mother Connelly's own buoyancy and optimism gave her an insight into the psychology of success. No one, she maintained, should be allowed to think herself a failure. Her cheerful, encouraging spirit was one of the most attractive traits in her character.[81]

It may, therefore, be argued that Cornelia's spirituality of suffering was not an unrelenting denial of all that was life-giving and pleasurable. Cornelia enjoyed life to the full: "a joyful spirit … is the mark … of the Society."[82] But the circumstances of her life were not always joyful. So Cornelia accepted her sufferings and failures as well as her joys as ways to encounter God. And Bisgood takes this spirituality and presents it in the language of convent culture—the language of mortification, renunciation, submission, detachment. Her biography of the foundress reinforces convent life as members of the Society were currently living it.

Holiness

Her spirituality of sacrifice is of a piece with Bisgood's constant—and evidently approving—references to detachment from natural pleasures and from human affections as an indicator of sanctity. Cornelia's mother died when Cornelia was fourteen, and Bisgood comments that at this time "Cornelia reached the first milestone on a way of progressive detachment

---

[79] Bisgood, *Cornelia Connelly*, 78.
[80] Aloysia Walker, quoted in Bisgood, *Cornelia Connelly*, 78.
[81] Bisgood, *Cornelia Connelly*, 167.
[82] Bisgood, *Cornelia Connelly*, 316.

from human affections."[83] How this squares with her passionate love for Pierce a few years later is not made clear. Instead, the early life of the foundress, about which Bisgood acknowledges that "very few details ... have come down to us,"[84] is presented in a traditionally hagiographical form that reinforces the chaste values of convent living. From the slender information she has, Bisgood makes some big (and unsupportable) claims to establish that Cornelia's saintly credentials stretch back into childhood:

> This girl in her teens showed a self-possession and a power of self-discipline unusual for her years. ...
>
> Already her ideals were pitched high, and she followed quite simply but determinedly the good, the true, and the beautiful under whatever form she saw them.[85]

Bisgood emphasizes the wealth of Cornelia's family, and claims that Cornelia was not only beautiful but "gifted far above the average, and in everything she touched she succeeded brilliantly."[86] This conforms to a hagiographical formula; Sheldrake, discussing traditional criteria for holiness, writes:

> Social élitism has also been present in perceptions of holiness. It is interesting to note that, between about 1000-1700, saints appear in a ration of approximately three to one in favour of élite classes. There was a disposition to equate moral with social nobility.[87]

To this we must add that saintly women were also invariably beautiful.

It seems indisputable that Bisgood's biography was intended to bear testimony to Cornelia's sanctity and to her suitability for canonisation, given Walsh's control over it, and given the Society's commitment at this time to the active promotion of Cornelia's cause. An assumption that the canonised saint must be seen to move from milestone to milestone along a way of progressive holiness underlies Bisgood's presentation of Cornelia's

---

[83] Bisgood, *Cornelia Connelly*, 4.
[84] Bisgood, *Cornelia Connelly*, 3.
[85] Bisgood, *Cornelia Connelly*, 4, 6.
[86] Bisgood, *Cornelia Connelly*, 4.
[87] Sheldrake, *Spirituality and History*, 61.

childhood. In accord with this model of saintliness Bisgood had also, necessarily, to demonstrate Cornelia's holiness as a wife and mother, before she could write about Cornelia the holy foundress. If, as I have argued, Bisgood was intent on reinforcing the values of convent culture, that would be no easy task for her.

In this context the references to masculinity with which the biography begins and ends cannot be overlooked. Walsh, in the introduction, calls attention to Cornelia's "masculine fearlessness and integrity of purpose [which] startled and unnerved Grant, exasperated Wiseman and outraged Ullathorne."[88] And in the final paragraph of the book Bisgood states that "Cornelia trained her religious to courage and virility."[89] In the body of the text Cornelia as sexually aware, sexually active woman, Cornelia as sexual partner, remains largely invisible, even if space and attention are given to Cornelia as mother in references both to her own children and to early members of the Society. Each of these elements (the choice of masculine epithets, the silence about sexual activity, and the emphasis on motherhood) situate the biography firmly within convent culture. Masculinity was unquestionably normative in the Church (and in society generally) in the 1950s, and both Walsh and Bisgood accept its appropriateness as an ideal for women religious.

Cornelia as Wife

Any examination of Cornelia as sexual partner, as wife, is inevitably coloured by the biographer's interpretation not just of Cornelia, but of Pierce. Bisgood describes the Connelly marriage as "so idyllic a love-match,"[90] and yet Pierce was a complex person whose choices and decisions brought real suffering to Cornelia. In biographies of her he is almost always painted as the villain.

In dealing with Pierce, Bisgood and other pro-Cornelia writers are faced with a dilemma: if they cast Pierce totally in the role of villain what are they to say about Cornelia's choice of him as her husband or, indeed, about

---

[88] Walsh, introduction to Bisgood, *Cornelia Connelly*, vii.

[89] Bisgood, *Cornelia Connelly*, 317.

[90] Bisgood, *Cornelia Connelly*, 107.

her continuing love for him? Bisgood's judgment of Pierce is uncompromising: "His mind was unhinged, and ... he was suffering from paranoiac delusions."[91] Nevertheless, Pierce "could not have been unworthy of Cornelia," and Cornelia must be above criticism:

> He could not have been unworthy of Cornelia who, ardent as she was, had nevertheless a balance and maturity of judgment which had always prevented her from being false to her own ideals.[92]

However, neither Cornelia's emotional outpourings in her early letters to Pierce, nor Bisgood's own comment that "she gaily flung aside practical advantage to follow the man she loved and admired above all,"[93] seem to justify such large claims about Cornelia's maturity and judgment.

Of the Connellys' early married life and their conversion to Catholicism Bisgood knew very little, because her biography was written before the circumstances of Pierce's pursuit of priesthood in the Roman Catholic church had been fully researched. Lacking facts, she builds up a picture of what she herself considers praiseworthy—even saintly—in a wife, in much the same way as she constructs Cornelia the laudable adolescent.

Her image is of Cornelia as a wife who was simultaneously proactive and submissive. On the one hand, she suggests that Cornelia played a leading part in the conversion and was in some way the stronger partner. She claims (inaccurately) that Cornelia's "interest and curiosity aroused her husband's,"[94] and that "she followed, or rather accompanied"[95] Pierce on the path to Catholicism. She depicts Cornelia as an independent woman in a partnership of equality. On the other hand, she presents Cornelia as passive, waiting, unsure what her husband is struggling with, not party to his decision, and suffering at his hands. What is clear from the documentation now, but was unknown to Bisgood, is that Pierce believed himself called by God to priesthood and was from the outset exploring the possibility of ordination within the Roman Catholic Church. It is thought

---

[91] Bisgood, *Cornelia Connelly*, 96.

[92] Bisgood, *Cornelia Connelly*, 6.

[93] Bisgood, *Cornelia Connelly*, 10. Is it too fanciful to hear echoes of Edward VIII's abdication speech here?

[94] Bisgood, *Cornelia Connelly*, 8.

[95] Bisgood, *Cornelia Connelly*, 10.

that Cornelia knew this too. Bisgood, however, imagines Cornelia as unaware of Pierce's dissatisfaction with the lay state, and of his growing desire for ordination. So she is obliged to discard her sense of the mutuality of the Connellys' relationship, and to present Cornelia as excluded from her husband's discernment and waiting passively for his decision, whatever it might be:

> The strain of the interior conflict was beginning to tell, and Cornelia, loving and intuitive, divined that for the first time in their married life he had anxieties which he was not sharing with her. She waited and prayed; but she never suspected the truth.[96]

The first definite step of the couple towards Pierce's ordination was the decision to refrain from sexual intercourse. Aware of Cornelia's "deep and strong affections," and of the fact that she was pregnant with her fifth child, Bisgood finds Cornelia's "calm detachment" at this time "astonishing."[97] But the evidence Bisgood presents for that cherished convent value "calm detachment" is negative and does not seem substantive: that Cornelia says little about the decision in her personal notebook. In fact, the extract from the notebook that Bisgood quotes could arguably be described as anguished rather than calmly detached:

> PRO. It is for the glory of God that we should save our souls. If we can save our souls more surely *that* way, and help others to do so too, this is fulfilling God's designs upon us and procuring His glory. CON. We are very weak. Those who are very weak are not fit for so perfect a state, and not more sure of saving their souls, therefore, not for the glory of God. We do not know ourselves and cannot judge if we are weak or strong.[98]

Bisgood calls this "a compelling syllogism, worked out remorselessly." In view of the fact that both the Connellys had Jesuit spiritual directors, this entry in Cornelia's notebook presumably reflects her efforts at discernment according to the rules of St Ignatius.[99] The suggestion that it may have been written in anguish rather than in calm detachment is strengthened by

---

[96] Bisgood, *Cornelia Connelly*, 30.

[97] Bisgood, *Cornelia Connelly*, 32.

[98] Quoted in Bisgood, *Cornelia Connelly*, 32.

[99] Compare *The Spiritual Exercises of St Ignatius*, n. 181.

knowledge of Cornelia's behaviour on other occasions when she was deeply distressed. For instance, when she received news of the death of Mercer, her eldest son, Cornelia was inconsolable; she sent to the school for a textbook and took refuge in the logic of geometry.

The argument for anguish is no more supported by the written text than Bisgood's claim for calm detachment. What is clear is that even in Bisgood's apparently objective account there is necessarily a good deal of subjectivity: she finds what she values herself writ large in the foundress. She presses the claim for detachment strongly. In the Connellys' exterior lives, she says, "no change was desirable or even possible .... So the peaceful routine ... proceeded without interruption." [100] When, a few paragraphs later, she has to acknowledge that Cornelia is anything but calm, she accounts for this in convent terminology, admiring "sublime impersonality" and opposing grace to nature. Cornelia "was raised by grace to this sublime impersonality. Yet there were times when nature reasserted itself." [101]

Before Pierce's ordination, Bisgood says, Cornelia wrote to her husband whom "she knew ... through and through," offering to resume "married life again before anything was known or any irrevocable step taken." [102] Not withstanding their Ignatian discernment, Cornelia is presented as distrusting her own insights at this crucial moment and following instead the traditional path of wifely obedience and submission:

> To the end of her life Cornelia always found peace in the thought that the call had come first to him, and that her part had been *merely* to yield to the dictates of her conscience, pressed to the utmost. Again he affirmed his own certainty, and again she surrendered her will to God's designs on him, and *drove down her misgivings, blaming herself for want of trust.* [103]

Cornelia did not cease to be wife and mother when she assumed the role of founder, and Bisgood draws a final picture of the Connellys' marriage when Pierce, abandoning both Catholicism and its priesthood in

---

[100] Bisgood, *Cornelia Connelly*, 32.

[101] Bisgood, *Cornelia Connelly*, 35.

[102] Bisgood, *Cornelia Connelly*, 39.

[103] Bisgood, *Cornelia Connelly*, 39-40 (my italics). Might not this equally suggest that to the end of her life Cornelia struggled with the notion that if she had trusted her own instincts things might have been different?

the 1850s, effectively ended his relationship with Cornelia. Now Bisgood has no doubts that Cornelia was the stronger, and she expresses her view in very black and white terms:

> Little as Cornelia's tact had allowed him to realise it, Pierce was in fact extremely dependent on her moral support. From the earliest days of their marriage, her loving admiration and encouragement had buoyed him up in every crisis …. Not only this, but her beauty and popularity had helped to build up his own personality and added to his welcome wherever he went. Her commonsense and evenness of character had controlled and disguised his own want of balance. Her advice had found the solution to every problem. And now circumstances of his own making had deprived him of all this, and he was beginning to realise what he had lost and to make desperate efforts to get it back. …
>
> But Cornelia now had no need of him.[104]

The Cornelia who became a founder had been shaped both by her experience of happiness within marriage and by her response to the disintegration of her relationship with her husband. Discussing Pierce's case against Cornelia in the Court of Arches, Bisgood suggests that Cornelia was clear-eyed about her husband's motivation:

> Throughout the whole controversy, Cornelia, who knew her husband through and through, remained convinced that his motive was a desire for power, and that his bitterness towards Wiseman … was motivated by the realisation that his wife had moved away from his own control and declared by her acts her independence of him, while placing herself under the jurisdiction of the Bishop.[105]

The suggestion of a power struggle between two men, in which Cornelia is merely a female pawn, is supported by a quotation from one of Cornelia's letters: Pierce's "sole object," she writes "would be to force me to begin a new Congregation under his guidance."[106] Pierce's court case for the restitution of conjugal rights notwithstanding, Cornelia is suggesting here that his motivation is power rather than sexual partnership or the desire to

---

[104] Bisgood, *Cornelia Connelly*, 105-106. Today this might be read as illustrating not just Pierce's dependence on Cornelia but the couple's co-dependence.

[105] Bisgood, *Cornelia Connelly*, 105.

[106] Quoted in Bisgood, *Cornelia Connelly*, 107.

re-establish the family unit. But it is noteworthy that she does not question his right to such power; she and Bisgood share a theology of obedience which does not sustain the questioning of authority. It does not occur to Cornelia to challenge patriarchal structures either at this time in relation to marriage or in her later struggles with bishops and other clergy.

After the early 1850s the Connellys' marriage was effectively over, and they had no further direct communication with each other. In Bisgood's presentation, Cornelia is a wife who supports her husband, suffers at his hands, and bears all that happens with "sublime impersonality." Her sexual passion does not even flicker across the page; her sanctity within marriage is scarcely differentiated from her sanctity as a woman religious.

Bisgood, however, wants to present a foundress who had qualities and strengths that she has not identified in the wife and mother, and she makes a strong statement about the change which took place in Cornelia when she gave up the role of wife and assumed that of religious leader:

> They [the first women to join the Society] were a very mixed group, but Cornelia's handling of them shows for the first time her extraordinary gift of influencing others. In fact, a noticeable psychological phenomenon appears at this point of her life—the sudden emergence of a strong and remarkable personality. Up till now she had been content to efface herself, to live under the shadow of her fascinating, ebullient husband. For ten years she had been the docile and adoring wife. Then followed a period in which she imposed upon herself a rigid self-discipline, and from 1842 for four years she remained almost in eclipse, patiently seeking God's will and awaiting its manifestation. The sad-coloured merino gown and black lace veil of the Trinità were symbolic ... Cornelia found her true self in the slums of Derby.[107]

Bisgood seems to be overstating her case, creating too sharp a dichotomy between "before" and "after." Cornelia's character was not "uncomplicated," as Bisgood claims,[108] and the biographical material, even as she herself presents it, does not entirely support this assertion of "the sudden emergence of a strong and remarkable personality."

[107] Bisgood, *Cornelia Connelly*, 78-79.
[108] Bisgood, *Cornelia Connelly*, 134.

In childhood, Bisgood says, Cornelia "possessed a power of reflection and strength of will which impressed even her elders," and "showed a self-possession and a power of self-discipline unusual for her years."[109] Bisgood stresses not just Cornelia's independence and self-determination as foundress, but her continued emphasis on duty and her submission to those in authority over her. "She wrote immediately declaring the complete conformity of herself and the Community with the declaration"; "in obedience she had surrendered to ecclesiastical authority."[110] Similarly, Cornelia's need for intimacy, love and friendship did not disappear when her marriage was over and her links with her children had become tenuous. Bisgood hints that she developed significant relationships with some of the early members of the Society. Describing the last months of Cornelia's life, she writes, "She longed to see her eldest daughters again." Naming Ignatia Bridges, who was in Paris, she comments, "This was a separation which she [Cornelia] felt keenly ... Mother Connelly was deeply attached to her." Even Bisgood, champion of calm detachment, observes, "It is comforting to see these human touches in one so utterly detached."[111]

Cornelia as Mother

Early in her biography, Bisgood introduces the very 1950s concept of "Catholic motherhood," a concept she says that Cornelia came to understand in Rome after her conversion:

> Cornelia learnt from her friend [Gwendalin Talbot] how a Catholic mother can combine her social and maternal duties with a life of intense piety and devotion to the poor.[112]

Only ten pages earlier she has described Cornelia as a clergy wife with two small children in Pierce's Natchez parish: "She gave herself to the needs of rich and poor alike with a joyous self-spending in which was not the shadow

---

[109] Bisgood, *Cornelia Connelly*, 3, 4. On what evidence Bisgood bases these claims is unclear.

[110] Bisgood, *Cornelia Connelly*, 194, 208. These two quotations are taken almost at random. There are numerous other examples.

[111] Bisgood, *Cornelia Connelly*, 303, 304.

[112] Bisgood, *Cornelia Connelly*, 17.

of insincerity or patronage."[113] How this differs from the "Catholic" motherhood of Gwendalin Talbot is not made clear. But what is apparent, in the descriptions of both Natchez and Rome, is Bisgood's own understanding of saintly motherhood, which is characterized by a combination of "intense piety" and "joyous self-spending" in the service of others.

However, a presentation of Cornelia the saintly mother cannot be straightforward for Bisgood because of the thorny problem of the break up of the Connelly family and Cornelia's subsequent loss of access to her children. Walsh addresses the issue squarely in the introduction:

> … the outstanding problem of her life and holiness concerns the accusation that she was "an unnatural mother who abandoned her children." The question is admirably dealt with by Mother Marie Thérèse in the pages of this biography.[114]

To establish Cornelia's holiness, it is apparently more important to refute the claim that she "unnaturally" abandoned her children than to assert what is known of her loving relationship with them.

Bisgood leaves no doubt that the suffering caused by the loss of her children was heart-wrenching for Cornelia. "She accepted it as God's will, but the conflict in the mother's heart was severe."[115] Discussing Cornelia's separation from her oldest son Mercer, taken by his father to school in England at the age of nine, Bisgood allows herself the authorial comment that his mother "must have longed to have him back with her again."[116] Of Mercer's death she writes: "The shock of his death completely prostrated his mother, who was ill at the time. She gave way to her grief and refused to be comforted."[117]

Yet this is not the whole picture. The Connellys are portrayed as accepting the social customs of the upper-class English Victorians whom they came to know: "Ady and Frank were left in kind Mrs Berkeley's

[113] Bisgood, *Cornelia Connelly*, 7.

[114] Walsh, introduction to Bisgood, *Cornelia Connelly*, v.

[115] Bisgood, *Cornelia Connelly*, 75.

[116] Bisgood, *Cornelia Connelly*, 38.

[117] Bisgood, *Cornelia Connelly*, 112.

capacious nurseries, while Pierce and Cornelia went on to Alton."[118] That Bisgood, perhaps familiar with such nurseries from her own childhood, accepts this without comment is not surprising. More difficult to explain— except in terms of convent values—is her acceptance of a spirituality which constrained Cornelia's love for her children and intimacy with them. Bisgood describes in terms of "self-abnegation and mortification" attitudes to the children which strike a modern reader as chilling:

> She [Cornelia] denied herself the consolation which the company of her little girl might legitimately have given her; even on one occasion she did violence to her mother's heart by refraining for a whole day from enquiring about the child, who was ill with some infectious ailment. Her letters to Mercer, now at Stonyhurst, tenderly affectionate as they are, betray at once her underlying anxiety about the temperamental little boy and the severe restraint she put on the expression of her love for her firstborn.[119]

Bisgood is at pains to defend rather than criticize Cornelia's spirituality, calling it a spirituality of renunciation, and even to present it explicitly as a model for members of the Society. Where Cornelia wrote tersely in her spiritual notebook "reject all useless thoughts," Bisgood expands the note in a way that now seems deeply dualistic. The useless thoughts, Bisgood claims, were:

> Thoughts of the children, of Pierce, of the lost home and its joys; memories of happy times in Philadelphia, Natchez, Rome, of innocent gaieties, sweet occupations and interests that filled the golden days, perhaps even— Cornelia was after all very feminine—of pretty frocks and the companionship of admiring friends. ...
>
> Little as she realised it, she was laying up stores of spiritual treasures for others besides herself.[120]

In this way Bisgood connects Cornelia's experience of motherhood with her role as founder. Cornelia is described as "the most solicitous and motherly of Superiors," concerned for "her daughters." Members of the Society are frequently referred to as children: Teresa Hanson is "one of

---

[118] Bisgood, *Cornelia Connelly*, 43.

[119] Bisgood, *Cornelia Connelly*, 38.

[120] Bisgood, *Cornelia Connelly*, 37.

Mother Connelly's most loving and faithful children"; the first members of the Society to go to America "shared a childlike affection for their 'ever dearest Reverend Mother'"; and, once in the States, they "were longing to see their Mother again." Cornelia thinks lovingly "of all her children especially those so far away in America."[121] Clearly some of this language emanates from the nineteenth-century women themselves: "We felt as safe and confiding as little children."[122] But some is Bisgood's own. She points out that Cornelia "was some years older than any of the others, and had passed through deep spiritual experiences. They all looked to her as a mother and guide."[123] She suggests that motherliness is an essential characteristic of the Society, and speaks of a "spiritual motherhood" which has superseded Cornelia's first call to her own children:

> The nuns of those early days had their own training directly from the Foundress and what they learned from her above all was motherliness. Cornelia Connelly had two vocations from God and the first was to the state of wife and mother; in that she had expected to live out her life. Then it would seem that in her second vocation all the gifts of love and sympathy which could no longer envelop her own lost children were poured out on those who were given to her spiritual motherhood.[124]

Bisgood suggests here that the Society was in some way a substitute child for Cornelia or, at least, provided scope for her motherliness. This notion is reinforced by the language Bisgood uses in discussing Cornelia's reaction to the suppression of her rule by Bishop Danell: "To see her ideals trampled down and her work set aside was like watching another child die."[125]

The references in the earlier quotation to Cornelia's "two vocations," and to the influence of Cornelia's experiences as a mother on her "spiritual motherhood," are powerfully reminiscent of the views of James Walsh. In an appreciation of Walsh written after his death, Elizabeth Mary Strub states:

---

[121] Bisgood, *Cornelia Connelly*, 222, 81, 215, 226, 306.
[122] Aloysia Walker, quoted in Bisgood, *Cornelia Connelly*, 79.
[123] Bisgood, *Cornelia Connelly*, 79.
[124] Bisgood, *Cornelia Connelly*, 170.
[125] Bisgood, *Cornelia Connelly*, 286.

He compared Cornelia to Our Lady in her passage from physical motherhood to spiritual motherhood through the cross .... [He] presented her as reflecting the fidelity of God in her own attachment to His will. He returned to the theme of spiritual motherhood and divine adoption as children.[126]

In his pamphlet, *The Vocation of Cornelia Connelly*, Walsh seems to understand the whole of Cornelia's earlier life only in terms of her work as foundress, and as a preparation for it. He evinces little imaginative awareness of what the loss of her husband and children cost Cornelia:

> The mother never saw her eldest son again. The other two children were grown up before any further meeting with their mother. All these events were accidental circumstances to her vocation; but they were certainly the test of her fidelity to it. ...

> We must reiterate that she had no longer any duty in justice towards Pierce. And with regard to the children, the vow is merely the explicit clarification of what was always implicit in their double vocation, namely, that God's claims, interpreted by the Church, must be paramount.[127]

Though Walsh was undoubtedly influential, Bisgood's own mistrust of natural pleasures and human affections cannot be overlooked. She may deal "admirably" with the question of Cornelia's loss of her children, as Walsh claims, but she does not deal with it at any length. She devotes less than a quarter of the biography to the first half of Cornelia's life. In fact, her account of Cornelia as wife and mother seems little more than an extended prelude to the life of Cornelia the foundress.

Cornelia as Founder

Like all the other biographers, Bisgood has to examine two facets of Cornelia's life during her years as founder: her response to the bishops who sought to exert control over the infant Society, and her own exercise of leadership and authority within the congregation. In each case Cornelia's attitudes are complex: she both obeyed and resisted the bishops; she was both deeply loved and fiercely rejected by members of the Society. So

---

[126] Strub, "James Walsh, Cornelia Connelly and the Society of the Holy Child Jesus," 187.

[127] Walsh, *The Vocation of Cornelia Connelly*, 20, 25.

Bisgood is faced with difficult, and significant, choices in her presentation of the material.

Bisgood herself held positions of authority within the congregation over a long period. She was a local superior and a member of the provincial council during the Second World War, when a good deal of real power necessarily devolved to the provinces. So her emphases and interpretations may reveal something of her own perspective on issues of power and obedience.

Cornelia and the Bishops

From the time Cornelia arrived in Derby, much of this biography revolves around her relationships with bishops, first with Wiseman and then with Grant and Danell, the two consecutive bishops of Southwark. Bisgood suggests that Cornelia's fundamental attitude to ecclesiastical authority was one of obedience; and the assumption in convent culture is that obedience is a certain road to finding the will of God.

Bisgood's description of her spiritual formation in Grand Coteau has prepared the reader to accept Cornelia's obediential stance. Guided by Mother Cutts at the Sacred Heart convent, Cornelia had "realised the value of obedience and the relinquishing of one's will."[128] Her spiritual director at that period, John Francis Abbadie SJ, is quoted as saying, "But in everything her obedience to me was perfect."[129]

When John Grassi first proposed in Rome that Cornelia should found a congregation, Bisgood describes Cornelia's response in terms of passivity:

> In the early spring she surrendered her will once again to the divine will, and patiently waited as from the hand of God for whatever should be decided for her.[130]

> Cornelia understood from the decision of her advisers that she had received her commission from God himself.[131]

By the time she arrived in England, Bisgood claims, Cornelia accepted explicitly that bishops were "the voice of God" for her. When Wiseman

---

[128] Bisgood, *Cornelia Connelly*, 36.

[129] Quoted in Bisgood, *Cornelia Connelly*, 24.

[130] Bisgood, *Cornelia Connelly*, 59.

[131] Bisgood, *Cornelia Connelly*, 66-67.

offered Cornelia a building in Derby which her common sense told her was totally unsuitable, she "brought forward objection after objection; Dr Wiseman demolished them all, and Cornelia recognised in his authority the voice of God."[132] With Grant and with Danell Cornelia is presented as even more acquiescent; and Bisgood perceives her obedience as more absolute because less questioning. In fact, Bisgood claims, Cornelia was practising obedience to a heroic degree:

> A brain so quick, a character so decisive as hers, must have found his [Grant's] hesitations torturing and his policy inexplicable; but she obeyed without asking for explanations and loyally accepted his decisions. Such obedience must often have carried her to an heroic level.[133]

When Danell suppressed Cornelia's rule and imposed his own on the Society, Bisgood describes Cornelia as "calmer and more silent than anyone present," though this must have seemed "the destruction of her life's work": "But it was God's will acting through ecclesiastical authority; and in God's Name she must salvage what she could from the wreck."[134]

The message that obedience to legitimate authority is necessarily obedience to God, that being obedient is doing God's will, is strongly reinforced. The references to "perfect" obedience in Grand Coteau and "an heroic level" of obedience in England must have reminded Bisgood's contemporaries of descriptions of sanctity in conventional hagiography. So Cornelia is established as holy, and her response to the bishops, which was highly praiseworthy in the terms of the convent culture of the 1950s, makes the foundress into a model for the current members of her congregation.

The element of personal discernment, of seeking and trusting what God is saying to oneself, is notably absent from this approach: this is a surprising omission given that both Cornelia and Bisgood were formed in the spirituality of the Ignatian Exercises. It is possible that Cornelia was more discerning than Bisgood's language suggests; but among religious women of Bisgood's era obedience was perceived as a more certain route to God than personal discernment. Further, Walsh's influence may be

---

[132] Bisgood, *Cornelia Connelly*, 72.

[133] Bisgood, *Cornelia Connelly*, 174.

[134] Bisgood, *Cornelia Connelly*, 285, 286.

perceptible in this emphasis: in his own writing he lays stress on Cornelia's obedience to ecclesiastical authority:

> For her, "Superiors" meant the Church—Christ in His sacerdotal function, with His priestly authority, His Pontifical power—the *pons*, the bridge between the Divine Will and the human conscience. For one walking the way of perfection, as Cornelia was at this time, the advice of her successive directors, ultimately ratified by the Holy See, was the voice of Christ. This was the voice to which she listened. ...

> Holy Church, in decreeing this separation between husband and wife, took all reasonable precautions concerning the truth of their vocation and the future welfare of the children .... In the full acceptance of vocation there is occasionally revealed to us the sacrificial love of Christ, the God-man, Who "learned His obedience in the school of suffering." On this love and this obedience rests the claim of Mother Cornelia Connelly to high sanctity.[135]

But this is not the whole picture. On several occasions Bisgood notes Cornelia's struggle to obey the decisions of others against her own contrary judgement. (She "drove down her misgivings, blaming herself for want of trust"; "she accepted it as God's will but the conflict in the mother's heart was severe"; "she had a nagging intuition that all was not well, but she attributed this to her own shortcomings.")[136] And she provides evidence of a more spirited and self-trusting response on Cornelia's part:

> Mother Connelly submitted, but not without protest. She considered it her duty to maintain as far as possible the rights of the Society, and so she put her point of view roundly before the Bishop.[137]

Cornelia was a woman of her time who accepted the authority of the hierarchical Church as a legitimate pointer to the will of God. Nevertheless, the emphasis on obedience in this biography reflects, to some degree at least, both Bisgood's convent assumptions and her own "languid" temperament. Discussing the endlessly convoluted matter of the St Leonards property, Bisgood allows herself the comment:

---

[135] Walsh, *The Vocation of Cornelia Connelly*, 17, 31.
[136] Bisgood, *Cornelia Connelly*, 40, 75, 270.
[137] Bisgood, *Cornelia Connelly*, 151.

It would have been more reposeful to take the easy way out, to accept someone else's ruling and shuffle off the responsibility; but would it have been *right?* [138]

Bisgood herself may have found something "reposeful" in obedience; during the writing of the biography she ceased to hold office in the Society, and this comment perhaps reflects something of her relief at no longer carrying responsibility. But, much as Cornelia valued obedience, there is little to suggest that she had any interest in the "reposeful," or in "yielding to the superior wills and intellects of men ... and so earn[ing] golden opinions." [139] As Bisgood acknowledges, Cornelia "dared to maintain her own principles and to have a mind of her own" [140] alongside her willingness to obey. This aspect of the founder's personality has always been a matter of pride in the Society, and so Bisgood is engaged in the difficult task of presenting Cornelia as both conventionally obedient and submissive, and as a woman with "a strong and remarkable personality." [141] Bisgood cannot conceal that the forceful Cornelia came into conflict with the bishops, and with other authority figures, on numerous occasions, or that she sometimes found it difficult to submit to the power of others.

There can be no suggestion that Cornelia ever sought parity with those who exercised ecclesiastical authority over her; she had embraced obedience by vow and, at the level of day to day practicalities, she recognised her need for ecclesiastical approval. Yet over and over again she crossed the men who might have supported her. In his introduction Walsh comments explicitly on her relations with Wiseman, who was "official sponsor of the new Congregation," but within two years became "Cornelia's antagonist in the dispute over the St Leonards property." In the same paragraph he names "as ranged against her at various times, besides Cardinal Wiseman, Bishops Grant and Danell of Southwark, Archbishop Ullathorne of Birmingham and Bishop Goss of Liverpool." [142]

---

[138] Bisgood, *Cornelia Connelly*, 134.

[139] Bisgood, *Cornelia Connelly*, 129.

[140] Bisgood, *Cornelia Connelly*, 129.

[141] Bisgood, *Cornelia Connelly*, 79.

[142] Walsh, introduction to Bisgood, *Cornelia Connelly*, vii.

Such a formidable list of opponents necessarily raises questions—questions which Bisgood attempts to address. In the Postscript she writes:

> It is difficult, humanly speaking, to understand why a woman of such charm, ability and goodness should have been the object of so much dislike.[143]

After describing those who disliked her as "the cranks ... the embittered and disappointed ... the prejudiced," Bisgood acknowledges that "upright and conscientious men, especially among the clergy, opposed her," along with a motley collection of parishioners, schools' inspectors and former members of the Society.[144] One tentative explanation Bisgood offers is that, among the bishops, as with Pierce, Cornelia may have been a victim in a male power struggle:

> Dr Ullathorne's prejudice against Cornelia Connelly may have been due partly to his instinctive opposition to the projects and policy of Cardinal Wiseman, especially concerning converts.[145]

Much more clearly expressed is Bisgood's assertion that it would have been uncharacteristic of Cornelia to remain passive and submissive:

> She was no passive, downtrodden victim of circumstances. On the contrary, it is obvious that she inspired a certain amount of awe even in her adversaries. She stood firmly on her rights ... and usually came off victorious.[146]

Here, though she does not elaborate, Bisgood is touching on issues of gender and power, as the comments of Wiseman and Newman that she records make clear. Wiseman complained to Cardinal Franzoni that Cornelia was "invested with a power which would require a *man* of consummate ability, wisdom and virtue to exercise it; how much less should it be confided to a woman."[147] Newman observed to William Mansell MP,

---

[143] Bisgood, *Cornelia Connelly*, 310.

[144] Bisgood, *Cornelia Connelly*, 310.

[145] Bisgood, *Cornelia Connelly*, 310-311.

[146] Bisgood, *Cornelia Connelly*, 313.

[147] Quoted in Bisgood, *Cornelia Connelly*, 254.

"She is a Yankee, I suppose this is the reason, but anyhow, although she is a very good woman, it is difficult for an Englishman to follow her."[148] Today the bishops would stand accused of sexism. Bisgood (to whom the word "sexism" would have been unfamiliar) only suggests that a good deal of the opposition Cornelia aroused among men stemmed from her actions and attitudes as an independent-minded woman. This comment is one of Bisgood's few explicit references to gender:

> In a period when what was expected of women, especially religious women, was a submissive yielding to the superior wills and intellects of men, she dared to maintain her own principles and to have a mind of her own. It might have been easier to submit and earn golden opinions ... [149]

Cornelia's complex and increasingly conflictual relationship with the bishops must be explained, in part at least, by the unquestioned nineteenth-century assumption that it was inappropriate for women to exercise power. Even in women's congregations it was customary for the priest, the bishop, often the male founder, and always the male Church to take responsibility for decision-making. Walsh, in his introduction, presents Cornelia as an innovator: "Her story makes a breach in the wall of religious custom as wide in its way as that of Florence Nightingale or Sylvia Pankhurst when they forced an entry into medicine and politics."[150] Whether or not the extravagance of the comparison can be justified, it does perhaps explain the bishops' instinctive resistance to Cornelia.

Cornelia's Leadership of the Society

For Bisgood patriarchal authority was normative, and it does not occur to her to ask whether Cornelia exercised power differently from a man, or whether she merely replicated the patterns of patriarchy within the congregation. Though she hints that Cornelia's model of leadership was less rigid than that of a man, Bisgood's primary concern is to present Cornelia as a natural leader who became a model superior—as that would have been understood within convent culture in the 1950s. According to

---

[148] Quoted in Bisgood, *Cornelia Connelly*, 311.

[149] Bisgood, *Cornelia Connelly*, 129.

[150] Walsh, introduction to Bisgood, *Cornelia Connelly*, v.

Bisgood, Cornelia had "a supernaturalised quality of leadership which carried the others along with her," and she exercised "a certain tranquil power"[151]; she had a "remarkable power of influencing others," and her leadership of the Society reflected "the ascendancy of her personality."[152] Sometimes her power and authority were exercised in a maternal way, with Cornelia's motherhood being directly acknowledged both by herself by and her "daughters"—and by Bisgood, who reinforces this language.[153]

As leader of the Society, Bisgood's Cornelia is "a woman of vision [who] never contented herself with anything less than the longest views," a person "quite ready to shoulder risks," a woman with the "power of swift decision."[154] On several occasions Bisgood emphasizes the spirit of freedom and mutuality that prevailed in the Society; Cornelia is presented consulting the community, sharing decision-making with them, and dealing with outside bodies as their spokesperson:

> She wrote to the two Superiors … telling them first to consult one another, and then after three days' earnest prayer to give her their opinion as to the "dismission of Miss Bowles." … She had [already] obtained the opinion of the three eldest Professed.[155]

> All the same, she informed the Bishop that "the members of the Community think we have not been properly represented in Rome, and that only one side has had their work done"; which was true.[156]

> Mother Connelly answered … the Bishop: "I shall be deeply grieved, and with our community unanimously, if your Lordship opposes our journey to America." … In this she was supported by the enthusiasm of the Community.[157]

There were, however, occasions when "her personal sway"[158] was questioned and, beneath Bisgood's approval of Cornelia, we can hear the dissatisfaction of some early members of the congregation. More than once

---

[151] Bisgood, *Cornelia Connelly*, 78, 79. No further explanation is offered for either epithet.

[152] Bisgood, *Cornelia Connelly*, 297, 259.

[153] See, for example, Bisgood, *Cornelia Connelly*, 222.

[154] Bisgood, *Cornelia Connelly*, 230, 237, 118.

[155] Bisgood, *Cornelia Connelly*, 147.

[156] Bisgood, *Cornelia Connelly*, 194.

[157] Bisgood, *Cornelia Connelly*, 212-213.

[158] Bisgood, *Cornelia Connelly*, 259.

"there was a tension of wills"[159] between Cornelia and other members of the Society; there were times when some seem to have found her more matriarchal than maternal. Emily Bowles, for instance, left the Society whilst Cornelia was consulting the local superiors about her "deliberate disobedience and insolence."[160] Bisgood is not sympathetic towards Bowles. In terms of convent culture she makes the perfect foil for Cornelia, a failure on every count. From her earliest days in the Society "religious obedience was not a word in Emily's vocabulary"; she was "embittered and disappointed"; "her feelings continued to govern her for the rest of her life."[161] Nevertheless, Bisgood records something of Bowles' view of Cornelia:

> [Emily] never seems to have written a letter during this period in which she did not refer to her [Cornelia] accusing her of "despotism," "overbearing waywardness," "cruelty and recklessness," and, above all, a want of integrity.[162]

As Bisgood says, these sound like the views of someone with an axe to grind. However, this was not the only occasion on which Cornelia's exercise of power was something less than "tranquil." In spite of "the gentle strength of her government,"[163] Cornelia was not always in tune with the feelings of others. When changes to the Rule were opposed by the communities in Preston, Cornelia "was wholly unprepared for the volume of disagreement that reached her."[164] Cornelia labelled her opponents in Preston a "cabal,"[165] and Bisgood condemns "a separatist spirit … and a smouldering disaffection"[166] among the Preston sisters. But she also acknowledges that what was at issue was Cornelia's style of leadership, her exercise of power:

---

[159] Bisgood, *Cornelia Connelly*, 80.

[160] Bisgood, *Cornelia Connelly*, 147.

[161] Bisgood, *Cornelia Connelly*, 80, 150.

[162] Bisgood, *Cornelia Connelly*, 150.

[163] Bisgood, *Cornelia Connelly*, 259.

[164] Bisgood, *Cornelia Connelly*, 265.

[165] See Bisgood, *Cornelia Connelly*, 268.

[166] Bisgood, *Cornelia Connelly*, 266.

> In Preston an underground feeling of restlessness under what was beginning to appear an arbitrary form of government welled up into the open.[167]

> The dissentients were ... anxious to curtail the authority and the tenure of the Superior General.[168]

> A note in Propaganda observes that they had asked if their communications could be sealed and sent direct as "they are afraid of Madame Connelly should they comment freely on the Rules."[169]

> The chief complaint was that her methods were too arbitrary and her power too great.[170]

Cornelia misjudged the situation: "She had thought that in spite of differences of opinion the Society was united under her."[171]

The preposition "under" is revealing of Bisgood's view of authority within the Society. On other occasions, too, she indicates by a single word or simple phrase her own unquestioning acceptance of a certain amount of autocracy in Cornelia. After the first general chapter a local superior was appointed at St Leonards where Cornelia, the superior general, was living. Bisgood comments: "the Foundress was practically a subject in the house where she had queened it for twenty-six years."[172] Discussing Cornelia's skills as an administrator, she writes: "In the ordinary day-to-day administration of temporalities she had not any adviser—but neither did she need one." Notwithstanding the members of the Society who "protested to ecclesiastical superiors against her arbitrary government,"[173] Bisgood's judgement of Cornelia's leadership is wholly favourable. Her summary of the foundress' style perhaps represents the ideal of leadership that Bisgood had striven to achieve herself:

> She was strict, she could be stern, she was unchangingly kind, but one characteristic was noted and appreciated by all: she was eminently just. She

---

[167] Bisgood, *Cornelia Connelly*, 265.
[168] Bisgood, *Cornelia Connelly*, 267.
[169] Bisgood, *Cornelia Connelly*, 269.
[170] Bisgood, *Cornelia Connelly*, 276.
[171] Bisgood, *Cornelia Connelly*, 272.
[172] Bisgood, *Cornelia Connelly*, 296.
[173] Bisgood, *Cornelia Connelly*, 313.

had the great gift of seeing all around a problem and grasping other people's point of view, and she ruled, not only with justice, but with equity.[174]

Bisgood's Vision

Bisgood's own unquestioning acceptance of patriarchy and hierarchy can be detected underlying her examination of Cornelia as foundress. Bisgood's ideal is that Cornelia will obey the bishops and that the members of the Society will obey Cornelia. The more unhesitating the obedience, the more "perfect" it is. And obedience will lead them all surely to the will of God.

But the biography contains a subtext which persists in spite of Bisgood's convictions about the nature and value of obedience. Cornelia's response to the power of the bishops, and her own exercise of power within the Society, cannot always be presented as praiseworthy in convent culture terms. Sometimes she "drove down her misgivings"[175] in response to the bishops (who took a remarkably detailed interest in the affairs of the Society and its members), and obeyed without demur. But sometimes "she dared to maintain her own principles and have a mind of her own."[176] Bisgood stresses Cornelia's constant determination to find "God's will acting through ecclesiastical authority,"[177] but she also records "her courage" in resisting the bishops' demands.[178]

It seems that Bisgood's concept of power is largely unexamined. She takes for granted a hierarchical correspondence between authority and obedience, and she stresses the importance of obedience as a way of knowing and responding to the will of God on a number of occasions. The obedience she praises is largely absolute rather than discerned obedience (an obedience that was called "blind" in Bisgood's day). But the biography also presents Cornelia as struggling to practise an obedience which is anything but blind, and to exercise an authority which is shared and communitarian.

---

[174] Bisgood, *Cornelia Connelly*, 169.
[175] Bisgood, *Cornelia Connelly*, 40.
[176] Bisgood, *Cornelia Connelly*, 129.
[177] Bisgood, *Cornelia Connelly*, 286.
[178] Bisgood, *Cornelia Connelly*, 195.

Bisgood's purpose appears to be straightforward: to relate Cornelia's life in such a way as to establish her credentials as a holy woman, a woman worthy of canonisation. And she seems to equate holiness with perfection. The biography has a tendency to the hagiographical, though it was based on the documentation being gathered at the time of writing in furtherance of the cause. There is little discussion of Cornelia's faults or shortcomings, except to suggest that she was successful in overcoming them.

Bisgood does not come to terms with Cornelia's sexuality. (The Cornelia who, on a number of occasions, referred to the vow of chastity as "accepted suffering" does not appear here.) She prefers instead to focus on Cornelia's motherhood and on the continuity that can be perceived between her physical and her "spiritual" mothering.

Bisgood does not ask the questions that a biographer might ask today about Cornelia's use of power and her response to it. She accepts a hierarchical and patriarchal concept of power: power is fundamentally God's and, as we are obedient to God, so we must be obedient to those in authority over us. But given the strength of this unexamined assumption, it is both exciting and enlivening to perceive traces of other attitudes to power and authority within her text.

Bisgood's interpretation of Cornelia's spirituality of suffering is fundamentally more rounded than her language of mortification, renunciation and self-denial might suggest. She stresses that it is God whom Cornelia is seeking, in sorrow and in joy. The spirit of the Society is a spirit of joy. But God can also be recognised and loved in suffering when suffering comes.

Bisgood herself emerges as an advocate of the values of convent culture, firmly rooted in the pre-conciliar Church. There is nothing in the biography to suggest any questioning of the *status quo*, any looking forward to the changes that Vatican II will bring, or any anticipation of major developments in the Society. But the world in which she lived was about to change out of all recognition, and with the changes would come the need for a different approach to Cornelian biography.

Chapter Six

EXPLORING A WAY FORWARD: THE *INFORMATIO*

The *Informatio*, published in 1987, is not a biography in the strict sense: it is a section of the material presented to the Sacred Congregation for the Causes of Saints in support of Cornelia's canonisation. Nevertheless it has an important place in this study, because the theological and cultural assumptions on which its approach to Cornelia is based differ radically from Bisgood's. Where Bisgood, twenty years earlier, conveyed a sense of the immutability of convent culture and its accompanying value system, the author of this text, Elizabeth Mary Strub, takes for granted the changes in the Church that followed Vatican II. Her writing presumes both the understanding of holiness promoted in *Lumen gentium* and *Gaudium et spes*, and the renewal of religious life encouraged by *Perfectae caritatis*.[1] Such a radical change makes an equally radical difference to the presentation of the life of the founder.

The *Informatio* marks a major departure for Cornelian studies in a number of ways. It is the first study written with full access to all the materials collected for Cornelia's cause; it is rooted in Vatican II; and it is shaped according to the procedures regarding canonisation introduced by the Church in 1983. Further, its author is from the USA, unlike all previous biographers of Cornelia; she is theologically educated and, as a former superior general, has reflected on the Society's current understanding of Cornelia's charism. Strub completed a ten-year term in office in 1986, and remained in Rome throughout the following year writing the *Informatio*.

A formal presentation to the historical section of the Sacred Congregation for the Causes of Saints consists of two substantial documents: a *positio* that summarises all the documentation available about

---

[1] *Lumen gentium* (1964), *Perfectae caritatis* (1965) and *Gaudium et spes* (1965) are documents promulgated by the Second Vatican Council. (*The Documents of Vatican II*, edited by Walter M. Abbott SJ [London: Geoffrey Chapman, 1967].)

the candidate, and an *informatio* that presents the evidence for the person's sanctity. An *informatio* is, therefore, persuasive and approbatory in tone and intent: "Everyone directly involved with a cause has reason to see it succeed."[2] The primary purpose of the *informatio* is not the narration of the candidate's life story, but a demonstration of his or her practice of heroic virtue. However, since the reform of 1983, *informationes* locate their proof of holiness and heroic virtue in a biographical context.

The *Positio* for Cornelia Connelly's cause was written prior to the reform of the canonisation procedure, and published in 1983. It is a three-volume text, produced by a group of Holy Child scholars under the leadership of Ursula Blake. Blake, who was qualified in both theology and Italian, worked for ten years in close co-operation with Monsignor Fabijan Veraja (at that time Aiutante di Studio of the historical section of the Congregation of Saints) to craft a *Positio* which conformed rigorously to the legal requirements of the congregation. But Elizabeth Mary Strub benefited from the reformed system when she wrote the *Informatio* in 1987, and though she was still restrained by church requirements, she was able to move towards a quite different presentation.

The *Informatio*'s Canonical Context

In order to appreciate both the constraints upon Strub and the creative way in which she responded to them, some grasp of the form within which she was writing is needed. An *informatio* is a legal, not a literary, document:

> In the thirteenth century [Pope] Gregory IX formalised the rules of procedure in cases of canonisation. It was the same Gregory IX who set up the tribunal of the Inquisition. This was no coincidence: like a good lawyer, Gregory was concerned to define both saints and heretics, the opposite ends of the Christian scale. He used similar legal methods in both instances: trials. The trial for sanctity required witnesses; it required judges; and it required the notorious devil's advocate, the equivalent of counsel for the prosecution.[3]

[2] Woodward, *Making Saints*, 382.

[3] Peter Burke, "How to Become a Counter-Reformation Saint," in *The Counter-Reformation: The Essential Readings*, edited by David M. Luebke (London: Blackwell, 1999), 130.

Gregory IX's process was modified during the centuries that followed, most notably by Urban VIII in the mid-seventeenth century, but the procedure remained rooted in the practices of the law court. Legal protocol influenced the construction of texts; for centuries the documentation sent to Rome on behalf of a candidate was a brief presented to a court. "What mattered was not the text but the legal dialectic, with all its adversarial rhetoric and bite ... the exchanges between the Devil's Advocate and the defence lawyer."[4]

In 1930 Pius XI recognised that this juridical process could not deal adequately with causes presented after everyone who had known the candidate had died. In such cases a system that depended upon the questioning of witnesses was clearly unworkable. He therefore developed another process, which took greater cognisance of historical documentation. (The Cornelian *Positio* follows the guidelines of the historical section he established within the Sacred Congregation.) And in 1983 John Paul II instituted a far more radical reform of the whole procedure in an apostolic constitution, *Divinis perfectionis magister*. He abandoned the legal system altogether in favour of "a historical-critical account of the candidate's life, virtues, and, in appropriate causes, martyrdom."[5]

However, although this new approach eliminated courtroom presentations, it did not alter the basic norms by which the Church measures sanctity—norms which have remained unchanged at least since the canonisation of St Bonaventure in the fourteenth century. The church's judgement of sanctity continues to depend on proof that the candidate has practised to a heroic degree both the theological virtues (faith, hope and charity) and the cardinal moral virtues (prudence, justice, fortitude and temperance). The written documentation which accompanies a cause provides the evidence on which the case is judged. The 1983 reform "did not eliminate the requirement of proving heroic virtue,"[6] even though the requirement is at odds with the demands of biography, the form on which

---

[4] Woodward, *Making Saints*, 391.

[5] Woodward, *Making Saints*, 91.

[6] Woodward, *Making Saints*, 391.

the new process is based. Thus the authors of *informationes* find themselves in a literary-theological morass:

> The burden [of proving heroic virtue] fell on the authors .... The result, as I have emphasized, is a hybrid genre in search of its proper form. The problem is ... a confusion of purpose .... [T]he manifestation of character, even a saintly character, depends on elements of plot and characterization which cannot be organized according to a recipe for proving moral virtue.[7]

Woodward maintains that the demands of biography and of moral theology, of telling the story and of proving virtue, create an unresolvable tension within the text. Because the virtues examined are prescribed by the Congregation, and are identical in every case, the uniqueness of the candidate's sanctity cannot be explored freely. Further, the rigid schema of virtues leaves no room for acknowledging the person's faults or limitations and so "fails to produce believable saints."[8] And the Congregation's underlying assumption that candidates for canonisation can sustain perfection in the practice of virtue precludes the exploration of a more developmental approach to holiness, which could reveal how the candidate "overcame his human failings and grew in the grace of God."[9]

In Woodward's judgement, therefore, Strub is constructing a text according to quite unsatisfactory guidelines, like all authors of *informationes*. However, he praises Strub's creative approach highly, describing her *Informatio* as "a spirited departure from the past—perhaps because it is the first conceived and written by a woman."[10]

Strub's work was shaped both by the formal requirements for the structure of an *informatio*, and by the need to demonstrate irrefutably that Cornelia was holy. The *raison d'être* of the *Informatio* was to gain official recognition of Cornelia by the Church. So Strub could not lightly take liberties with the formal requirements of the Congregation, and thereby risk alienating the very authorities she was setting out to convince. Her approach in the *Informatio*, therefore, especially where it differs from the

---

[7] Woodward, *Making Saints*, 391.
[8] Woodward, *Making Saints*, 396.
[9] Woodward, *Making Saints*, 395.
[10] Woodward, *Making Saints*, 274.

norm, may reveal how her theological, spiritual and cultural convictions influenced her understanding and presentation of Cornelia.

Strub's Innovative Approach

Strub's predetermined task in writing the *Informatio* was to summarise the arguments and evidence contained in the *Positio* and to present, virtue by virtue, the case for proceeding with Cornelia's cause. Though she was obliged to conform to the structure prescribed by the Congregation, she found herself instinctively resisting the pressure to "mince [Cornelia] into spiritual lessons."[11] Woodward quotes her as saying:

> I don't see Cornelia as just a nun or a wife or a mother, but a woman who was a saint in all three stages of her life ... I want to present the evidence for holiness according to her own inner logic and experience of grace.[12]

More recently Strub has spoken of her "attempt to synthesize rather than analyze—to see the whole person, not a sum of virtuous parts."[13] This desire to adopt a holistic approach necessitated a modification of the usual format. She expanded on the requirements of the Congregation, inserting a chronological account of Cornelia's life, precisely "because I wanted to ... contextualise her values and virtues." She acknowledges:

> There was an innate resistance in me to the virtue approach, but since I had to go on that way I concocted an approach or method .... Here my own bias came into play. What I considered virtuous another might find questionable.[14]

In its published form, the Cornelian *Informatio* consists of three major sections—the history of the cause, the biographical synopsis, and the evidence for Cornelia's holiness arranged virtue by virtue.

An account of the history of the cause and an explanation of the delay in presenting it are required in all historical cases. The delay in Cornelia's

---

[11] Woodward, *Making Saints*, 391, suggests that John Henry Newman's complaint about hagiographical biographies—that they "do not manifest a saint but mince them into spiritual lessons"—was apposite to modern *positiones* and *informationes*.

[12] Woodward, *Making Saints*, 274.

[13] E-mail, 4 November 2000.

[14] E-mail, 4 November 2000.

case is a delicate matter, because it seems to hinge on disapproval of her among nineteenth-century bishops, and on a continuing "sceptical cynicism or cynical criticism"[15] among some of the Southwark clergy who gave testimony to the Diocesan Tribunal between November 1968 and January 1969. Peter Gumpel SJ, the relator of the cause, defends Cornelia unequivocally in his formal presentation, suggesting that her unwavering loyalty to legitimate hierarchical authority was "an outstanding sign of heroic virtue."[16]

The inclusion of the second section—the biographical synopsis, which is not normally provided—is defended by Strub on the grounds that Cornelia's life was complex and, as Woodward says, "relentlessly episodic."[17] She stresses that the insertion of the synopsis into the *Informatio* was her own idea:

> The next thing I did was to make for myself as full a chronology as possible of every event in Cornelia's life referred to in the *Positio*. I did this because I wanted to see what was going on in Cornelia's life not just sequentially but also simultaneously in order to contextualise her values and virtues. The *Positio* does not proceed chronologically, so I needed my own summary. I remember going to Paul [Molinari SJ, postulator of the cause] with this chronological account and persuading him it should be included in the *Informatio*.[18]

In this Strub was innovative: the addition of a biographical account highlights her desire to be more holistic than the canonisation process normally allows, and to locate the proofs of Cornelia's holiness more firmly in the ongoing events of her experience.

But the third section, which presents the evidence for Cornelia's holiness, shows an even greater divergence from the norm. In this section Strub focuses on two issues not laid down by the Congregation, before she turns to the proofs of Cornelia's heroic practice of each required virtue.

First, she offers an overview of what she calls Cornelia's natural gifts, and explores her character, stressing that it was this particular person with

---

[15] Elizabeth Mary Strub, *Informatio, Positio for the Canonisation Process of the Servant of God, Cornelia Connelly (née Peacock) 1809-1879*, Sacred Congregation for the Causes of Saints, Prot. No. 953 (Rome: SHCJ, 1987), xv.

[16] Strub, *Informatio*, [xxii].

[17] Woodward, *Making Saints*, 253.

[18] E-mail, 4 November 2000.

these particular characteristics who became holy through co-operation with grace. This section, entitled "Character and Natural Gifts of Cornelia Connelly," begins unequivocally: "To understand the work of grace in Cornelia, it is a help to know her as the human person she was."[19] The conviction that grace builds on nature is central to Strub's theology of holiness, and to her presentation of Cornelia, and she returns to it in her final paragraphs:

> Cornelia's gifts—her attrait for God, her spiritual alacrity, her active zeal, her unfailing responsiveness to grace, her capacity to confront and surmount every obstacle in the way of God—were partly of nature, partly of grace.[20]

Secondly, Strub departs even more radically from the prescribed format when she identifies the "core of Cornelia Connelly's holiness" as something quite different from her practice of individual virtues. She argues that Cornelia's particular, specific holiness was shaped by her experiences at Grand Coteau around the time of the death of her son, John Henry. She presents holiness as something other than a list of virtues, and asserts that Cornelia's holiness as a foundress was rooted in her experience as a wife and mother:

> It is noteworthy that Cornelia's holiness was given its definitive shape while she was living a married life. By degrees her context would shift, she would make religious vows and her life's devotion would centre more heavily in the Incarnate Word, the Holy Child. But her love for God which was ignited at Grand Coteau would continue to express itself in all the same characteristically active ways.[21]

So Strub argues for a unity within Cornelia's several vocations, a progressive growth in holiness through the various stages of her life.

Only after these holistic presentations does Strub turn to categorizing Cornelia's holiness according to the schema of virtues laid down by the Congregation. And even as she introduces the more systematic section of

---

[19] Strub, *Informatio*, 99.

[20] Strub, *Informatio*, 262.

[21] Strub, *Informatio*, 117. This central and most original aspect of Strub's presentation is analyzed more fully later in the chapter.

her work, she stresses again "the essential unity and coherence" of Cornelia's spirituality:

> The exercise which follows of analyzing Cornelia's virtues and the many forms her goodness takes serves not only to underline once more the essential unity and coherence of Cornelia's personality but also to sound the depths and lay out the riches of someone who in her own person clearly points to the depth and richness of God.[22]

Strub's adaptation of the form of the *informatio* needed the approval of the relator and the postulator of the cause. In addition to her text, the published *Informatio* carries two prefatory essays—a report by Peter Gumpel SJ, the relator, and a presentation by Paul Molinari SJ, the postulator. These two priests had formal responsibility for the cause; as Gumpel explains: "By the very fact that the Relator authorises the publication of a *positio*, he declares that he is in full agreement with the latter and that he assumes full responsibility for it."[23] It is noticeable that both their reports justify "the liberties with the conventions"[24] which Strub has taken. Molinari explains that, though this *Informatio* aims to present a more unified and holistic account of Cornelia's spiritual growth, it "respects the understandable demands of a systematic presentation (in keeping with the requirements of the Congregation for the Causes of Saints)."[25] Gumpel makes it clear that Strub's arrangement of material and her theological approach, though somewhat unusual, reflect current thinking about the limitations of the schema of virtues:

> It is common knowledge that a number of highly competent theologians who are conversant with the work of our Congregation question the wisdom of dealing with the individual virtues by following the classical system of the Scholastics. They are of the opinion that by dividing and subdividing the virtues, one runs the risk of losing sight of the spiritual unity of the life of a Servant of God. They fear too that this schematic approach impedes one from highlighting and grasping the most typical and personal elements in the spirituality of the person whose life is under examination. ...

---

[22] Strub, *Informatio*, 121.
[23] Strub, *Informatio*, [vii].
[24] Woodward, *Making Saints*, 391.
[25] Strub, *Informatio*, [xxxv].

> I mention the matter only so as to underline that it is with my full
> approbation that the sections devoted to the heroicity of the virtues of
> Mother Connelly follow essentially, but not in a servile manner, the classical
> and traditional system. Care, however, has been taken to underline the
> intrinsic unity and coherence of her entire spiritual life, and this has entailed
> some changes and transpositions which are inducive to this end.[26]

Gumpel and Molinari are attempting to bridge the gap between Strub's preference for a holistic presentation of Cornelia and the Congregation's demand for a systematic approach, a demand that had to be met if the cause was to succeed. Strub's instinct was to produce the kind of *informatio* called for by Woodward: "an exercise of Christian imagination brought to bear on the raw data of a human life transformed by grace."[27] But she was constrained, not only by the prescribed formula, but also by expectations that she would present her material using scholastic terminology.

Strub's Approach to Traditional Language and Categories

Strub could not afford to lose sight of her objective: to present Cornelia's life and demonstrate her holiness in a way that would convince the people who receive the text at the Congregation for the Causes of Saints. The language that she employs is, therefore, sometimes formal and traditional. And this seems to be particularly the case when she is being creative and innovative. For instance, she chooses to summarise Cornelia's experience using the classic terminology of mystical theology in the section where she explores "the core of Cornelia Connelly's holiness as formed at Grand Coteau"—her most radical departure from the congregation's norm:

> Looking back over this period, it is possible to see that the graces of
> Cornelia's thirty-second year were at the same time purifying—her vine was
> trimmed and cut to the quick; illuminative—she was given to understand
> John Henry's death as her share in the Paschal Mystery; and unitive—she
> was joined to God by desire and love and she was faithful to that unitive gift
> in ordinary time and in seasons that were extraordinary.[28]

---

[26] Strub, *Informatio*, [xxvi].

[27] Woodward, *Making Saints*, 395.

[28] Strub, *Informatio*, 117.

It may be that Strub is deliberately employing these terms to convince her readers at the Congregation that Cornelia's experience is consonant with scholastic categories. But this is not an isolated instance: Strub frequently calls attention to the "unitive" quality of events in Cornelia's life:

> Always after this episode, suffering would be embraced by Cornelia as unitive and therefore as mysteriously joyful. …
>
> … one of Cornelia's special insights—her own version of contemplation in action: because one's natural duties are willed by God, they are unitive. …
>
> There, with him, she found her life's object and purpose—union with him. In that union of love with Christ suffering, Cornelia knew joy. Staying with the suffering was a way of staying with the suffering Christ until he blessed her with union.[29]

A major characteristic of personal holiness is surely union with God; the argument here is not that Strub should have avoided this terminology, but that her recourse to it may have been politic.

Strub's use of the language of perfection is even more revealing of her dilemma, her struggle to hold the middle ground between the assumptions of an earlier period and her own convictions. The earlier biographers of Cornelia all perceived some correlation between holiness and perfection, and tried to establish that Cornelia reached a state of perfection which raised her above the struggles and temptations of ordinary Christians. This understanding of holiness is at variance with Strub's more developmental, holistic stance; so she never speaks of Cornelia's having "achieved" perfection, only of her "pursuit" of it:

> It would be a mistake to imagine Cornelia as morose or morbid in her pursuit of perfection. …
>
> It is possible to watch Cornelia stretching toward perfect love in her prayers and in her actions. …

---

[29] Strub, *Informatio*, 112, 114, 139, 146.

> She gave herself to the active pursuit of perfection, doing all that lay in her power and "waiting in patient hope for the increase that God [would] surely give."[30]

Strub never claims that Cornelia reached perfection in her heroic practice of virtue; instead, and the difference is subtle, she speaks of Cornelia remaining *consistent* in her relationship with God:

> At Grand Coteau her spiritual physiognomy became what it was to remain until her death. The inner face which she turned toward God became as distinctive and clearly defined as her beautiful profile. Age and life experience served only to accentuate the most marked of her soul's features. She remained interiorly consistent with the person she had become at Grand Coteau, meeting the incoherence and absurdity of much that was to befall her with the inner coherence of her unequivocal "yes" to God. ...
>
> In a turn-about of John Henry's story, Cornelia was the real victim led into the Temple of the Lord by Pierce. It was entirely consistent with her formation in "accepted suffering" that, feeling the sacrifice so keenly, Cornelia could say she was "ready" to make it with all her heart if God wanted it ... Cornelia was consistent. ...
>
> Cornelia's exceptional balance, integration and consistency as a human person derives from her being fixed in God. Her life holds together only in God.[31]

This use of the term "consistency" leaves Strub free to imply that Cornelia had adopted an unvarying stance before God, but also that she was developing and growing, still subject to struggle and temptation.

On occasion, however, the desire to hold the middle ground leads Strub into the use of expressions which are difficult to comprehend. She writes of the role of mortification in Cornelia's life, and explicitly of the effect of the "passive purifications" arising from John Henry's death and from Pierce's discernment that he was called to priesthood in the Roman Catholic Church: "What they achieved in her was a supernaturally natural ease in maintaining a basic equilibrium amidst unheard of provocations."[32] This

---

[30] Strub, *Informatio*, 114, 139, 213. Cornelia herself spoke of perfection as something to be aimed at rather than achieved: "Aim at the most perfect always—God alone forever—Excelsior." (CC7:54, quoted in Strub, *Informatio*, 257.)

[31] Strub, *Informatio*, 103, 116, 119.

[32] Strub, *Informatio*, 234.

sentence, in all its awkwardness, highlights the tension in Strub's work, the lack of congruence between the ideas that she was exploring and the language in which she was presenting them. This tension is further revealed by her tendency to juxtapose apparently static, passive presentations with much more dynamic explorations of the same theme. It is as if, having satisfied the Congregation with her first approach, Strub finds the need to re-express her point in language more consonant with her own stance. So, for instance, two passages just a few paragraphs apart explore Cornelia's response to grace. The first equates sanctity with heroic goodness, and speaks of the soul rather than of the person:

> The dispositions she took to Grand Coteau opened her to grace which raised her from ordinary goodness and pointed her soul toward sanctity, toward heroic goodness.

Then, almost immediately, Strub repeats something of the same theme in language which could not be more different, or more dynamic:

> One of Cornelia's most marked traits was her susceptibility to grace. She was so promptly and wholeheartedly responsive, so incapable of half measures that she fairly "ran with ardour" along the way her director pointed out.[33]

Strub's language shifts backwards and forwards between passively traditional, and more spirited, active, even racy, expressions. But the underlying sense consistently reflects her conviction that holiness cannot be understood apart from the context in which it is lived.

Holiness Rooted in Experience

Strub returns to her view that Cornelia's holiness was rooted in experience over and over again, in spite of the pressure upon her to categorize it virtue by virtue. She makes this assertion, not only in the innovative holistic sections, but also in the conventional passages which detail Cornelia's heroic practice of specific virtues. And she relates it explicitly to Cornelia's understanding of the Incarnation. Cornelia's charism, her particular gift for

---

[33] Strub, *Informatio*, 105.

the Church, was incarnational; it was an understanding of the significance of God become human, and, Strub claims, it necessarily drew upon Cornelia's understanding and experience of being human:

> The genesis of Cornelia's devotion to the Incarnation is certainly to be found in her life experience.
>
> Because she was dedicated to Christ in his human reality, Cornelia was a down-to-earth realist .... Sanctity was to be found within the everyday duties of one's state in life; ordinary events mediated God's will, and the natural order glorified him.[34]

For Strub, Cornelia's life, and its impact on her writing and teaching, take precedence over any categorization of virtue. In fact, Strub seems to find it almost impossible to remain within the terms of reference laid down by the Sacred Congregation. In the sections she devotes to Cornelia's practice of the virtue of charity (love, Strub calls it), she elucidates Cornelia's understanding of the Incarnation, showing how her theology and spirituality emerge from reflection upon life events. The Society today perceives the preface that Cornelia wrote for the Constitutions as a key to its charism, and Strub makes a direct connection between this text and events in Cornelia's life:

> This definitive statement by Cornelia on God's loving mercy in the Incarnation came to birth within an experience of multiple loss. It was 1853. Mercer had just died; Cornelia was painfully ill; Pierce had apostasized; Adeline and Frank were beyond her reach. She knew she was being sent to Rome on a pretext ... and she was not sure she would be allowed to return to England and to the Society, then only eight years old. Finally, sensational publicity had robbed her of her reputation during and after the Connelly v. Connelly case. Small wonder that Cornelia depicted the Child who was the manifestation of God's merciful love, and its source, as a suffering child ...[35]

Strub constantly asserts her conviction that Cornelia's holiness was integral to her living of everyday life; in fact, this almost becomes Strub's definition of holiness: "She lived her ordinary life with a heightened

---

[34] Strub, *Informatio*, 178, 180.

[35] Strub, *Informatio*, 167.

attention to the opportunities for meeting God in the present." Or, as Strub expresses it again, more conventionally: "The faith by which Cornelia lived prompted her to take a consistently supernatural attitude toward everything and to respond to all of life's reality as to God."[36]

Strub's insistence on contextualising Cornelia's practice of virtue enables her to explore a dynamic, developmental concept of being virtuous. Cornelia did not gain possession of a virtue and then remain unwavering in its practice. Rather, Strub claims, it is possible to trace in her a spiritual development and a growth in holiness. This theme too is grounded in Cornelia's understanding of the incarnation: "She was particularly conscious of the dynamism of the growth principle concealed in Jesus' infancy."[37] And it is illustrated by Cornelia's attitude to the spiritual growth of others:

> Understanding growth as the personal response of the individual to the personal leading of the Holy Spirit, she encouraged, nurtured and challenged aspirations, never frustrating them or forcing them into a uniform pattern. ...

> Cornelia's respect for persons was most often expressed by a characteristic trust—in them and in God's way with them ... [38]

Central to Strub's presentation is her conviction that Cornelia's holiness was revealed in choices made over and over again across a lifetime. There is no evidence for a single, road to Damascus conversion after which Cornelia achieved perfection; there are only daily choices, and gradual growth and change.[39] In a rare authorial comment, Strub reveals her personal view of developmental holiness: "It is not the graced moment alone that works the transformation but the moment pondered, acted upon and nurtured."[40] And Strub notes this process frequently in Cornelia's life:

---

[36] Strub, *Informatio*, 115, 124.

[37] Strub, *Informatio*, 187.

[38] Strub, *Informatio*, 137, 138.

[39] It should, however, be noted that Cornelia spoke of a "conversion" experience which occurred during her first retreat, Grand Coteau, Christmas 1839: "At her first retreat of three days she was converted and ... she said that all subsequent retreats only completed this one, in which she said that the sketch of her interior life was drawn" (D64:37).

[40] Strub, *Informatio*, 109.

By the time she left there [Grand Coteau] in 1843 to join Pierce for the return journey to Rome, Cornelia was already a holy woman. She had become holy not as a result of any single intervention of divine grace or act of generosity on her part but because she had cherished God's word as life spoke it and had clung with the tenacity of extraordinary love to God's will mediated through a series of shattering events. …

This [Cornelia's choice to practise the third degree of humility] was not a facile burst of fervour; it was a solemn choice confirmed by a lifetime of repeated choices. …

Always ready to venture all for God, she trusted in the God-given dynamism of life to carry her initiatives forward into life eternal. …

It is clear from her writings that she thought of life as a journey, a progression through a series of stages presided over by the overshadowing Spirit.[41]

Whilst conventional hagiography presents the saint on an unswerving trajectory towards holiness and towards God, Strub's Cornelia constantly suffers setbacks and has to start again:

By the power of the risen Jesus, Cornelia was enabled to rise up in spirit again and again through a series of new beginnings and through the contradictions and reverses of her life.[42]

The approach Strub takes in the *Informatio* suggests that her concept of holiness differs from that of Cornelia's earlier biographers. In spite of the requirements of the Sacred Congregation, she avoids any suggestion that perfection is an achievable state, or that it is possible to practise particular virtues perfectly. Strub's model of holiness leads her to explore the ways in which Cornelia responded to the movements of God's grace and was transformed by them throughout her life. This is a major shift in biographical presentation of Cornelia, a legitimate twentieth-century rereading of her life made possible by a different approach to the theology of holiness.

Emphasis on Ignatian Spirituality

Strub's understanding of holiness is, in fact, thoroughly Ignatian—a heightened awareness of the possibility of finding God in all things. As

---

[41] Strub, *Informatio*, 103, 150, 213, 223.
[42] Strub, *Informatio*, 213.

there is a deep Ignatian seam in Cornelia's spirituality and writing, author and subject are in harmony here. But Strub gives more attention to the Ignatian influence on the founder than to the influence say, of St Francis de Sales or of St Francis of Assisi, although the lives and writings of these saints were not without significance in Cornelia's spiritual development and in the shaping of her charism. The *Informatio* barely mentions the name of Francis de Sales, despite the record in Cornelia's spiritual notebook, from December 1847, of the influence of de Sales on the nascent Society:

> I am about to prepare myself before God to make the vows of Poverty Chastity & obedience according to the spirit & to the letter of our rule with the intention of carrying out the Rules of St Francis of Sales as I shall interpret them according to the double objective of our Congregation of the Hy Cd Jesus ... [43]

I argue here that all Cornelia's biographers impose their own interests, concerns and assumptions on their retelling of her story. Strub's and Flaxman's emphasis on the Ignatian tradition in her spirituality, to the exclusion of other strands, is a good illustration. In studying the Cornelian materials they came directly under the influence of the Jesuits: of Paul Molinari and Peter Gumpel in Rome, and, more significantly, of James Walsh in Britain. Strub has noted Walsh's impact on their approach to Cornelia, and explicitly links their biographical work with their experience of the full Ignatian Exercises:

> But we all came out of a common experience of the Institute for SHCJ Studies which was very much the brainchild of James Walsh .... Once he became involved with CC's story he lost his heart to her ... James' legacy to all of us was twofold—insistence on sound historical research and a deep appreciation of Cornelia's spirituality. We held a number of workshops together, organized a 30 day retreat around Cornelia's response to the Ignatian tradition ... [44]

Strub's comments make it clear that for Walsh, and for the SHCJ whom he influenced, "a deep appreciation of Cornelia's spirituality" was bound up with an understanding of the Ignatian tradition, and also with a personal

---

[43] CC21:60.
[44] E-mail, 22 November 2000.

experience of the Exercises. So, having come to value the Exercises in her own spiritual development, Strub highlighted their centrality in Cornelia's.

The period when the SHCJ was retrieving and reclaiming its Cornelian heritage was also the period when the Jesuits were rediscovering the Exercises in an individually guided form. The two strands became intertwined because Walsh and Molinari were involved with both. Though members of the Society were responsible for writing the *Positio* and the *Informatio*, their approach and their interpretation of the materials were strongly influenced by their Jesuit mentors. This is confirmed in the presentations by Gumpel and Molinari which preface the *Informatio*. Gumpel writes:

> While fully recognising the merits of Sister Elizabeth Mary Strub, it is, however, equally my duty to acknowledge that this *Informatio* owes much to the recognised competency and to the zeal of Fr Paul Molinari SJ, the Postulator of the Cause. Fr Molinari's work for the Cause of Cornelia Connelly, over a period of twenty-seven years, has been of inestimable value.[45]

And Molinari:

> In a special way I want to recall the invaluable contribution made to the Cause by Fr James Walsh SJ. James Walsh … animated and sustained the work of research. He perhaps more than any other person studied the life and writings of Cornelia Connelly, highlighting the richness of her charism and spirituality.[46]

Emphasis on how Ignatius influenced Cornelia is not misplaced (there are significant Cornelian texts demonstrating that it was strong), but a full exploration of "the richness of her charism and spirituality" would investigate more seriously the influence of Francis de Sales and Francis of Assisi on its development and formulation. Its exclusive focus on the Ignatian tradition makes Strub's exploration seem less than complete, and, I suggest, reflects her own experience and spirituality.

Strub writes about Cornelia's experience of the Exercises, the importance of the third degree of humility in her personal spiritual growth, and her understanding and practice of Ignatian discernment. In the final paragraphs of the *Informatio* she says, simply and comprehensively:

---

[45] Strub, *Informatio*, [xxv-xxvii].

[46] Strub, *Informatio*, [xxxi]. The patriarchy inherent in these comments is discussed in the next chapter.

Cornelia understood the dynamic of the Spiritual Exercises and was able to
lead others through the Exercises with confidence and skill, both in their
full and abbreviated forms. Her spiritual direction was clear, strong and
incisive, yet always respectful of the prerogatives of the Holy Spirit in those
with whom she dealt.[47]

While Strub neglects any discussion of Francis de Sales, she
acknowledges the influence of Francis of Assisi on Cornelia's thought, in
the section on her understanding of poverty which Strub heads "Poverty
with Christ poor: love to the limit":

> Cornelia was strongly attracted to Francis of Assisi. ...
>
> Cornelia, like Francis, was drawn to the stable of Bethlehem where God was
> strong in weakness and where, having nothing, he possessed all hearts. ...
>
> Her joy had a Franciscan character .... This joy was the fruit of her poverty
> and an expression of her freedom of spirit. ...
>
> From the first, she thought of Francis as a co-patron of the Society with
> Ignatius.[48]

What Cornelia drew from Francis de Sales and Francis of Assisi was not
in conflict with the Ignatian strand in her spirituality and writing. On the
contrary, Strub notes that, "Francis [of Assisi] found his way into the Society's
constitutions by way of Ignatius' rules on poverty rather than directly."[49] And
the *Positio* makes a similar link between de Sales and Ignatius:

> His teachings belonged in many ways to the Ignatian school of spirituality in
> which he had been educated, but in them Cornelia found a gentler spirit, a
> mystical dimension of unitive love ....[50]

The absence of any fuller investigation into Cornelia's dependence on
the spiritualities of Francis de Sales and Francis of Assisi is explained, at
least in part, by the importance of Ignatian spirituality in Strub's own
experience, and by the enthusiasm for all things Ignatian which
characterized the group of SHCJ scholars who came under Walsh's

---

[47] Strub, *Informatio*, 261.

[48] All these quotation are taken from *Informatio*, 197.

[49] Strub, *Informatio*, 197.

[50] *Positio*, 756.

influence. It is a further demonstration of the biographers' tendency to present Cornelia in the light of their own interests and experience.

However, the influence of Ignatius on Cornelia is not central to Strub's presentation as a whole. At the heart of the *Informatio* is the section entitled "The Core of Cornelia Connelly's Holiness as Formed at Grand Coteau." It has already been noted that this section is a major departure from the prescribed format; and its content is as original as its form. All Cornelia's biographers acknowledge the huge significance of the death of John Henry at Grand Coteau in her life and in her spiritual development. But no earlier writer attempted anything approaching Strub's analysis of the event as a "graced moment ... [a] moment pondered, acted upon and nurtured."[51] In this innovative section, Strub arguably satisfies Woodward's plea that an *informatio* should be a "primary exercise of Christian insight and imagination brought to bear on the raw data of a human life transformed by divine grace."[52]

An "Exercise of Christian Imagination"

This section of the *Informatio*, fourteen pages of closely reasoned textual criticism and theological argument, is based on a terse entry in Cornelia's spiritual notebook. First Cornelia recorded the date, 2 February 1840. Then she drew a symbol, something between a crown and a large intertwined M and A, which Strub says is "a monogram for Mary."[53] Then, down the middle of the page, she wrote:

Jesus

Marie

Joseph.

I.B.H.M.L. Connelly.

Fell a victim on Friday—Suffered 43 hours

& was taken "into the temple of the Lord"

on the

Purification[54]

---

[51] Strub, *Informatio*, 109.
[52] Woodward, *Making Saints*, 396.
[53] Strub, *Informatio*, 110.
[54] CC21:5. The manuscript is reproduced opposite the foreword.

The entry refers to the death of Cornelia's two-year-old son, John Henry (John Baptist Henry Maria Louis),[55] who was accidentally knocked into a vat of boiling sugar. Cornelia nursed him for forty-three hours, until he died, on the feast of the Purification.

Strub analyzes this page of the notebook word by word and line by line; she "proceeds to tease out meanings as if she were explicating a poem."[56] She employs a combination of literary and theological analysis:

> John Henry's name is fourth in a list including the members of the Holy Family. His name is placed on the page as a link between Cornelia's family, also called to present one of its own members in the Temple, and the Holy Family .... Next, she identifies John Henry with Jesus who was *the* Friday victim. John Henry "fell a victim" and Jesus too fell on his way to death ... John Henry's forty-three hour agony was Jesus' passion brought home to her and Mary's compassion to be shared. Finally, John Henry "was taken" by Cornelia, as Jesus was by his Mother, "'into the temple of the Lord' on the Purification." There is a note of conscious offering on Cornelia's part—a bringing of the child-victim to the Father as Mary carried Jesus into the Temple in obedience to the divine law.[57]

Strub "goes on to argue that out of Cornelia's response in faith to her son's death, her friendship with God was deepened and a spiritual personality formed."[58] She sees this tragic experience as fundamental, not just to Cornelia's personal spiritual development, but to her charism and to her particular choice of the title "Holy Child" for the congregation that she founded. From the entry in Cornelia's notebook, and from the information that has come down to us about the events surrounding it, Strub argues that:

> John Henry became for her a sign that Jesus' passion would always lead her back to the Child. In fact, Cornelia came to the Holy Child as the centre of her Society's devotional life by way of suffering and separation—by way of her own Calvary .... Her personal tragedy was illuminated and transposed by the Passion of Jesus explicating the Infancy of Jesus. ...

---

[55] "I" in Cornelia's text stands for the Latin "Ioannes."

[56] Woodward, *Making Saints*, 276.

[57] Strub, *Informatio*, 110.

[58] Woodward, *Making Saints*, 277.

> John Henry's death and its circumstances was at once the most terrible and the most pregnant of Cornelia's life experiences. It was the sword that pierced her own heart and at the same time it let loose a flow of "thoughts" that would quicken her religious family, because the event and its meaning to Cornelia are at the core of her charism, her holiness, her mission and her self-understanding. Through it God set the bent of her soul. It is the pivot on which her spiritual life turned.[59]

Strub's examination of the seminal nature of this personal tragedy for Cornelia's spirituality and for her charism comes out of her own reading of the original entry in the notebook, and is not derived from the earlier biographers. Many present-day members of the Society find in Strub's account an authentic and inspiring description of their founding myth. It is unequivocally Woodward's "primary exercise of Christian insight and imagination brought to bear on the raw data of a human life transformed by divine grace."[60]

And yet some questions must be raised. It is not possible to know now, with any certainty, what happened in Cornelia's heart during the long hours when she nursed her dying child (even she herself may not have known fully). As later generations, we have to deduce "the hidden movement of grace" exclusively from "external evidence."[61] By Strub's own account, "Cornelia was inarticulate about her interior life and left only hints and tantalising clues ...."[62] So, this major argument around which the *Informatio* hinges, this claim to show "the core of Cornelia Connelly's holiness," depends upon the flimsiest of documentation—a terse, even cryptic, entry in Cornelia's spiritual notebook. Nowhere does Cornelia spell out her response to the event; indeed in later life she seldom spoke of this child at all. Woodward's "raw data of human life" are, therefore, summary; and the "insight and imagination" are commensurately free-ranging. Are we coming closer to Cornelia here, or are we only learning more about Strub through her personal reading and interpretation of events in Cornelia's life?

---

[59] Strub, *Informatio*, 111.

[60] Woodward, *Making Saints*, 396.

[61] Woodward, *Making Saints*, 274.

[62] Strub, *Informatio*, 106.

In her account of these ten crucial months, Strub seems several times to overstate her case. She appears to suggest that the death of John Henry, and the events which surround it, were the beginning of Cornelia's relationship with God, when it is known that Cornelia had taken prayer and spiritual growth extremely seriously at least since the time of her conversion to Catholicism in 1835. Strub writes:

> [H]er love for God ... was ignited at Grand Coteau. ...
>
> Cornelia's first transforming encounter of love with Jesus was set in the context of the Paschal Mystery. Her first response to God's love in Jesus was sacrificial. Love led Cornelia to desire and to choose to be with Christ suffering.[63]

Similarly, she restates the view of the earlier biographers that the reception of Cornelia's sister Mary into the Church, on the day following John Henry's death, offered her a joyful resurrection experience after the sorrow of the child's suffering and death:

> After John Henry's death life did not stop for Cornelia to nurse her pain. She was swept forward to a kind of resurrection in a joyful family event. Her sister Mary, now living with her, was received into the Church, made her first Communion and was confirmed on February 3 1840.[64]

This is an imaginative interpretation of events, and it is attractive to anyone who wishes to show Cornelia passing through a paschal experience of suffering, death and resurrection. But the facts equally support the imaginative scenario that, while the whole family was overwhelmed by the little boy's painful death, the reception into the Church could not be delayed because the bishop who was to perform the ceremony was about to leave the remote outpost of Grand Coteau. In fact, this seems the more likely explanation; and it would appear to be supported by the next entry in Cornelia's notebook, and even by Strub's own comments:

> Within the week, Cornelia's journal entry: "off. mortification. Throw all on Confessor. Vow of obe. offered," indicates that she had seen her director

---

[63] Strub, *Informatio*, 117, 139.
[64] Strub, *Informatio*, 112.

and was struggling. As she would do later, here she proposed to bolster her resolve with a vow (which was not accepted). One can surmise that she feared grief or self-pity was driving her in on herself ... [65]

Raising these questions does not imply disagreement with Strub's interpretation. My intention is rather to highlight that what is being presented is precisely that: an interpretation. Strub, like all her predecessors, is crafting a story. As Woodward comments:

> [H]istorians today ... recognise that "facts" exist only in relation to an interpretative scheme, a story. I think, therefore, that the saint-makers would gain greater conceptual clarity about their craft—and its relationship to biography in general—if they would recognise that they do what all historians do: they tell a story. A documented story, to be sure, but a story nonetheless.[66]

Woodward is impressed by Strub's *Informatio* because, by inserting the biographical synopsis, it acknowledges the importance of story. But he is even more impressed by a theological insight into holiness which underlies Strub's presentation of Cornelia. In the consciously holistic section "The Core of Cornelia Connelly's Holiness as Formed at Grand Coteau," Strub shows that Cornelia's holiness is rooted in her response to "the gift of God's love"; she argues that it was Cornelia's lively relationship with God which moved her to practise virtue. In short, Cornelia was virtuous because she was holy, not holy because she was virtuous.

In spite of its limitations, Strub's *Informatio* is undoubtedly "an act of the religious imagination."[67] Describing Cornelia's "unique transformation through the grace of God's love,"[68] Strub has applied her own theological insight to Cornelia's story, and has succeeded in presenting it creatively, even while writing within the constraints of the Sacred Congregation's guidelines. She is rightly praised by Woodward as the writer of an excitingly different *Informatio* in which "the argument for [Cornelia's] holiness represents a significant departure from the past."[69]

---

[65] Strub, *Informatio*, 112.

[66] Woodward, *Making Saints*, 390.

[67] Woodward, *Making Saints*, 397.

[68] Woodward, *Making Saints*, 391.

[69] Woodward, *Making Saints*, 278.

Cornelia's Faults and Limitations

However, Strub does not entirely escape the censure that Woodward heaps on *informationes* and *positiones* generally. One of his major criticisms of the approach required by the Congregation is that it precludes any discussion of the candidate's limitations, weaknesses, failures and personal sins, and so fails to demonstrate fully the power of God's grace. Woodward argues that the process devised by the Congregation offers us less than human models of sanctity, because it leaves no room for discussion of change or growth, or for the acknowledgement of flaws.[70]

Woodward believes that the prerequisites of the canonisation process have steered Strub away from any serious examination of Cornelia's faults and limitations. In the end, therefore, he is not perfectly satisfied with the Cornelian *Informatio*:

> ... as a whole [it] still remains something less than a full-scale study in spiritual development because no account is provided of the moral faults or other weaknesses of character others saw in her. For all her trials and hardships, the Servant of God still inhabits a moral Eden where serious personal sin has yet to spoil the landscape.[71]

Whilst there is justification for Woodward's complaint—the *Informatio* patently does not make a serious study of Cornelia's weaknesses—there are indications within the text which suggest that Strub recognises Cornelia's limitations and acknowledges the validity of some, at least, of the criticisms levelled against her. Whilst Strub was not at liberty to explore these issues fully herself, she points the way forward towards a less constrained view of Cornelia, towards a fuller, freer, more human presentation.

In his prefatory report, Peter Gumpel comments upon the constant opposition that Cornelia met throughout her life, drawing attention to the dissension that arose within her congregation, and to the hostility she encountered among the English bishops. He praises the "care and honesty" with which these issues are addressed in the *Informatio*, and then adds:

---

[70] Woodward, *Making Saints*, 393, 395, 396.
[71] Woodward, *Making Saints*, 278-279.

> Naturally nobody pretends that Cornelia Connelly was infallible or that she
> was always right in all her decisions. Such a claim neither can nor should be
> made with regard to any Servant of God. The point in question is whether
> she honestly tried with all the means at her disposal to discern the Will of
> God and to follow it loyally once she was convinced that she understood
> what Our Lord was demanding of her.[72]

But the truth is that many of the biographers have come very close to pretending, if not that Cornelia was infallible, at least that all her decisions were—had to be—justifiable. Her faults, her brushes with hierarchical authority, and her independence of mind and spirit have troubled them, and they have felt obliged to explain them away or justify them in order to bring their presentation into line with their sense that holiness equates with perfection.

Gumpel and Strub are consciously exploring a different model of holiness and are, therefore, freer to contemplate a less than perfect Cornelia. In the biographical synopsis, Strub records the confrontations that Cornelia entered into with one person after another; and she notes the reservations expressed about her by bishops and priests, Jesuits, laymen and members of her own Society. These events and opinions are recorded in the *Informatio* largely without comment: Strub allows them to stand, generally resisting the temptation, familiar to the earlier biographers, to defend or to explain away.

When Cornelia left Derby and accepted the accommodation offered in St Leonards, for instance, we read within a few pages of her uncomfortable relationships with a growing number of clergymen. These are not the complaints of one difficult person, but the responses of each successive priest with whom Cornelia comes in contact:

> Sing [parish priest in Derby] ... accuses her of arrogance, insolence and
> high-handedness. ...
>
> Cornelia is the object of his [Mr Jones'—owner of the St Leonards
> property] growing mistrust and hostility. ...
>
> So begins the cooling of Wiseman toward Cornelia until he finally turns
> against her.[73]

---

[72] Strub, *Informatio*, [xvii].

[73] Strub, *Informatio*, 16, 21, 22.

Cornelia's struggles with Pierce, and the growing antagonism of the convent chaplain, Samuele Asperti, towards her, are also recorded on the same pages.

Even allowing for nineteenth-century gendered assumptions about behaviour, accusations of "arrogance, insolence and high-handedness" constitute serious criticism. To these complaints may be added Wiseman's to Cardinal Barnabò (recorded by Strub in both English and Italian) about "the dominating and ungovernable character of that American lady" ("*il carattere dominante ed ingovernabile di quella Signora Americana*"), and the damning indictment of Cornelia by William Cobb SJ in a letter to his provincial: "a married woman who can find no other order … in the Church to suit her but must found her own …."[74] And this is by no means exhaustive; Strub summarises the criticisms levelled at Cornelia:

> The impact of her force of character and, especially in later years, her direct, forthright speaking of the truth pleased some and alienated others. In the eyes of her critics and enemies, Cornelia was called by turns "autocratic," "ungovernable," "insolent," and "obstinate."[75]

Strub's brief is to demonstrate incontrovertibly Cornelia's heroic practice of the theological and moral virtues, and so it is understandable that she sometimes feels impelled to defend Cornelia, suggesting, for instance, that the allegations laid against her are "misinterpretations": "Cornelia put the truth to people with a directness that was sometimes misinterpreted as rudeness or arrogance."[76] But the truth cannot be avoided that this *is* precisely how many people experienced her. And when Strub asserts that "it pained her deeply to be thought disobedient or high-handed,"[77] she is highlighting in Cornelia what is, in fact, a common human experience—a lack of congruence between her intentions and the way in which her behaviour was perceived and judged by others.

Strub readily acknowledges that Cornelia was not above criticism. She suggests, for instance, that communication was not Cornelia's strong suit, and that her failure to discuss some matters had serious consequences. Her lack of

---

[74] Strub, *Informatio*, 35, 132, 74.
[75] Strub, *Informatio*, 102.
[76] Strub, *Informatio*, 249.
[77] Strub, *Informatio*, 132.

communication with Emily Bowles exacerbated the situation in Liverpool. ("Emily construes silence as consent.")[78] Her unwillingness to discuss the Preston nuns' problems with proposed changes to the Constitutions contributed to a near schism. "Cornelia interprets their silence as satisfaction with her earlier answer. They consider her silence dishonest and evasive."[79]

Strub also identifies the more personal fault of stubbornness in Cornelia, though she links it with determination and strength of character:

> In her struggle to obtain permission from Grant for this foundation [Towanda] Cornelia has shown her most determined, most persistent and perhaps even most obstinate side. ...
>
> Circumstances often forced Cornelia to act with strength and firmness .... A woman of determination, rectitude and strong principle, Cornelia sometimes appeared inflexible, even stubborn.[80]

Within the guidelines of the Sacred Congregation, it was not possible for Strub to explore Cornelia's limitations and failings more fully. She does, however, express reservations about Cornelia from time to time. While praising Cornelia's prudence, she points to the disastrous outcome of some of her decisions:

> This is not to say that when she exercised her prudence, her judgement was necessarily correct .... In regard to Pierce ... [b]oth her refusal to see him and her move to St Leonards brought on disaster .... She had to take a stand with Wiseman over his plan to create a marine residence for himself at one end of the convent. Her prudent effort to avoid scandalous talk precipitated a rupture in their relationship which was never mended.[81]

And later Strub acknowledges:

> It is hard to know, even by hindsight, whether Cornelia's efforts to deal prudently with opposition within the Society worsened or eased a conflictive situation which was bound to come to a head in any case.[82]

---

[78] Strub, *Informatio*, 31.
[79] Strub, *Informatio*, 67-68.
[80] Strub, *Informatio*, 44, 102.
[81] Strub, *Informatio*, 224-225.
[82] Strub, *Informatio*, 227.

Again, describing Cornelia's passion for justice, Strub comes close to naming it as anger. But anger is not listed among the Sacred Congregation's virtues, and so she speaks only of justice, though she acknowledges that Cornelia's passion was sometimes read very differently by her contemporaries:

> Her veneration for truth amounted to a passion which had a flaming quality about it. All forms of deception repelled and saddened her because they were an affront to God …. Her towering sense of justice and her reverence for the sacredness of truth put steel behind her sweetness, even to the point of rendering forgiveness difficult when it appeared to compromise truth or tolerate falsehood. Her uncompromising attitude toward what she deemed falsehood could take the form of indignation which risked interpretation by her enemies as insolence and intransigence and by some of her sisters as hardness.[83]

Woodward claims that "no account is provided of the moral faults or other weaknesses of character that others saw"[84] in Cornelia. But an examination of the text proves otherwise. Strub does not deliberately emphasize the flaws, inconsistencies and contradictions. But neither does she blindly deny them or attempt to justify them. Nevertheless, there is surely truth in Woodward's observation that, "For all her trials and hardships, the Servant of God still inhabits a moral Eden where serious personal sin has yet to spoil the landscape."[85] Serious personal sin has not figured in any biography of Cornelia. Though Strub adopts a more developmental approach to holiness, she explores in Cornelia a movement from natural goodness to graced goodness, not from sinfulness to virtue.

Holiness in the *Informatio*

In the concluding paragraphs of the *Informatio*, Strub explains precisely how she understands Cornelia's holiness: "Cornelia's holiness turned on two points: her desire for God and her receptivity to grace. Her desire was great …. Her receptivity was total."[86] This is a large claim—and it certainly leaves no room for Woodward's "serious personal sin." But it is a summary of all

---

[83] Strub, *Informatio*, 241.
[84] Woodward, *Making Saints*, 278.
[85] Woodward, *Making Saints*, 278-279.
[86] Strub, *Informatio*, 259.

that Strub has been exploring in the body of the text. Her presentation of Cornelia's is based on a concept of holiness which has diverged fundamentally from the understanding of the earlier biographers. She is not intent on demonstrating that Cornelia achieved and maintained a state of perfection, nor that she was perfectly, heroically obedient, patient, or zealous. Instead, she illustrates Cornelia's growth and development through the responses to God's love made in the ordinary choices of every day. Cornelia's holiness, Strub says, was "not the result of any single intervention of divine grace," but rather the outcome of having "cherished God's word as life spoke it and [having] clung with the tenacity of extraordinary love to God's will."[87] For Cornelia:

> Ordinary events mediated God's will, and the natural order glorified him. ...
>
> Everyday tasks were transformed into practical holiness so that nothing need be lost to eternity.[88]

Because Strub's underlying concept of holiness is rooted in the theology of Vatican II, because Strub is herself from the USA, and because she wrote the *Informatio* immediately after having spent ten years as superior general of the Society, she presents Cornelia from a new perspective. The Cornelia Strub describes:

> ... shared with her fellow countrywomen an independence of mind, a breadth of vision and a self-initiating will not typical of her English counterparts. A description of American womanhood given in 1866 fits Cornelia: force of character, intellectual vigour, capacity for affairs, high spirits, courage ... [89]

It is the holiness of a lively, independent, self-motivated woman that Strub attempts to describe. Her writing was circumscribed by the requirements of the Sacred Congregation for the Causes of Saints, but she points a way forward to a more thoroughly human presentation of Cornelia.

---

[87] Strub, *Informatio*, 103.

[88] Strub, *Informatio*, 180, 223.

[89] Strub, *Informatio*, 99.

Chapter Seven

RECASTING INTERPRETATIONS[1]

During the past fifty years, methods of examining texts have been adopted by feminist theologians that have enabled them to read against the grain, to ask new questions, and to retrieve hidden or neglected implications which can provide a fuller picture of the lives and contributions of our foremothers in the faith. One method which has been widely used is the threefold approach of critique, recovery and reconstruction. Women scholars have *critiqued* the sexist and patriarchal traditions in Christianity; they have challenged the credibility of claims to objectivity and neutrality in theology, and they have questioned the validity of the universal male subject. Because they believe that theological discourse is enhanced by a variety of voices, they have tried to *recover* the submerged stories of women in Christian tradition so that these can be added to the wealth of our communal experience. Finally they have called for a *reconstruction* of theology which takes into account the full personhood of women as well as of men.[2]

This development in theology has not happened in isolation: women theologians have been part of a movement, drawing on the writings of feminist theorists and philosophers, which has influenced the research of women scholars in many disciplines. Feminist biographers have based their critique of the androcentric nature of the biographical tradition on the same theories, and have challenged received practice in much the same way as women in theology have done, questioning both the loss of women's stories and the submergence of women's vitality beneath stereotypical femininity

---

[1] This phrase is borrowed from Eleanor L. McLaughlin, "The Christian Past: Does It Hold a Future for Women?" in Christ and Plaskow, *WomanSpirit Rising*, 95.

[2] "It should be noted that these feminist hermeneutical tasks are not necessarily sequential or chronological, nor are they ever completely finished." Mary Ann Hinsdale, "Heeding the Voices: An Historical Overview," in *In the Embrace of God: Feminist Approaches to Theological Anthropology*, edited by Ann O'Hara Graff (Maryknoll, NY: Orbis, 1995), 22.

in the stories that have been told. They have explored what it might mean for a woman to tell the story of another woman without using the "objective" white, middle-class, male voice that has dominated life-writing for so long,[3] and they have begun to identify and employ some feminist approaches to biography.

This chapter, drawing on new questions being raised in both spirituality and biography, explores what can be learnt from a reading of feminist biographers' spiritual and social subtexts; it attempts to understand the concerns, assumptions and intentions of the biographers (as these are revealed by their use of source materials, and by their omissions, emphases and interpretations); and it asks how their assumptions have shaped the ways in which Cornelia's story has been told. This approach may not bring us closer to the original Cornelia, but it should enhance our understanding of the multiple presentations of her in the biographies. "Historical resources must be revisited and reread continually in order to bring newly discovered perspectives to bear on past interpretations."[4]

Biographers' Contexts

Two major events that occurred in the 1960s created a watershed in Cornelian biography: firstly, attitudes in theology and spirituality were revolutionised by the Second Vatican Council; secondly, Cornelian studies were enhanced by the systematic collation and editing of the original source materials in preparation for Cornelia's cause. It does not seem too much of a simplification, therefore, to consider together first the biographers who wrote before this period, and then those whose work was influenced by these developments.

Buckle, Bellasis, Gompertz, Wadham and Bisgood

The earlier biographies, from the seminal and influential work of Maria Joseph Buckle in the 1890s to the polished production of Marie Thérèse Bisgood in the 1960s, span a period of huge social change: the impact of the First and Second World Wars on Western society creates an almost

---

[3] See Carolyn G. Heilbrun, *Writing a Woman's Life* (New York: Ballantine Books, 1988), 40.
[4] Hinsdale, "Heeding the Voices," 34.

unbridgeable gulf between Buckle and Bisgood.[5] Nevertheless, the first five biographies belong to a remarkably coherent period in Roman Catholicism and in women's religious life. All these biographers (including Juliana Wadham) seem to have written unquestioningly from within the Catholic subculture. They take for granted that their readership will share their value system, have a familiarity with the customs of religious life, and understand unexplained allusions to Roman Catholic practices.

Mary E. Hines provides a thumb-nail sketch of the prevailing ghetto mentality of the Catholicism of this period, emphasizing the way in which the Church viewed itself as being in opposition to the "world":

> In the years preceding Vatican I and to the eve of Vatican II, the official Church had adopted an attitude of deep suspicion toward the world, consistent with its negative evaluation of modernity. Pius IX's "prisoner of the Vatican" posture in protest against the seizure of the Papal States epitomized this attitude of salvation through withdrawal from the world. The world, particularly the modern thinking symbolized by the theories of Freud, Marx and Darwin, was viewed as evil and dangerous, even an occasion of sin. The world of grace, and the world of human history were viewed as separate realities. The Church was the realm of grace, sometimes even identified with the kingdom of God on earth.[6]

This conceptual framework, which shaped the Catholic world generally, was even more strongly influential within religious life. Hines notes the high status of religious within Catholic culture:

> Consecrated religious, people who "left" the world most definitively, seemed the most perfect Christians and religious life intrinsically a more perfect state.[7]

The convent culture out of which the biographies were written, and which they were consciously and unconsciously reinforcing, was deliberately out of tune with "the world" and its developments. In fact, convent culture was "other worldly" in a social as well as a theological sense: it was a

---

[5] Susan O'Brien's suggested phases in the development of women's religious life (before 1914; World War I to the 1960s; 1960s to 1990s) were noted in chapter one.
[6] Mary E. Hines, "Community for Liberation," in *Freeing Theology: The Essentials of Theology in Feminist Perspective* edited by Catherine Mowra LaCugna (New York: HarperSanFrancisco, 1993), 164-165.
[7] Hines, "Community for Liberation," 165.

subculture that retained many of the standards, values and attitudes of Victorian society (especially as regards women), alongside a spirituality which offered personal perfection as a goal and proposed withdrawal from "the world" into a life of self-denial as the best means to achieve it. Convent culture had a gendered perspective, being more fully subscribed to in communities of women than of men. It mirrored the traditional assumptions of Church and society regarding gender. Women were of a lower status than men; that there was some correlation between sinful weakness and women's bodies; the women who entered religious communities were at once to be honoured by men and subordinated to them.

The biographers' unquestioning acceptance of this anti-world, anti-body subculture influenced their readings and interpretations of the Cornelian documentation, and their presentations of Cornelia's life. They used her story to reinforce the values of religious life as they were living it, and to validate the patterns of life and ministry which had become established within the Society at the time when they were writing. In this, of course, they were no different from any other biographers: it is a general tendency of the whole biographical genre to reflect and confirm the social structures and values out of which the writing emerges. What is read into and out of a life is dependent upon the perspective of the writer.

Because the Cornelian biographers accepted the values of convent culture, they read those values into and out of Cornelia's story. Those parts of her life and writings that stressed the need for self-control, mortification, obedience, struck them as being of particular importance and significance. They valued and emphasized, for example, Cornelia's submission rather than her independence; her willingness to subordinate her own judgment to that of others (especially clerics) rather than her passion and vitality. Their desire to demonstrate that Cornelia was holy, even a saint, led them not only to emphasize her striving for perfection, but also to construct her life as an unswerving trajectory towards the perfect.

This approach, reflecting their spiritual and theological convictions, was reinforced by prevailing assumptions in biography. Like spirituality, biography is culturally embedded, reinforcing the values of a particular social context: "Patterns for telling one's life originate outside one's life experience; they are imported from the cultural storehouse."[8] Into their work, the biographers of Cornelia imported from the storehouse not only a whole set of religious and spiritual assumptions, but also conventional attitudes to biography. None of them was a professional biographer or had undertaken a serious study of the genre. Their understanding of biography had been acquired from general reading; they took as normative the patterns developed in male biography, and stereotypical approaches to the telling of women's stories.

The traditional model of telling women's stories attempted to find "beauty even in pain" and to transform "rage into spiritual acceptance." Today this approach is perceived as "less than honest .... Above all ... what has been forbidden to women is anger, together with the open admission of the desire for power and control over one's own life."[9] The first biographers of Cornelia are guilty of all these failings. But they were not deliberately "less than honest"; they were interpreting Cornelia's life according to their own understanding of perfection and holiness.

Every biography is a construct, an attempt to piece together, to make coherent, the events of an individual's life. Roland Barthes called biography "a novel that dares not speak its name"[10]; and Northrop Frye asserted that biographers' selection of material is "inspired by a fictitious impulse to select only those events and experiences ... that go to build an integrated pattern."[11] The pattern does not arise from within the life; it is superimposed on the subject's fractured and disparate life events by the biographer. But the dominant patterns in male biography ("destination, a 'significant' (public) life, solitariness, 'universal' themes, and the suppression of the personal") do not fit women's lives. The "chronological, linear narrative, which is well suited to accounts of career and of war, resonates less readily with women's daily lives."[12]

Nevertheless, the influence of these assumptions and patterns on Cornelia's biographers is clear. The biographers perceive Cornelia as

---

[8] Long, *Telling Women's Lives*, 18.
[9] Heilbrun, *Writing a Woman's Life*, 12, 15.
[10] Heilbrun, *Writing a Woman's Life*, 28.
[11] Long, *Telling Women's Lives*, 18.
[12] Long, *Telling Women's Lives*, 18.

foundress of the congregation, and retrospectively shape her life as if this were the destiny to which it always tended. All that they narrate, even about her early life and her experiences as a married woman, is written with an eye to the foundress she is to become. These biographies are essentially lives of a Reverend Mother Foundress rather than a woman, much as a biography of Nelson written during this period would have been the life of an admiral, or of Gladstone that of a politician.

Buckle's assumptions about what was appropriate in biography are particularly important. Her influence on all subsequent Cornelian biography cannot be exaggerated: her choice of emphasis and anecdote casts a long shadow across every other account. But she herself possessed only a sketchy knowledge of Cornelia's life before the founding of the Society; it was Cornelia the foundress whom she knew and whom she wished to portray. As foundress Cornelia was inextricably linked with the Society, and Buckle deliberately employed the power of Cornelia's words and actions to reinforce and validate what Buckle herself valued and approved of in the life of the Society as it changed after Cornelia's death. This use of biographical material to give support to current patterns of life and ministry, and to prevailing value systems, is also evident in the works of Bellasis, Gompertz and Bisgood. Even Wadham is not entirely free from this approach, presenting Cornelia primarily as foundress, and as the establisher of an educational system from which Wadham herself had benefited.

An important aspect of the biographers' context is their concern not just with Cornelia, but with the Society in which the founding charism was being systematized and institutionalised. After Cornelia's death, other SHCJ assumed responsibility for interpreting, developing, and shaping the charism, and for protecting it from distortion. Writing the life of the foundress was a contribution to the creation of the Society's myth, and a genuine expression of its charism. The tendency of institutions at this second stage of their development is to simplify and formalise—an instinct particularly noticeable in Angelica Croft, the second superior general. If the Society was to establish its credentials and gain hierarchical approval, Cornelia's scandalous and unconventional life had in some way to be tamed. And this was true not only of her personal story, but also of her original founding impulse. Her wide ranging vision for a congregation devoted to all the spiritual works of mercy was gradually focused more exclusively onto the task of education, and thereby made more quantifiable. The same tendency towards retrenchment has been noted in other congregations: "In general a sisterhood in the 1860s tended to be a more radical organisation than the same sisterhood in the 1890s."[13]

The early biographers of Cornelia were influenced by this general development. But the two factors that were particularly significant in shaping the context of the first group of biographers were their unquestioning acceptance of the values of convent culture, and their interest in crystallizing the charism into a system—a less fluid and more manageable construct. These spiritual and religious preoccupations were reinforced by the patterns of conventional biography which these biographers applied to Cornelia's life.

Strub and Flaxman

Elizabeth Mary Strub and Radegunde Flaxman wrote for a Society and for a Roman Catholic world radically different from the context of the first biographers. Their work is informed by late-twentieth-century cultural attitudes, by the documents of Vatican II, by the revolutionary changes in religious life which followed the Council, and by their own detailed study of quantities of original Cornelian source materials which were not available to the earlier biographers. But it would be too simplistic to suggest that a neat caesura divides these two later biographers from the others. Their training as religious had been similar to that of the earlier biographers; and they had personal experience of convent culture in the pre-Vatican II Church. They were writing at a historical and cultural turning-point. In church terms, they straddled the pre- and post-Vatican II worlds. Thus, their use of the Cornelian materials was informed by the approaches of their predecessors, for all the differences in emphasis and tone.

The positions of responsibility and authority which Strub and Flaxman held in the Society in the years immediately after Vatican II ensured that they not only gained an understanding of the radical changes through which they were living, but also explored ways in which the Society's

---

[13] Susan Mumm, *Stolen Daughters, Virgin Mothers: Anglican Sisterhoods in Victorian Britain* (London and New York: Leicester UP, 1999), xiii.

charism and founding myth could be handed on within the new culture. Both women carried responsibility for the formation of new members, and both served on the general council of the Society. Undoubtedly, these experiences influenced their approaches to the biographical task.

Whilst these two later biographers were without question daughters of the Council, the factor which most significantly shaped their work and differentiated it from that of their predecessors was the introduction of the cause of Cornelia's canonisation. The introduction of the cause led to the collation of all the known Cornelian resources, to Strub's and Flaxman's meeting with Paul Molinari and James Walsh, and to the establishment of the Institute of Holy Child Studies in which they were both involved.

Walsh and Molinari shared with the members of the Society their own enthusiasm for the new approaches in Ignatian studies, and encouraged Strub and Flaxman to apply similar principles to the study of Cornelia. They showed them how to undertake research, and educated them in the intricacies of work for the Sacred Congregation for the Causes of Saints. On a personal level, they deepened the women's commitment to Ignatian spirituality and the Exercises. Their influence, especially Walsh's, was enormous—so much so that the relationship that was established now seems deeply patriarchal. Walsh and Molinari were the experts who gave generously of their knowledge and enthusiasm; Strub, Flaxman and the other members of the Institute were the neophytes with everything to learn. It is startling to realise that as recently as the 1980s serious women scholars needed such support and encouragement from sympathetic clerics. Today, so short a time later, our expectations and assumptions are very different.

Both of these biographers, but especially Strub, wrote with the explicit intention of furthering the cause of Cornelia's possible canonisation. Strub was constrained by the criteria laid down by the Congregation for the Causes of Saints, and was not free to structure her work as she wished. She was obliged to present Cornelia as a model of specific virtues and as a striver for perfection. Strub's own theological training, and her ongoing contact with current theological thinking during her years in Rome, heightened her awareness that this approach had limitations. Further, the new insights into Cornelia (and especially into the significance of the events of her life at Grand Coteau) that Strub and the other members of the Institute of Holy Child Studies were exploring did not fit easily into the

Congregation's pre-defined structure: and the tension is apparent in Strub's writing. Ultimately, despite the pressure of the Congregation's requirements, she pointed the way towards a fuller and freer exploration of Cornelia the woman.

Flaxman's biography, unlike Strub's, was written for publication—the first general biography of Cornelia to appear for thirty years. Flaxman and Strub had lived and worked together over a number of years, and seem to have stimulated each other's research interests. Flaxman was able to draw on the *Positio*, and on Strub's exploration of Cornelia's spiritual development as outlined in the *Informatio*. But, because she was writing for a more general readership, Flaxman's approach differed substantially from Strub's.

Flaxman undertook an impressive amount of research, and in her biography she presents, for the first time, a detailed account of Cornelia's social and cultural context: life in Philadelphia after the declaration of independence; the world of the English Catholic aristocracy resident in Rome; the life of the Church in England following the Second Spring revival and the restoration of the hierarchy; approaches to the education of working girls and women in nineteenth-century England, and so on. The tone of the work is "objective"; the structure she adopts is largely chronological; the focus of her writing is Cornelia's public persona rather than her inner world.

Flaxman does not seem to have been influenced by the methods of feminist scholarship, whether theological or biographical. She does not share the feminist biographers' interest in presenting the inconsistencies and self-contradictions of their subjects. Neither does she bring into the frame, as they do, the significance of her own relationship with her subject, or indicate that she recognises the necessarily partial and particular perspective from which she is writing. On the contrary, Flaxman's work has all the appearance of being "definitive," of being an attempt to write "the standard biography." It is apologetic in tone and defensive of Cornelia, frequently justifying or explaining away her flaws, weaknesses and poor judgments.

In this attitude to Cornelia, Flaxman is a direct inheritor of the approaches of the earlier biographers. And yet her work differs substantially from theirs in content. Not only is her biography more broadly based and more solidly researched, but what she praises in Cornelia and holds up for admiration is quite different from the characteristics chosen by her predecessors. Where they emphasized Cornelia's submission to ecclesiastical authority, for instance, Flaxman highlights her independence of spirit. It is unthinkable that an earlier biography could have been entitled *A Woman Styled Bold*.

The ways in which Flaxman's biography is in harmony with the previous biographies, and the ways in which it differs from them, neatly pinpoint the moment at which she was writing. On the one hand, the structure of her work is not influenced by emerging feminist theories or by postmodern scholarship; on the other hand, its content—the exploration of the social and cultural background, the drawing out and emphasising of different Cornelian characteristics—clearly reflects the attitudes and interests of the late-twentieth century.

Flaxman's approach, therefore, like that of the other biographers, is determined to a considerable degree by the historical moment that forms its context. Each author's historical, social and cultural context, as much as her own interests, personality, preferences and prejudices, determines the ways in which she reads the documentation and interprets Cornelia's life. The context in which each biography is written defines its range of plausible interpretations, and makes some views literally unthinkable.[14] Context goes a long way towards explaining the biographers' treatment of the source materials: what they choose as important, what they omit, and how they interpret.

Omissions and Interpretations

In beginning to discuss the omissions and interpretations in the Cornelian biographies, I place myself, as feminist scholars do, within a research framework. My standpoint, my particular historical context, determines my perspective—a perspective as provisional as all those which have preceded it. My approach to the biographies is influenced by my reading in feminist biography and spirituality, and by attitudes to saintliness and to the telling of women's stories which are current at the beginning of the twenty-first

---

[14] See Heilbrun, *Writing a Woman's Life*, 28-29.

century. More robust and complex versions of the lives of our foremothers in the faith are looked for today if their "life stories [are] to serve as encouragement and guidance for our own lives in the presence of God."[15] My purpose here, therefore, is to raise questions about some of the accepted interpretations of Cornelia's story which, because they are rooted in cultural assumptions that are no longer current, are ceasing to have relevance or credibility today.

Cornelia's Family of Origin

Today most biographies verge on the psychobiographical; initial questions, reflecting popular psychology, are likely to concern the significance and influence of the subject's family of origin: "Where should [the biography] begin? With her birth … ? [What] is the subject's relation—inevitably complex—with her mother?"[16] If these are important questions, any biographer of Cornelia will fall at the first hurdle, because information about Cornelia's parents, about her relationships with them, and about her childhood generally, is extremely sparse. Each biographer in turn explains that "Of her parents and her early life very little has come down to us … Of her childhood little is related."[17] In spite of this, the biographers all assert that Cornelia was a beautiful child from an unusually happy home:

> All the children were gifted with talents and beauty, but the youngest daughter [Cornelia] seems to have been the most generously endowed with both …. It is pleasant to dwell upon her in her sunny childhood, fair and spirited and joyous, loving and beloved. …
>
> The little dark-eyed girl grew up lovely and spontaneous … merry and very intelligent … the joy and often the consolation of the household. But very few details of this happy childhood have come down to us. …
>
> Cornelia Augusta Peacock, the last of seven children, is born in Philadelphia into a happy family in comfortable circumstances. …

---

[15] McClendon, *Biography as Theology*, 179.

[16] Heilbrun, *Writing a Woman's Life*, 27.

[17] Gompertz, *The Life of Cornelia Connelly*, 2, 3. Compare Bisgood, *Cornelia Connelly*, 3, "very few details … have come down to us"; Flaxman, *A Woman Styled Bold*, 8, 9, "What little information there is … we have only one anecdote."

> Yet what little information there is … conveys the certainty that hers was a happy, secure childhood that formed her to love and trust.[18]

These accounts all have a whiff of hagiography about them. Like princesses in fairytales, female saints are stereotypically happy and good and beautiful and wealthy. The language that all the biographers use is suspiciously synthetic: Gompertz goes so far as to describe the dark-haired, dark-eyed Cornelia as "fair." Yet the only document that the *Positio* produces to support this standard presentation of the young Cornelia is a paragraph in a letter written by Cornelia after the death of her sister, Mary, who joined the Society of the Sacred Heart:

> My dearest Sister, from her earliest childhood was remarkable for her gentleness and amiability which were accompanied by an almost unvarying cheerfulness of mind. She was very fond of birds and flowers and these claimed her chief attention when she was not studying her lessons or writing. Her character was very docile and freed from self confidence and she generally exalted others far beyond herself and beyond their merits, especially her younger Sister [Cornelia] whom she praised quite undeservedly though she intended no fault in doing so.[19]

Cornelia's language, as she records this memory of her sister, is consciously hagiographical ("she intended no fault in doing so"); and yet this, and an assertion by Cornelia's niece, Mary Gaenslen, that "Aunt Mary told us there was never an unpleasant word spoken in their family,"[20] are the sum total of the evidence for a happy carefree childhood. Against this is the knowledge that "some months before his fiftieth year," Cornelia's father, who speculated in property, "was confined in a nursing home belonging to a Mr Sebastian Himmelsporker" and died there when Cornelia was nine. At this time his "debts exceeded his assets."[21] Cornelia's mother, who had been married twice, died when Cornelia was 14, "after a severe and lingering illness."[22] A father in debt and confined to a nursing home, and a mother

---

[18] Gompertz, *The Life of Cornelia Connelly*, 3, 4; Bisgood, *Cornelia Connelly*, 3; Strub, *Informatio*, 3; Flaxman, *A Woman Styled Bold*, 8.

[19] D9:164-165, quoted in the *Positio*, 21.

[20] *Positio*, 1230, n. 21.

[21] *Positio*, 4.

[22] *Positio*, 6.

suffering from a lingering illness, do not usually make for a happy and carefree childhood. And a psychobiography today would certainly not overlook the fact that in all her many letters to her siblings, throughout the rest of her life, Cornelia never once made a single reference to either parent.

The mythologized version of Cornelia's life goes on to relate how this beautiful and gifted young woman, from one of the best families in Philadelphia, fell deeply in love with the local curate, who was socially and financially beneath her, and married him in spite of family opposition. Not only does this enhance and dramatize Cornelia, but it also sows seeds of doubt about Pierce from the very beginning of the story. Yet once more, the few known facts do not fully support this account. Flaxman is here the pioneer:

> Although American-born like Pierce, her [Cornelia's] ancestral roots were less fully American than his, her immediate family situation less stable and its members less prominent. In these ways, at least materially, Pierce was more advantaged than she.[23]

Lacking information about Cornelia's family of origin and early life, the first biographers provided a romanticised, hagiographical picture. The feminist biographer today cannot reproduce this, but neither has she the material that would form the basis of a well-researched psychobiography. So all she can do is to acknowledge the lacuna.

Cornelia as Wife

In current feminist thought the categorization and definition of a woman according to degrees of relationship with the men in her life (daughter, sister, wife, mother) are automatically suspect. But Cornelia as wife and mother, and the representation of her marriage and motherhood in the biographies, have been perceived as extremely important, at least in terms of her possible canonisation. In 1963, Paul Molinari explained the theological rationale:

> The Church will never proceed to her [Cornelia's] canonisation just because she founded a religious community and will never limit herself to exalt

---

[23] Flaxman, *A Woman Styled Bold*, 8.

Cornelia's life on account of the trials she underwent as a nun. The really deep meaning of every canonisation consists principally and always in this: the whole life of a person, from the moment of conversion to God up till the moment of death, is held up as a masterpiece of God's grace in our world and as a true example of this person's heroic correspondence to God's gracious invitation to loving surrender.[24]

So, Molinari argues, the kind of wife and the kind of mother Cornelia was cannot be overlooked in the canonisation process. Molinari and Peter Gumpel (the relator of the cause) both address this issue directly, making the formal claim that Cornelia was "an exemplary wife and mother,"[25] as well as "an outstanding religious and foundress, and above all, a woman entirely open to God's demands and his unfathomable and mysterious ways of love."[26] Yet, every biographer from Buckle onwards has been aware of, and has attempted to counter, the scandal of Cornelia's marital difficulties and the widespread criticism of her as an "unnatural mother."

Molinari's defence of Cornelia as exemplary wife is set within the context of his understanding of priesthood and religious life as higher vocations than marriage:

We must understand that God's ways are not our ways and God can indeed ask sacrifices and does in fact ask sacrifices that exceed our narrow conceptions. The vocation of a married person to the more perfect state of the priesthood or the religious life is, therefore, a possibility.[27]

Nevertheless, he claims that, before she became a religious, Cornelia "lived an exemplary family life, and was intensely happy in it," and that she had "*a truly heroic love for her husband*" [his italics].[28] Because of this, and in spite of her pursuit of a "higher vocation," he argues that she "is a shining example" to married people:

[24] Paul Molinari, "Commitment to Love: A Reply to Cornelia Connelly's Critics," *Homiletic and Pastoral Review* 64 (October 1963), 21-29, here 29.

[25] Peter Gumpel, "Report by the Relator of the Cause," in *Positio*, [xi]; Paul Molinari, "Presentation by the Postulator of the Cause," in *Positio*, [xxxvii].

[26] Molinari, "Presentation," [xxxvii].

[27] Molinari, "Commitment to Love," 23. That priesthood and religious life are "more perfect states" than marriage continues to be asserted in the writings of John Paul II.

[28] Molinari, "Commitment to Love," 26, 28.

> She is, in our own days, a valid and highly opportune example also for married people in so far as she has taught us that Christian love between husband and wife should always intend the greater spiritual benefit of the married partner and that, for the achievement of this higher and God-willed spiritual good, it should never shrink back even from the greatest personal sacrifices once these are seen to be the will of God.[29]

Molinari's argument is that Cornelia was a theologically exemplary wife because she sacrificed her happiness with her husband to what was perceived to be a call from God for Pierce to embrace a higher vocation. Even if this argument continues to be considered theologically valid, it has to be acknowledged that, for many people today, the consequences of the decision as they unfolded in the Connellys' lives prove a serious stumbling block both theologically and emotionally. Cornelia's choice, whilst arguably praiseworthy within her context and maybe even contributory to her sanctity, no longer strikes people as exemplary; people today would not take it as a model to imitate.

Gompertz,[30] however, writes entirely from within the position outlined by Molinari: priesthood and religious life are higher callings than marriage, and Cornelia's holiness is demonstrated by her willingness to sacrifice life with her husband and children. Gompertz summarises this view in an extravagantly worded passage on the second page of her biography:

> Physical torture even pagans have braved for love or duty, but it has been left to the saints to show an equal courage in the greater sufferings of the soul. Divine Love is the secret of their power. Cornelia Connelly had tasted the happiness of perfect human love. She was loved more devotedly and in more varieties of relationship than falls to the lot of most women. But when God took possession first of her intellect and then of her heart, her love for Him became an impelling force which stopped at no sacrifices and ever goaded her on to greater activity in His service.[31]

Gompertz' claim that the Connellys experienced "perfect human love" seems fanciful, but the first years of their marriage were happy. Evidence is

---

[29] Molinari, "Commitment to Love," 29.

[30] Space does not allow for a detailed exploration of each biographer's treatment of the themes explored in this section; instead, Gompertz is quoted as representative of the earlier group of biographers, and Flaxman as representative of the later group.

[31] Gompertz, *The Life of Cornelia Connelly*, 2.

provided by, among others, Cornelia's sister Mary, a rather effusive letter writer: "They are and always have been about the happiest couple that ever breathed."[32] Discussing Pierce's decision to seek ordination in the Catholic Church (which she wrongly believes he concealed from Cornelia), Gompertz confirms the quality of the marriage:

> [T]hese were the questionings ... which he had of necessity to hide from the wife who had hitherto shared his every thought. We have her testimony that the union between them had been unclouded. ...

> Mrs Connelly's attitude towards her husband at this time was one of generous admiration. At the beginning she was absolutely free from any feeling of reproach or mistrust towards him. She had always been a devoted wife, and the fidelity and intensity of her love had ... grown with the years.[33]

Even within Gompertz' schema—writing the life of a foundress, accepting a theology of the superiority of the call to priesthood and religious life—the enormity of the sacrifice which Cornelia was called upon to make is evident. She had been happy in her marriage, and she had a great deal to lose:

> We cannot but marvel at the grace that was given her, utterly to put aside her own wishes, feelings and most sacred rights, and to think of nothing but the Will of God.[34]

Yet Gompertz' theology traps her into describing Cornelia's feelings for her husband as "obstacles to perfection." After Pierce's and Mercer's departure from Grand Coteau for Europe (Mercer was nine), Gompertz pictures Cornelia struggling to die to her feelings for her husband and son, literally to forget about them; and she presents this struggle as a path towards personal perfection:

> Her chief enemies were her thoughts and affections, which would, in spite of herself, follow her husband and her little son across the ocean; or dwell on memories of what had passed away. While determined to overcome these obstacles to perfection, she reminds herself in words that foreshadow the

---

[32] D2:53, Mary Peacock to Adeline Duval, 1835.

[33] Gompertz, *The Life of Cornelia Connelly*, 31, 35-36.

[34] Gompertz, *The Life of Cornelia Connelly*, 35.

future motto of her Society, that it is actions that count, not sentiments. She knows that her old self must die, and she condemns it to death without mercy. All must be for God, nothing for the indulgence of imagination or memory.[35]

Gompertz writes emphatically from within the convent culture. Cornelia's struggle to set aside her marital and maternal feelings, and her motivation for doing so, are described in language which would have found echoes in the spirituality of every member of a religious congregation in the 1920s. After describing Pierce's ordination, Gompertz idealizes Cornelia's radical choice even further. Here is a woman that the religious of the 1920s can admire and desire to emulate:

> Never at any time was she even tempted to regret the sacrifice she had made of her life to God …. With her there was no rapine in the holocaust.[36]

Gompertz presents Cornelia as exemplary. But those who will follow her example are more likely to be women religious than wives struggling to remain faithful to their husbands. Flaxman, writing seventy years later, perceives the experiences of the married Cornelia rather differently.

Though Flaxman describes the beginnings of the Connellys' married life in Natchez as "three happy years,"[37] she believes that their circumstances were far from easy. Pierce's ministry was "unusual, hard and depressing"; he was lonely, isolated and "under great strain." "In such circumstances a wife's support was important."[38] When the Connellys decided to abandon Episcopalianism in favour of Catholicism, Flaxman quotes a stereotypically nineteenth-century comment from one of Cornelia's letters: "I am ready to submit to whatever my beloved husband believes to be the path of duty."[39] This image of a submissive and dutiful Cornelia, if it had not won approval from the earlier biographers, would certainly have been passed over by them without comment. But it is not consonant with Flaxman's basic view of Cornelia as *a woman styled bold*, and so she is obliged to contest it. In an authorial comment following the

---

[35] Gompertz, *The Life of Cornelia Connelly*, 47.
[36] Gompertz, *The Life of Cornelia Connelly*, 84.
[37] Flaxman, *A Woman Styled Bold*, 20.
[38] Flaxman, *A Woman Styled Bold*, 20-24.
[39] Flaxman, *A Woman Styled Bold*, 33.

quotation, Flaxman asserts that, the letter notwithstanding, Cornelia was a woman of independence and spirit:

> The way in which Cornelia here expresses her relationship with her husband calls for comment. By nature she was by no means submissive. Her decision to marry against opposition was an independent choice. She was naturally spontaneous, strong, warm. She was also clear-headed, but the age in which she lived demanded submissiveness from wife to husband. In all things temporal his was the final say. Both law and society agreed with him and the wife had no rights. A girl would be bred to this concept and to a future in which as wife she could not dream otherwise. Cornelia's family was no exception. "Be a Catholic, or whatever will make you happiest," Addie wrote to her, "follow the path of duty strictly. Be advised by your dear good partner, he is your earthly guide."[40]

The presentation of Cornelia as the exemplary wife is problematic for all the biographers, because none of them is sympathetic towards Pierce or his choices. Flaxman's comments about him are particularly stinging. Of his decision to give up his living in Natchez, for instance, she writes: "Publicly he had deprived himself of his parish and incidentally of income for his wife and children. If this was indeed heroism for the sake of truth it was also an ill-judged and precipitate action."[41] Flaxman wishes to present a Cornelia who is as independent of her husband as possible. Consequently, she makes much of Cornelia's decision to be received into the Catholic Church in New Orleans before the family sailed for Europe, whilst Pierce, with his intellectual and theological questions still unresolved, waited until they arrived in Rome. She speaks of this choice of Cornelia's as "pivotal," as "a quantum leap out of dependence into freedom":

> No event in Cornelia's future among many that were momentous would be more pivotal than this. By breaking away from her husband's plans in a matter so intimate to their relationship as religion, this nineteenth-century wife made a quantum leap out of dependence into freedom. Henceforth she is more and more herself, and at the same time more and more free for God, whatever her husband may ask of her.[42]

---

[40] Flaxman, *A Woman Styled Bold*, 33.
[41] Flaxman, *A Woman Styled Bold*, 26.
[42] Flaxman, *A Woman Styled Bold*, 37.

"Quantum leap" seems an exaggerated claim when Flaxman acknowledges, in the same paragraph, that "it was 'with full sanction and approval of her husband' that [Cornelia] was received into the Catholic Church." Nevertheless, it is clear from Flaxman's presentation that submission, duty and obedience are not central to her concept of the exemplary—or holy— wife. In a decidedly twentieth-century way, Flaxman sees Cornelia's dependence on her husband as something she will grow out of. She speaks of an early letter of Cornelia's to Pierce as "the spontaneous expression of a strong but still dependent love."[43] And she offers an interpretation of Cornelia, left at Grand Coteau after the departure of her husband and son for Europe, which fundamentally contradicts the view of Gompertz quoted above:

> It would be surprising were there no sense of being abandoned, no temptation to envy and blame her husband and reach out possessively to her children, even to cry out against God, "Why me?" But what we have in this second notebook … is not that side of the picture. Instead, there is evidence of a sustained generous effort to put herself, come what might, into God's hands.[44]

Flaxman allows us—in a way unthinkable in the earlier biographies—to contemplate the possibility that Cornelia felt resentment, even self-pity. She emphasizes the struggle, the cost to Cornelia of the decision to break up their home and become a religious:

> The presence of her little boy [Frank], "trying to say everything: with pretty curling hair & rosy cheeks & saucy chin," her last child, was a piercing reminder of all that was lost to her. …
>
> At the very beginning [of the notebook] she writes that every day she will "give P[ierce], self, children, all" into the care of the Mother of God. … At the end of the retreat made with the nuns she offers (and deliberately initials and dates) "to support all kinds of adversities" if that is what God chooses for her. The earnestness with which she strove to respond is evident in the notebook.[45]

---

[43] Flaxman, *A Woman Styled Bold*, 29.

[44] Flaxman, *A Woman Styled Bold*, 85.

[45] Flaxman, *A Woman Styled Bold*, 86.

Flaxman, from her own context, reads into the source material an account of a woman coping with the disintegration of her marriage which might well be exemplary and encouraging for people in similar situations in the late-twentieth century. Flaxman's Cornelia arguably has "a truly heroic love for her husband," as Molinari suggested, but Flaxman's understanding and presentation of Cornelia's heroism differs radically from his or from that of Gompertz.

However exemplary Flaxman sees Cornelia's married life as having been, it was not till the deed of separation had been signed and Pierce had been ordained that Flaxman's Cornelia finally came into her own, that her potential began to be realised:

> Here was the moment of closure on years of uncertainty, on the kind of experience which would have led many a woman to breakdown. They had been years marked by prolonged deliberation, prayer and waiting, by great love and extraordinary trust in God. They were also years of confused feelings, of shifting roles and—most of all—of conflict within herself which she had never been able to alleviate, as would a late-twentieth-century wife, by effective decisions of her own. This was a moment of unseen beginning when potential began to stir and action call. She was like one of those whose life so far had always been in the half-light and who now stood waiting in the wings till the new scene was set.[46]

For late-twentieth-century readers this development and use of Cornelia's gifts is more satisfying, more godly, than her behaviour either as a docile and submissive wife or as a woman who, in Gompertz' words, was willing "utterly to put aside her own wishes, feelings and most sacred rights, and to think of nothing but the Will of God." But, given this attractive picture of the new possibilities opening up for Cornelia as her marriage effectively ends, has Flaxman's Cornelia lost her value as an exemplary wife?

Cornelia as Mother

Paul Molinari and Peter Gumpel, in their prefatory essays to the *Positio*, assert that Cornelia was exemplary as a mother as well as a wife. Molinari's article, "Commitment to Love," speaks of Cornelia's "very maternal and extremely delicate love for her young children," and of her realisation that

---

[46] Flaxman, *A Woman Styled Bold*, 103.

"God in His infinite wisdom and goodness was asking her to make a most painful sacrifice, the sacrifice of her children whom she dearly loved."[47] If we view this sacrifice "in the light of faith," he argues, we may have every confidence that there will be no resulting damage to the children:

> In the light of faith it is further not difficult to see that this sacrifice of what is dearest to one's heart is, at the same time, not only a secure means of personal sanctification, but also an unimaginable source of apostolic fertility. God is not outdone in generosity. In His way He will not only bless the future life of the person who, on His explicit demand, has entered upon a higher state of perfection, but He will also supply (though not always in a way visible to our human eyes) for the needs of that parental care and love that the parents concerned will no longer be able to give their children.[48]

The tell-tale parenthesis, "though not always in a way visible to human eyes," suggests that Molinari recognises that objections might be raised over the fate of the Connellys' children. He does not explain how God, in this specific case, supplied the children's need for maternal care and love. But, at least by implication, he acknowledges that the decisions of the parents could have an adverse effect upon the children's general welfare. In this he takes a broader view than James Walsh who, in his two articles in *The Month* in 1959, focuses exclusively on what he called "the religious perversion" of the children—the loss of their Roman Catholic conviction and practice. And for this Walsh places the blame squarely on Pierce:

> Doubt is sometimes cast on the genuinity of Cornelia's vocation because it occasioned the religious perversion of her three children .... But the fact is undeniable—that the children's perversion and the deprivation of all communication with their mother was wholly the result of their father's broken promises.[49]

Neither Molinari nor Walsh makes a substantial case for the claim that Cornelia was an exemplary mother. And the facts are difficult: of her three children who survived to adulthood, Mercer lived with her until he was

---

[47] Molinari, "Commitment to Love," 28.
[48] Molinari, "Commitment to Love," 24.
[49] Walsh, *The Vocation of Cornelia Connelly*, 20, 24.

nine; Adeline until she was seven (followed by another four years in Sacred Heart boarding schools where her mother was also present on the premises); and Frank until he was five. Afterwards her influence over the children was severely restricted. Mercer died at the age of twenty, not having seen his mother since he was thirteen, or having had any correspondence or contact with her after he left Stonyhurst aged sixteen. Adeline saw Cornelia only once in later life, in 1877, when she was already 42; and by that time, according to Gompertz, "all intimacy had vanished …. For her mother she had little more than politeness."[50] Frank met his mother twice after the age of five—in 1867, when he was 26, and again in 1872. "His visits merely added to [Cornelia's] sorrow."[51]

For readers of Cornelia's story today, the question of the children is possibly more significant than it was at an earlier period. Certainly, Gompertz' treatment is no longer perceived as acceptable. She speaks of Cornelia as "an affectionate and devoted mother [whose] love was fully returned by her children," and she describes her separation from them as a "cross."[52] But she presents the mother's love for her children as "natural" rather than "spiritual," and suggests, with apparent approval, that Cornelia "conquered" it:

> Once again in this separation the clash of natural and spiritual claims had become acute for the mother, and once again she silently conquered.[53]

When Pierce removed the children from their schools, intending "to hold them as hostages … as the best means of getting hold of their mother," Gompertz speaks of the conflict between "natural and spiritual claims" in Cornelia, and of her heroic resistance to the ties of natural affection:

> For the last time the natural and spiritual claims upon her met in violent conflict, and she saw how impossible it was to serve two masters. The temptation to recover her children at any cost pursued her, and with it came the inspiration to new heroism. She dared not trust her own heart lest in its overmastering love for them it might prove a traitor to her solemn obligations. …

[50] Gompertz, *The Life of Cornelia Connelly*, 183.
[51] Gompertz, *The Life of Cornelia Connelly*, 183.
[52] Gompertz, *The Life of Cornelia Connelly*, 101.
[53] Gompertz, *The Life of Cornelia Connelly*, 102.

> Nerving her soul as usual by meditation on the Passion and on the Mother
> of Sorrows, she made [a] vow [to be directed by the convent chaplain in the
> matter] and forced her heart to be at peace.[54]

Gompertz never seems to have reflected upon the consequences of
these choices for the Connelly children. She is writing a biography of a
Reverend Mother Foundress who happened to have children, and whose
relationship with her children "furnished her with many opportunities for
sacrifice."[55] This is the language of convent culture, and the foundress is an
example to be emulated by Gompertz' contemporaries in the Society, who
were encouraged to make a radical break with the lives they had led before
entering the congregation. But in the early-twenty-first century, the
biographer's lack of concern for the effect of the Connellys' sacrifice upon
their children is heart-wrenching.

Gompertz describes one incident which took place at Grand Coteau
after Pierce and Mercer had left for Europe. Adeline had become a boarder
at the Sacred Heart school, and Cornelia was living with Frank at Bishop's
Cottage:

> Her little daughter Adeline seems to have furnished her with many
> opportunities for sacrifice. She left her entirely to the care of the nuns, often
> denying herself the pleasure of her company …. It happened one day that
> the child developed an infectious disease and was hurriedly isolated by the
> nuns. Her mother, who was teaching in the school, could not be with her.
> The next morning Mrs Connelly refrained, in a spirit of mortification, from
> making enquiries. Everybody thought that someone else had surely told her
> how the child was, and consequently she went through the whole day
> without any information. This little incident she afterwards related herself
> to help another, and encourage her to bear the torment of anxiety.[56]

In spite of anecdotes such as this, Gompertz, like all the biographers,
asserts that Cornelia was a devoted and affectionate mother. Gompertz
speculates—though she offers no supporting evidence—that in this we
may see the influence of Cornelia's own mother: "it *must have been* from her

---

[54] Gompertz, *The Life of Cornelia Connelly*, 155.

[55] Gompertz, *The Life of Cornelia Connelly*, 48.

[56] Gompertz, *The Life of Cornelia Connelly*, 48. The implications of suggesting that Cornelia's sacrifice was
misplaced and that it had an adverse effect on the children are explored in the next chapter.

that Cornelia inherited much that was great and noble, and above all, her exalted idea of a mother's office".[57] Though she has stressed Cornelia's heroic suppression of her natural feelings for her children, Gompertz acknowledges that:

> Her heart still yearned for her own little ones. She was full of compassion for them in their loss of their home and she tried as far as she could to make them happy by her bright loving letters and presents suited to their years.[58]

Cornelia's letters to Mercer, at school at Stonyhurst, are quoted extensively by the biographers. To a reader today they appear tendentious, moralising, and lacking in empathy for the difficult situation in which Mercer found himself. He was an American adolescent at a nineteenth-century English public school; his father was a priest and his mother a nun; and he was obliged to be grateful to the Earl of Shrewsbury, who was paying the fees. Gompertz describes him as "a source of anxiety":

> His school reports were not satisfactory, and the faults she [Cornelia] had so often warned him against were growing. He was moody and unpractical, as well as passionate, and began to resent reproof. There was too a strain of duplicity in the boy which astonished and pained her. …
>
> He had dangerous defects of character … and his school career had been disappointing.[59]

Gompertz does not speculate in the main body of the text on the reasons for Mercer's difficulties, and presents Cornelia as more concerned about his "perversion" from Catholicism than about his happiness:

> To Mother Connelly the loss and perversion of her children was the deepest sorrow of her life. …
>
> [Mercer's] death … was a terrible grief to Mother Connelly. She had always hoped that early impressions and the religious education he had received at Stonyhurst would bring the boy back to the Church.[60]

---

[57] Gompertz, *The Life of Cornelia Connelly*, 4. My italics.
[58] Gompertz, *The Life of Cornelia Connelly*, 126.
[59] Gompertz, *The Life of Cornelia Connelly*, 126, 183.
[60] Gompertz, *The Life of Cornelia Connelly*, 183, 186.

Gompertz comments: "It is strange that a boy of sixteen, brought up as Mercer had been, should have so easily abandoned his religion."[61]

Sympathy for Mercer is relegated to a long footnote. And the sympathy is hedged, firstly by the assumption that he had some "natural" character defects, and secondly by an attempt to defend Cornelia's approach to her son:

> One cannot help feeling a pang of sympathy for Merty. A possible cause of his disimprovement suggests itself to those who have had experience of boys. Even in the best conducted schools they are quick to ridicule anything "queer" about a companion. A boy whose father and mother had become priest and nun, and who had actually spent his vacation in a convent, may have had a good deal to suffer on that account. To Merty's sensitive, brooding disposition the strain would have been great and might have brought on an almost morbid depression. In any case he seems at this time to have been angry and sick at heart, and to have resented his mother's inexperience of the ways of British schoolboys. ...
>
> Although her letters strike us as too supernatural for the capacity of a child, we must remember that Merty had been brought up from infancy in a very spiritual atmosphere. Remarks in the letters show that for some years at least he had responded sympathetically to his mother's treatment.[62]

The post Gompertz held, as lecturer in psychology at the college in Cavendish Square, perhaps explains her attempt at a psychological assessment of Mercer. But it also raises the question as to whether her overriding purpose—to present Cornelia as a suitable candidate for canonisation—in some way curtailed any more rigorous examination of the mother-son relationship.

The Cornelia of Gompertz' biography can only be considered an exemplary mother in the terms of Molinari's theological argument—in that she trusted God to supply the parental love that she could no longer offer. If, as Gompertz suggests, Cornelia's primary concern was not her children's human happiness but their eternal salvation, she must have agonised over their "perversion" and her own partial responsibility for it.

---

[61] Gompertz, *The Life of Cornelia Connelly*, 183.
[62] Gompertz, *The Life of Cornelia Connelly*, 129 (footnote).

Flaxman's presentation of Cornelia as mother is in marked contrast to that of Gompertz. Flaxman is sensitive to the criticisms necessarily raised about the Connelly children by a reading public aware of childhood psychological trauma and its long-term effects. Flaxman addresses explicitly those points in the story which she recognises will be problematic for her readers. She defends Cornelia against the accusation that she "gave up" her children; and she offers a stout explanation of the educational arrangements the Connellys made when they entered upon their marital separation:

> Although later Cornelia refers to having "given up" her husband for the work of God, she never spoke of having given up her children. On the contrary, when in regard to them fearful injustice and suffering overtook her, she maintained the opposite, passionately. …

> The arrangements made for the Connelly children would have excited not critical comment but congratulation. What was largely missing in their milieu was the notion of parental responsibility and the educational significance of the family for the proper maturing of a child. And disregarded was the crisis which mothers had to face when their children, especially their sons, were "lost" to them at so early an age. Whether or not the Connellys really approved of this state of affairs, they were victims of their milieu as much as anyone else. What they went along with when they separated was what they would have sought to do had there been no separation.[63]

Nowhere does Flaxman enter into discussion about the exemplary nature of Cornelia's motherhood. But the picture she paints is fundamentally more human than that of Gompertz, and consequently more attractive and imitable. Flaxman carefully avoids the suggestion that Cornelia sacrificed her children for a higher good; instead, Flaxman reflects on "the psychological confusion she must have been in" when Cornelia arrived in England in 1846 and learnt that the children were to be sent away to school.[64] She speaks of Cornelia's "suffering of the heart,"[65] and

---

[63] Flaxman, *A Woman Styled Bold*, 93, 92.
[64] Flaxman, *A Woman Styled Bold*, 113.
[65] Flaxman, *A Woman Styled Bold*, 315.

acknowledges that she must have experienced doubts about the fate of her children, must have been prey to guilt and anxiety.[66]

Flaxman recognises, as Gompertz did, that the loss to the children of their Catholic faith added to Cornelia's pain:

> The children ... were to be uprooted from the ways of the faith she had taught them to love. ...

> Throughout Cornelia's life as religious and foundress the one suffering always with her was the apostasy of her husband and the loss of her children.[67]

But, alongside this concern for the children's loss of faith, Flaxman stresses a human ache and desire and "desperate longing" for their company, for contact with them and influence over them:

> During the years since Pierce had first asked her to free him it had been through the heart's natural affections that she had chiefly suffered. ...

> Behind all that clamoured for attention every day, ... and deeper than any of this, lay the hidden ache for husband and children.[68]

Adeline's being sent away to school at New Hall "was affliction for Cornelia"; the decision was "most painful and unacceptable," but "remained to be obeyed" because Wiseman had decreed it. As for five-year-old Frank, "it was longer before Cornelia brought herself to give him up. [But] if Wiseman was insisting, it was a question of when, not whether."[69]

When Flaxman comes to examine the vow that Cornelia made after Pierce abducted the children, she avoids Gompertz' dualistic tension between the natural and the spiritual, and focuses on Cornelia's strong desire for contact with the children. But her underlying theology does not differ greatly from that of Gompertz:

> It must have been the dictates of feeling with which most of all she had to wrestle .... [Her vow] was prompted by Pierce's traitorous removal of the

---

[66] Flaxman, *A Woman Styled Bold*, 191.

[67] Flaxman, *A Woman Styled Bold*, 190, 315.

[68] Flaxman, *A Woman Styled Bold*, 130, 272.

[69] Flaxman, *A Woman Styled Bold*, 112-113.

children, a searing moment of truth for the mother: he would do even this to gain his end. The temptation to temporise with God's claims must have hung over her .... She thus fortified herself against the desperate longing to give up everything for the sake of the children—which Pierce had probably counted on.[70]

Flaxman sets the struggle for the children, and Cornelia's subsequent loss of contact with them, within the context of apparently happy nineteenth-century family relationships. She presents Cornelia as full of parental pride in her children and their achievements:

> The children constantly occupy her: Ady can now "just get up by a chair alone"; she cannot get Mercer to keep his little spectacles on for even ten minutes at a time. ...
>
> "Our little Ady has grown so much that you would scarcely know her I think. She speaks Italian quite as well as French and her English is not neglected. On St Peter's day (dear Papa's feast), she played a little duet on the piano with me and sang some pretty little verses." ...
>
> "Our dear little Frank," she wrote to her sister, was doing spelling and Bible story and repetition with her and found it very hard "*to keep still.*"[71]

Flaxman writes with less detachment of Mercer at Stonyhurst, "an anxiety-ridden, very insecure adolescent." She notes the deterioration in his grades at school, and acknowledges that "for the twentieth century" his mother's letters "smack altogether too much of advice, virtue and piety."[72] But by the 1990s, something more than this mildly-worded criticism was needed.

Though neither Flaxman nor Gompertz make much of it, a serious block to Cornelia's continuing role as an exemplary mother lies in the legal status of women in nineteenth-century England and America. As Flaxman explains:

> The only "person" in the marriage was the husband, and his wife and children were viewed as his property. With that as her legal status the wronged married woman had little hope in law on which to ground a petition .... He would generally retain her property along with custody of

---

[70] Flaxman, *A Woman Styled Bold*, 130-131.
[71] Flaxman, *A Woman Styled Bold*, 44, 94-95, 105-106.
[72] Flaxman, *A Woman Styled Bold*, 155-156.

the children *and* whatever they might inherit …. Had Cornelia challenged … she risked a decree which would bar her irretrievably from the children.[73]

Cornelia's relationship with her children after the decree of separation had been signed was, therefore, wholly dependent upon a promise Pierce made to her "that everything done with regard to the children would be with her consent."[74] When he foreclosed on this agreement, she had no redress. The very basis for her relationship with her children differs so radically from that which pertains in the West today that it is difficult to see how she can, in any simple way, be offered as a model of maternal behaviour.

Cornelia as Religious

Cornelia's arrival in Derby with three companions on 13 October 1846 was an auspicious moment: it marked not just the beginnings of the Society of the Holy Child Jesus, but the first foundation of a new congregation of religious women in England since the Reformation.[75] The nascent Society, however, immediately faced a number of difficulties. They had to contend with considerable public feeling against the growth of religious communities—in the popular imagination convents were akin to religious brothels—and in March 1851 Charles Newdegate, an evangelical member of Parliament, tried to introduce the forcible registration and inspection of convents in his Religious Houses Bill. But of even greater consequence for the nuns themselves was the fact that women's religious life was in a state of flux. Prior to the nineteenth century, almost all religious women had lived within enclosure. So, active women religious, and especially those establishing themselves in a Protestant country, had few role models to draw on. They were involved in a process of exploration and experiment.

Cornelia's understanding of the practices of religious life had been acquired largely through contact with the Society of the Sacred Heart (founded in Paris in 1800). She had been given privileged access to their community life both at Grand Coteau and at Trinità dei Monti. But she had not absorbed their approaches and customs unthinkingly or uncritically.

---

[73] Flaxman, *A Woman Styled Bold*, 146-147.

[74] Flaxman, *A Woman Styled Bold*, 130.

[75] Some French congregations—the Sisters of Notre Dame and the Society of the Sacred Heart among them—had already established communities.

Ultimately she had been deeply unhappy at the Trinità. On 12 November 1845 she wrote to her sister, Adeline Duval:

> And now my dear Ady to explain at once why I did not answer your letter immediately the truth is it would then have passed through the hands of the Superioress here and would probably not have been such as would have pleased her for I considered myself obliged to announce to her nine months ago that I doubted very much that I should ever enter the order of the S Heart tho I had no doubts about my vocation to a religious life ... I bless our dear Lord again and again that I have been prevented so wonderfully from taking any promise or obligation upon me with respect to this french order for it is not the one for our country. Our own dear country women must be led to a perfect life by meekness and sweetness and not by fear.[76]

By the time Cornelia came to England, then, she had formed opinions about the principles and practice of religious life; but there were no fixed patterns into which the new congregation automatically slotted. Much was *ad hoc*. The Constitutions of the Society awaited approval by the Church, and Cornelia modified them constantly as her understanding of her congregation grew. Vows taken in the Society were of uncertain value, and the sisters learned gradually, and sometimes painfully, the implications of a vowed life. Relations with the hierarchy (only re-established in England and Wales in 1850) were often uneasy, as the bishops as well as the nuns teased out the nature of their mutual obligations.

The biographers, however, are sometimes tempted to write as if Cornelia and the early members of the Society shared their own fixed understanding, and their own secure living, of religious life. This illustrates again that each biographer is situated in her own moment—a moment different both from the world of Cornelia which preceded it, and from our own world today. Before Vatican II, twentieth-century writers of religious biography conveyed a sense of permanence, of certainty, of unchanging (and perhaps even unquestionable) values, which reflected the Catholic culture of the time. Consequently they emphasized the more settled and hierarchical aspects of mid-nineteenth-century religious life. Today, when religious life is once more

---

[76] CC1:51-52.

in a state of flux, the less settled, more uncertain, exploratory aspects of the life are ripe for retrieval.

Beyond Objectivity

A biography is more than a compilation of the written sources; it is a conscious construction of the subject's life. The biographer's ideal may be an objective, value-free presentation, but, in reality, that is not possible. Any close examination of the structure of a biography reveals the author's dependence on assumptions current at the time of writing. Flaxman's Cornelia differs markedly from the Cornelia presented by Gompertz, and the difference lies not in the "facts" but in the subtleties of emphasis and interpretation. So context largely determines the kind of biography that can be written.

The concern of this chapter has not been anachronistic criticism, let alone condemnation, of the biographers. Its purpose has been to show how the attitudes, approaches and assumptions that underpin biographies are quickly outmoded and, consequently, why the constant retelling of a life story is necessary:

> We have … given up the arrogance of believing that we can, once and for all, get our foremothers right. Second readings thus come with the territory …. For only by telling … our stories anew can we glimpse the truths that emerge not once and for all but all in their own good time.[77]

My final chapter attempts to raise the questions that are of concern today in postmodern, postcolonial, feminist society, and it tries to envisage the biography that might emerge from the addressing of those questions.

---

[77] Hall, "Lives Through Time," 155.

Chapter Eight

RE-READING CORNELIAN MYTHS AND COUNTER-MYTHS

This lengthy analysis of the existing biographies begs the question as to whether a new biography, drawing on the insights of contemporary theory in biography and spirituality, could avoid the limitations and pitfalls that have been identified. And the answer is that a more accurate biography of Cornelia is probably not possible: any new biography will be shaped by the author's context just as its predecessors were. However, a different biography might be written by an author more conscious of contextual influence. Repudiating any interest in being comprehensive, let alone definitive, the biographer could deliberately present Cornelia's story in terms of her own positionality, interests and preoccupations.

Feminist biographers attempt to articulate their intentions, and to make their ongoing relationship with the subject a significant part of their text. The convention that required the author to remain magisterially silent, that created a single, linear projection, and that slanted the whole telling of the story towards whatever was perceived to be the major event or achievement in the subject's life, no longer satisfies them. They engage personally with their subject and focus on the complexity and messiness of the subject's life, choosing to emphasize rather than to suppress detail and ambiguity.

A biography of Cornelia that took cognisance of these feminist approaches would abandon any (overt or covert) intention of demonstrating her holiness or potential for canonisation; its concern would be a presentation of a complex human being rather than of a putative saint. Cornelia's limitations, inconsistencies, self-contradictions and complexity would be addressed, not glossed over or explained away because they did not fit with the narrator's model of holiness. The author's relationship with Cornelia would be articulated, and the biography would draw on the tools of current criticism—a hermeneutic of suspicion, for instance—to re-examine the earlier, pre-critical narratives. So a new appreciation of the original story, and of Cornelia herself, might be achieved.

The preceding chapters have gone some way towards examining and deconstructing the existing biographies of Cornelia. For all their limitations, these texts form the dominant narrative of Cornelia's story, a narrative that we cannot simply reject or abandon because it is a major source of information about her. However, even as we remain reliant upon it, we can re-examine its form, and the myth that it has created and perpetuated.

The myth of Cornelia was established in the first biographies, and every subsequent retelling of the story has been held in thrall by it. Each successive biographer has found herself constrained by the mould that her nineteenth-century predecessors created. The pre-existing biographical format made it difficult to approach the story very differently, to ask new questions, or to see implications that the earliest biographers did not see. Strub and Flaxman made the greatest changes, praising in Cornelia what earlier biographers had glossed over or explained away. But even they retained the formulaic structure of Cornelia's life, the founding myth of the beautiful bride, loving mother and obedient daughter of the Church who, through her generous response to a series of events not of her making, was transformed into the saintly foundress. It is not possible to abandon this tradition entirely; each succeeding biographer remains dependent upon it even as she develops and changes it.

However, the primary documentation reveals that, in Cornelia's own lifetime, another myth was also current—a myth promoted in the press and subscribed to by many of the bishops and clergy. It was the myth of Cornelia as an unnatural mother, an unchristian wife, and a scandalous and disobedient religious. The earliest biographers, aware of this myth, constructed Cornelia's story in response to it. They deliberately created a counter-myth of a "perfect" woman who was a suitable candidate for canonisation. They were concerned to show that the congregation had been founded by a saint, but they were also reacting to the strongly-held contrary view of Cornelia.

This chapter is an attempt to free Cornelia's story, to some extent at least, from the restraining hand of the earlier biographers, and from their presentation of her as a "perfect" model for others (a notion that has little meaning today in a culture dominated by the provisional). It will examine both the myth and the counter-myth, and bring out the ways in which assumptions about gender and power underlie them both. Gender and power are themes of particular interest to women today, and their presence in Cornelia's story has not previously been highlighted.

All lives are lived, and all accounts of lives are written, in a gendered environment. Whenever we speak of women, gender constructs are inevitably present in our minds. So a feminist biographer will be alert to gender emphasis and influence within source materials:

> Understanding women's experiences, or accounts of them, requires one to read the code of gender. The reader must recognise how women and men write gender into their accounts, and into their accounts of lives. Personal narratives of women provide a portrait of gender arrangements that are invisible in the dominant discourse and that yield to a gender-sensitive reading.[1]

Obviously, Cornelia conducted her correspondence, directed her schools, trained her novices and so on, against the background of her own largely unexamined acceptance of the gender assumptions of Victorian society. This chapter considers how far those gender assumptions determined and curtailed her experiences and responses, and what part they play in the presentation of her story.

Victorian Assumptions about Gender

It is rash to make sweeping generalisations about any period, but it does not seem grossly unfair to suggest that, during the years when Cornelia lived in Britain, women were not expected to act as independent, autonomous human beings; respectable women largely confined themselves and their activities to the private sphere. And there, in the home, they were defined in relation to the men on whom they were economically dependent: father, brother, husband, son. William Rathbone Greg suggests something of the neat reciprocity of this arrangement, at least as Victorian men perceived it;

---

[1] Long, *Telling Women's Lives*, 9.

there are, he wrote in 1869: "two essentials of women's being; they are supported by, and they minister to, men."[2]

Two widely read literary works articulated Victorian assumptions about gender: Coventry Patmore's verse narrative about his first wife, "The Angel in the House" (1854), and John Ruskin's essay "Of Queens' Gardens," which appeared in *Sesame and Lilies* in 1865. Ruskin discussed gender categories and explored the role of women in relation to men, before expounding his educational scheme for girls. His essay has been called a "repellent little work," which presumed that women would be "self-denying to a pathological degree":

> He judged that woman's "intellect is not for invention or creation, but for sweet ordering, arrangement, and decision .... Her great function is Praise." Woman must be "wise, not for self-development, but for self-renunciation." "All such knowledge should be given her as may enable her to understand, and even to aid, the work of men: and yet it should be given, not as knowledge,—not as if it were, or could be, for her an object to know; but only to feel, and to judge." "Speaking broadly, a man ought to know any language or science he learns, thoroughly—while a woman ought to know the same language, or science, only so far as may enable her to sympathize in her husband's pleasures, and in those of his best friends."[3]

A contrary view of Ruskin's essay claims that when it was published "the book was widely perceived as an attack on middle-class complacency and the limitations of the syllabus customarily taught to girls by governesses at home."[4] As such it may have interested Cornelia, especially as it was written by a friend of Coventry Patmore, whom she knew well. His daughter Emily was at school at St Leonards and later entered the Society.[5] Patmore's "Angel in the House" celebrated a woman whose sole purpose in life had been to serve men. ("Man must be pleased; but him to please/ Is woman's pleasure .... ") Elizabeth Langland, who categorizes Ruskin's view of girls' education as "idealistic and naïve in the extreme," observes that the title, "The Angel in the House,"

---

[2] Quoted in Mumm, *Stolen Daughters, Virgin Mothers*, 181.

[3] Judith Flanders, *A Circle of Sisters* (London: Viking, 2001), xix.

[4] Matthew Sweet, *Inventing the Victorians* (London: Faber, 2001), 179.

[5] Letters between Cornelia and Patmore are extant, as well as accounts of his visits to St Leonards and Mayfield.

... served as a convenient shorthand for a type generally celebrated in tracts and novels, the selfless, virtuous, pure, and spiritualised deity, who presided over hearth and home and whose presence was a refuge from the storms of commercial strife.[6]

According to the poem, the "natural" order of things dictated that women were subordinate, subservient, obedient. Yet at the same time they exerted a high moral influence within the family. These two facets of women's life, taken together, rendered their economic independence, their education and enfranchisement not only unnecessary, but even undesirable.[7]

The unrealistic, idealistic views of Patmore and Ruskin reflected and influenced the prevailing climate of opinion. But practice did not entirely coincide with theory. Though an upper-middle-class woman had to *appear* angelic, in practice, within the private sphere, she exerted a great deal of power and authority, financial as well as moral, if she were responsible for a household of any size. And, gradually, even the theory was eroded: by 1866 John Stuart Mill was petitioning parliament on the subject of women's suffrage. However, a surprising number of influential women opposed any disturbance of the *status quo.* Beatrice Webb, Octavia Hill, Florence Nightingale, George Eliot, Charlotte Brontë and Elizabeth Barrett Browning all resisted the extension of the franchise to women.[8] Even the free-thinking Frances Power Cobbe castigated the exercise of authority by women as "almost by definition 'irresponsible'."[9] And Cornelia, in spite of the extraordinary events of her life, was fundamentally conventional, accepting rather than challenging the current *mores.*

The unexamined assumption of Victorians generally, and to a considerable degree of Cornelia herself, was that women should not assert

---

[6] Elizabeth Langland, *Nobody's Angels: Middle-Class Women and Domestic Ideology in Victorian Culture* (Ithaca and London: Cornell UP, 1995), 69.

[7] It need hardly be remarked that a whole class system underlay this gender stereotyping; Ruskin and Patmore were speaking of upper middle class women only. For a woman to become an Angel in the House an infrastructure supported by servants had to be in place. Working class women at this time were employed in dangerous occupations in newly developing industries.

[8] David Newsome, *The Victorian World Picture* (London: John Murray, 1997), 253. Edward Burne-Jones' wife, Georgiana, who was a committed socialist, found Mill's work "too exaggerated on the unpopular side of the subject." (Flanders, *A Circle of Sisters*, 124.)

[9] Mumm, *Stolen Daughters, Virgin Mothers*, 195.

themselves against men. Many of the women Cornelia knew must have found the obligations of domesticity and upper-class family life stifling, just as Florence Nightingale and her correspondents did. But there is no evidence that they questioned in any direct way the prevailing, separate-spheres mentality—unless their becoming members of a religious congregation may be deconstructed as an act of resistance or rebellion.

As religious, these women worked hard in difficult circumstances, in contradistinction to the accepted ideal that upper-middle-class women should do as little productive work as possible. Competence, self-reliance and independence were disapproved of in Victorian women; amateurism, ignorance and emotion were encouraged.[10] Women were commonly judged to be without the psychological balance and physiological stamina needed for serious academic pursuits:

> ... the discrepancy between what women were capable of doing and what they were permitted to do was perhaps greater in the mid-nineteenth century than at any other period in the modern era.[11]

In any case, before the Married Women's Property Act of 1870, only the most determined woman could have hoped for a separate intellectual existence. Prior to the Act, on marriage a woman ceased to have any right to her own property. Without her husband's consent, she could neither make a will nor keep her own earnings or inheritance. In law she was one and the same person as her husband: she and her children belonged to him. The married woman was "classed with criminals, lunatics and minors—legally incompetent and irresponsible."[12]

Women's status gradually changed, but in the mid-nineteenth century the vast majority of women as well as men accepted the curtailed life which Victorian gender assumptions imposed on them. Upper-middle-class women were programmed to be wives, the bearers of children and the holders of the moral high ground. Economically and legally they were

---

[10] See Mumm, *Stolen Daughters, Virgin Mothers*, 59, for an exploration of this as a particular issue for women religious.

[11] Mumm, *Stolen Daughters, Virgin Mothers*, 166.

[12] Martha Vicinus, *A Widening Sphere: Changing Roles of Victorian Women* (Bloomington: Indiana UP, 1977), ix, quoted in Flanders, *A Circle of Sisters*, xviii.

dependent upon their male relatives, to whom very different standards of behaviour applied, and for whom educational, career and travel opportunities existed beyond the wildest dreams of their wives, sisters and daughters.

In this context Cornelia was an anomaly; she could not be easily pigeon-holed or readily assimilated. She arrived in Britain as a married woman and a mother, who had set aside those biological roles so revered by Victorians in order to found a religious congregation. As founder she not only assumed a position of authority uncustomary among Victorian women, but also developed her innate administrative and managerial gifts, which would otherwise have found no other outlet than the supervision of her husband's household.

She was a woman; and she was failing to conform to the gender expectations of her contemporaries, some of whom were outraged by aspects of her behaviour that they perceived as deliberately flouting convention. Their response to her was necessarily coloured by their assumptions about "woman," assumptions that the first biographers shared. The biographers consequently angled their telling of Cornelia's story to defend her against the accusations that she was a disobedient wife, an unnatural mother, an arrogant and self-willed religious, and so on; but they did not question the underlying assumptions about gender and gender roles.

All gender constructs are lived out as roles (daughter, sister, wife, mother) which carry with them corresponding power and responsibilities, and Cornelia lived out the roles and exercised the concomitant power in a greater variety of ways than most women. She was a daughter and a daughter of the Church, a sister and a religious sister, a mother and a mother superior. Much of the confusion that surrounded her can be traced back to her transitions between these roles, and to the resulting mixed messages about sexual scripts and gender assumptions. This chapter, therefore, explores first Cornelia as daughter and sister, and then Cornelia as wife and mother.

Cornelia as Daughter and Sister

The lack of information about Cornelia's childhood has already been discussed. The earliest biographers fill this lacuna with assertions that fitted the myth they were deliberately creating, assertions that seem now to have been based on the flimsiest of evidence. They claim that Cornelia's childhood was extremely happy—despite the fact that her father died when she was nine and her mother when she was fourteen, and that nowhere does Cornelia make any reference to either parent. The contemporary reader might prefer to learn that the Peacock family was dysfunctional, and an argument could be made for that. But, without supporting documentation, it would be just as mythical as the assertions of the earliest biographers. All that can be said is that Cornelia the child, Cornelia the daughter, is largely lost to us.

Cornelia's role and influence as a sister is more accessible. She was the youngest of nine siblings (including a half brother and sister born during her mother's first marriage), who formed a tightly knit group. This is evident not only from Cornelia's own correspondence, but from other details of family history. We know, for instance, that the two oldest girls, Isabella Bowen Montgomery and Adeline Peacock Duval, who were already married at the time of their mother's death in 1823, took the two youngest sisters, Mary and Cornelia, into their own homes at that point. We know also something of the interfamilial connections of their brother Ralph. He inherited the property of their oldest half brother John Bowen (a vast but apparently unprofitable estate in Jamaica), and, from 1848 on, himself assumed the name John Bowen. In 1850 he compounded the complications further by marrying Elizabeth Murphy, the widow of another brother, George, who had died of yellow fever.

Cornelia was the first member of her family to become a Roman Catholic, and the extant correspondence reveals both the initial resistance of her siblings to this decision, and her own unconcealed desire to persuade the rest of them to follow her example. Adeline, George and Mary became Catholics; Ralph embraced Unitarianism; and Isabella seems to have remained an Episcopalian. Mary, perhaps the closest of Cornelia's siblings to her, entered the Society of the Sacred Heart at Grand Coteau. Of Pierce's three brothers, only John became a Catholic, and he disclaimed the influence of example, saying he had been "a Catholic at heart" for years before Pierce's conversion.[13] After Pierce abandoned the Catholic

---

[13] D59:107.

priesthood, John seldom mentioned his name. But he remained committed to Cornelia, "my very dear old friend, my sister by marriage to the miserable man I am compelled to call brother."[14] After Cornelia's death, he collected family material for Angelica Croft in preparation for any future biography.

Cornelia's affection for, and openness with, Adeline, Mary and Ralph is apparent in all her correspondence. The letters she sent to Adeline and Mary from Rome in 1836 are typical, not only in their loving spontaneity but in their earnestness about religion:

> What is the reason dear Mary that you tell me nothing about the <u>dear children</u> nothing about <u>any of the family</u>—the very thing that you used to complain of yourself. Do you expect either of the boys this Spring? Tell them to take the same love for themselves that I send to you. Talk about religion now, and tell me too <u>all</u> your own feelings for who should you tell them to if not to your little sissy who loves you even more than ever …. Dear Mary you may imagine poor little American me seated at a table surrounded by Princesses Earls and Countesses!

> My darling dear sweet Addie, I thank you for ever for your sweet letter it was like an ice cream on a summer day excepting that it lasted longer …. Oh Addie you dear little pet how I could hug you up …. I pray for you all every night and all ways in my thoughts—and I am sure we all have your prayers—but for you dear Molly I began a novena <u>last night</u>—oh you naughty girl not to have the strength of mind to act according to your conscience yes yes don't pretend to me … come come my dear act like a woman with a head and a heart …. Oh Mary act with single heartedness and the almighty will bless you with a faith and a peace that will enable you to go through with happiness all the misery that troubles of this life [*sic*].[15]

Ralph's Unitarianism distressed Cornelia. She addresses him as "my poor dear mistaken brother dear to me as ever," and urges him, "in the name of the Father and of the Son and of the Holy Ghost," to trust "the combined wisdom of the wisest of the Holy Apostolic Catholic Church."[16] She never succeeded in converting him, but he entrusted his daughters' education to her. Mary, Cornelia and Isabella Bowen travelled from San Antonio, Texas, to attend the Holy Child school at Sharon, Philadelphia. Later, Cornelia and

---

[14] D59:85.
[15] CC1:62-63; CC1:45-46.
[16] CC1:68.

Isabella sailed to Europe to complete their education at St Leonards. These nieces, and the daughters of Adeline Duval, continued to correspond with Cornelia, and so the family affection extended into the next generation.

In terms of the creation of myth, public or private, this material was scarcely drawn upon. Though some of the family letters were available to Buckle, their cumulative effect only became clear when they were gathered together as part of the formal documentation for Cornelia's cause. And in terms of gender, what do they reveal? Little more than that Cornelia acted within the assumptions of her culture. She expressed love and concern for her family of origin, and, with all the enthusiasm of a convert, desired that her siblings embrace what she herself had come to see as divine truth. The effervescent tone of the correspondence notwithstanding, she was exercising the conventional role of Angel in the House.

Another question is how far Cornelia's assumptions about sibling relationships influenced her approach to life among the sisters of the congregation that she founded. Letters show that she wrote to her religious sisters with the same freshness, interest, enthusiasm and spiritual openness as she did to her family, but the role she assumed in the Society was, from the beginning, more that of mother than of sister.

Cornelia as Wife

When Cornelia arrived in England she was 37 years old and had been married for over sixteen years, but little evidence remains of her attitudes to gender and sexuality in the early years of her marriage. Her letters to Pierce suggest that, as a young wife, she aspired primarily to doing what her husband wanted and to winning his approval. The earliest surviving letter, dated 22 September 1835, begins, "Dear love my more than life what a baby I am." Having explained matters of business, Cornelia writes, "If I did wrong you must never allow me to open your letters again but I think & hope love that you will say it is all right." And she ends, "I have written you too much—but not enough yet—my own life ever forever your devoted love CC."[17] Surely Ruskin and Patmore would have approved of such a wife. But there is always in Cornelia, to use Virginia Woolf's image, the granite as

---

[17] CC1:1-6.

well as the rainbow. Between the endearments and the immature self-abnegation, this long letter is filled with Cornelia's comments on activities and business arrangements, her proposals for their future and her insights into, and encouragement of, her husband's activities.

Cornelia was born in the United States, in the aftermath of Independence. How that context shaped her assumptions about womanhood and marriage is not clear. However, it is interesting to note that Abigail and Louisa Adams, whose husbands occupied the White House in the early years of the nineteenth century,[18] were strong advocates of marriage as a partnership of equals:

> Like Abigail, Louisa insisted that the relationship between men and women should be that of partners. The two contended that, while individuals in a marriage had different makeups, they deserved to be seen as equals … John and Abigail Adams were speaking literally when they referred to each other as partners. … Marital partners were to live on an equal footing.[19]

The Adams' conviction that marriage took place between equals who "needed each other, as [they] filled roles which nature and civilisation had assigned them,"[20] fits more satisfactorily with Cornelia's practice than does the concept of the Angel in the House. Cornelia was Pierce's partner as they struggled together to discern God's invitation to him (and consequently to her). "Our propositions," she called them.[21] Later, in England, she was angry that he broke the promises he had made to her when they were thinking it through together. She protested that he "carried off my children … though he had promised me before he became a Priest that whatever he did in their regard should be subject to my consent." And she complained about his control of her dowry "which he is using against [me] & contrary to <u>his promises</u>."[22]

During her life time, Cornelia the sexually experienced woman was of more interest to the creators of the anti-Cornelian myth than to her

---

[18] John Adams was President from 1800-1801, and his son John Quincy Adams from 1825-1829. Cornelia married Pierce in 1831.

[19] Paul C. Nagel, *The Adams Women: Abigail and Louisa Adams, their Sisters and Daughters* (Cambridge, Ma: Harvard UP, 1999 [1987]), 5. Abigail Adams famously called on her husband to enshrine women's rights as well as men's in the American constitution: "Remember the ladies."

[20] Nagel, *The Adams Women*, 5.

[21] CC21:21.

[22] CC43:9.

sympathetic biographers. It is not without irony that knowledge of this deeply personal and private aspect of her life is provided by documents in the public domain, documents written by Pierce and others with the specific intention of discrediting Cornelia, the bishops and the Catholic Church.

When Pierce published his pamphlets in the 1850s, his cause was taken up with enthusiasm by an English Protestant press. From Cornelia's annotations of the texts, and from a legal document which she seems to have had drawn up in direct response to them, something of her personal feelings—her pain, her anger, her hurt—can momentarily be glimpsed. This evidence is crucially important: without it there would be no way of knowing anything of the passion concealed behind the conventional sentiments expressed elsewhere. There would be nothing to refute the opinion of the leader writer of the *Morning Herald*, 5 September 1853, that her heart had hardened into stone.

In 1853 Thomas Hatchard brought out the second edition of a pamphlet, *Case of the Rev. Pierce Connelly*. A new preface had been added, as well as correspondence about the Connellys that had previously been published in *The Times*.[23] The pamphlet also included further responses by Pierce, W. H. Bellamy, the Rev. Hugh Stowell and the leader writer of the *Morning Herald*. The purpose of the pamphlet was "to give the public a more clear and intelligible idea of the relative positions of Mr and Mrs Connelly ... leaving the facts to speak for themselves."[24] Some sense of its highly emotive approach to this purportedly objective task may be gained from part of the new preface:

> When Rome once depraves the heart, or bows the will, it is not often that the work is done by halves. Admitting, for the sake of argument, that with Mrs Connelly it has been complete, and that the fountain of all natural affection has been, by priestly art, so dried up within her—as that she can forget her children whom she has borne, as well as the husband whom she has sworn, before God, to obey—even then would Mr Connelly be justified, as husband or as man, in allowing her, his wife, to remain—shut out from all private intercourse with himself or his children, the daily

[23] And carried in a number of other newspapers, including *The Morning Herald, Standard, St James' Chronicle, Bell's Weekly Magazine, The Morning Advertiser, John Bull* and *Britannia*.
[24] CC43:iii.

closeted companion of unscrupulous professors of LIGUORIAN morals, any and every hour being rife with opportunities for their reduction into practice? Can he, ought he, while she retains the title of his "wife," ought he to allow it? No honest English woman but would give an indignant answer in the negative. Could her true position in the sight of GOD and Man, as wife and mother, in all its reality be fully and fairly present to the mind of Mrs Connelly herself, the answer might safely be left to her.[25]

This farrago of prejudice demonstrates that the public anti-Cornelian myth was created and promoted by men who had strongly held and vehemently expressed views not only about religion but also about gender and gender roles. In fact, this pamphlet is as illuminating of Victorian attitudes to gender as anything written by Ruskin or Patmore. It is a jingoistic appeal to the proper sentiments of every English Protestant gentleman, and communicates an absolute conviction that a husband's rights are sacrosanct, inviolable and "paramount."[26] Rhetoric and invective are employed to stir up readers' anti-Catholic prejudices and their deep suspicions about convents. The pamphlet contains innumerable veiled references to the nastiness of Roman Catholic cultic practices, its tone throughout promoting disapproval and distaste. It presents Pierce as a personification of Protestantism and Cornelia of Roman Catholicism, so that the story of the breakdown of their marriage can be read as a struggle between the destructive power of Rome and the legitimate power of Protestant England.[27]

Over and over again the pamphlet reveals the author's gendered perspective, his assumptions about the rights of men, and his attitudes to women.[28] In the time-honoured tradition of sensation journalism, his text is titillating and replete with sexual innuendo. The hints of dark deeds behind convent walls might have been plucked straight from the pages of a Gothic novel.[29] The author speaks of the "unnatural excitements of conventual

---

[25] CC43:vi. Alphonsus Liguori (1696-1787) was a seminal Roman Catholic moral theologian.

[26] CC43:vii.

[27] See, for instance, CC43:viii.

[28] The pamphlet was published anonymously, but the author is now known to have been W. H. Bellamy, the secretary to the Duke of Manchester. The Duke was the chairman of a committee established to raise funds for Pierce.

[29] Convents are described as "sanctimonious prison-houses ... those barred and battlemented dungeouns, with which, under the name of cloistered nunneries, Rome is darkening our land."

life,"[30] describes Cornelia as "the bond-slave and thrall of those by whom she is surrounded and guarded,"[31] and calls attention to the fact that Pierce has been "obliged to leave his wife exposed to those priestly arts of seduction, which, he declares, she has herself avowed to him have ere now been tried upon her."[32] Throughout the text sexuality and power are constantly linked—not to say confused—and the conviction that men's power over women is God-given is asserted strongly: "A law higher than all human law gives to a husband authority over his wife. She is HIS, to cherish and rule over until death, and the law of England here, as elsewhere, but echoes the Divine."[33]

From Cornelia's response to this vitriolic text we learn something of her attitude to sexuality, and to the gendered assumptions of the world in which she lived. She was both angered and hurt by the pamphlet. The comments she made in the margins of her copy seem to be spontaneous reactions. If so, they provide a rare opportunity to overhear her inner dialogue. The words "False" and "Quite false" occur frequently, as well as comments such as "A strange invention," and "I do not know what this means ...."

A letter of Pierce's, included in the supplement, implied sexual misconduct by the Roman clergy with Cornelia:

> Sir, if you mean ... to say that my wife denies having ever communicated to me any attempt made on her chastity by a Romish priest, I am compelled, however reluctantly, to charge you, before all the world, with direct falsehood. My wife has NOT made any such denial ... [34]

Cornelia wrote in the margin: "I positively deny that I ever charged any Priest Confessor or otherwise with making any such attempt."

The leader writer of the *Morning Herald* called upon its readers to support Pierce in seeking "liberty for his wife from a thraldom to which mere bodily captivity, even in a gaol, so it were an English one, would be

---

[30] CC43:vi.
[31] CC43:9.
[32] CC43:13.
[33] CC43:20.
[34] CC43:36.

comparative freedom."[35] Cornelia pencilled in reply: "But Mrs C knows better what she wishes for herself than the *Morning Herald* can know." In another place the newspaper commented rhetorically on letters written by Cornelia and Emily Bowles that Pierce had made public:

> What an insight into the working of that detestable "system" do these letters of Mrs Connelly and "Sister Emily" unfold! The gradual drying up of the natural affections; the cold-blooded, deliberate severance of nature's holiest ties; the cautious exhibition of Rome's subtlest poison; the slow dropping of her "leprous distilments" upon heart and brain, until one becomes weakened or dried up, and the other hardens into stone![36]

Cornelia was stung into a particularly revealing response: "The affections do not so easily <u>dry up</u> but they mount up to Him who alone is capable of filling the heart." Her feelings had not dried up: the marginal notes testify to her pain and hurt and anger. They are expressions of her frustration at her own powerlessness and inability to defend herself, or to refute the statements made against her by men confident of the unassailable correctness of their gender assumptions.

Ultimately, however, Cornelia asserted that, whatever others might think or write, however disempowered she was by her female status, she knew herself to be a strong woman, capable of independent thought, decision-making and action. The *Morning Herald* mocked the ending of a letter she had written to her daughter, Adeline, "God give you the virtues of a STRONG woman": "What a tale of strength tried and found wanting! of hopeless, helpless subjugation in HERSELF does this reveal!"[37] And Cornelia responded in the margin: "Oh! No not in the least found wanting but by the grace of God increasing as she reads these lines."

The role that the pamphlet and newspaper reports assigned to Cornelia was that of the stereotypically hopeless, helpless, subjugated woman. Her responses suggest quite the opposite: that this experience was leading her to take up a more independent stance as a woman in a man's world than she might otherwise have done, to be less docile and submissive and more

[35] CC43:20.
[36] CC43:38.
[37] CC43:39.

determined to seek God in the way that seemed right to her, in spite of the suffering the pamphlets caused. Her granite determination was not altogether new; as early as 12 September 1846 she had written to her brother Ralph: "It is very little consequence to me what anyone says about me"[38]—hardly a conventional sentiment for a respectable mid-nineteenth-century woman.

Cornelia's response to Pierce's pamphleteering, and to the media interest in their affairs, was to have drawn up what appears to be a formal, legal document containing her version of events.[39] This text states that the Connellys' decision to abandon marriage for a life of chastity originated with Pierce alone, and that Cornelia co-operated only reluctantly. The implication is that Cornelia herself had no wish to abandon either sexual activity or family life:

> The Proposal to live apart in perfect chastity and the subsequent formal separation of Mr and Mrs Connelly and his taking Holy Orders and her becoming a Nun were all at the instance of Mr Connelly himself and were consented to by Mrs Connelly at his request and in furtherance of his own personal views and wishes. His taking Orders in the Roman Catholic Church was his own deliberate and long-sought act from which he did not "hold out" for many years or at all. He was never asked to consent but on the contrary he sought the consent of his wife and *she consented only after repeated requests on his part*.[40]

The whole document is a series of forceful, clearly expressed statements of Cornelia's view of events. It confirms that she sacrificed her marriage and family life, "acceded to his proposal," only to enable her husband to pursue "the then declared wish and intention of Mr Connelly to take Holy Orders in the Roman Catholic Church." Cornelia's own subsequent journey from the Trinità to Derby was entirely dependent upon Pierce's choices and decisions. Even the plans for the establishment of the Society, which Cornelia had drawn up in Rome, had "the full knowledge and approval of her Husband." In all this Cornelia is a woman of her time who "naturally" acquiesces in the wishes of her husband. No extant

[38] CC1:68.
[39] CC42:11 following.
[40] CC42:18. Italics mine.

material suggests that she wanted to separate herself from her husband and children or to avoid sexual activity. But there is plenty of evidence, sexual stereotyping notwithstanding, that even as she tried to follow the path of wifely or womanly obedience, she could not totally set aside her own judgment, her own intelligent response, her need to seek the truth and to act out of her own discernment and independent thought. And the attitudes of the pamphleteers to the gendered superiority of men pushed her into articulating her position more clearly.

We learn more about Cornelia the wife from the anti-Cornelian myth than from the pro-Cornelian biographers, for whom the disintegration of Cornelia's marriage, and what that cost her, were of less importance than the growth of the Society. Further, not even Strub and Flaxman make much attempt to read any of the material from Pierce's point of view. Pierce's immaturity and lack of spiritual insight serve as a foil to Cornelia's maturity and sanctity. Complexity, contradiction and confusion are not included in the pro-Cornelian myth. Flaxman's Cornelia, as early as 1836, has become "the stronger of the two .... It is no longer her need of him but his of her that strikes the reader."[41] And yet, long after the marriage was effectively over, Cornelia's experience as a wife continued to have a complex and not always positive impact on her life. It had major repercussions on her relationships with bishops and priests.

Cornelia as Daughter of the Church

Even a cursory examination of her writings reveals that Cornelia placed a high value on obedience to rightly ordered authority, and that her desire was to be a dutiful daughter of the Church. But the myth that the bishops subscribed to, and articulated in their correspondence, was that she was disobedient, self-willed, arrogant and ungovernable. The discrepancy between her intention and their perception reveals the power of unexamined assumptions, especially when those assumptions concern gender. The control of religious women by clerics in the nineteenth century was inextricably linked with sexual politics and with expectations about

---

[41] Flaxman, *A Woman Styled Bold*, 58, 57.

gender roles. A study of Cornelia as a daughter of the Church reveals the contrary judgments of myth and counter-myth.

Cornelia and the Stereotype

In Britain Cornelia was unconventional, whatever her natural inclination. It is hard to imagine how much more "other" she could have been: she was an American, a Roman Catholic, a nun; she was beautiful, sexually experienced and intelligent; and her husband, an apostate priest, very soon involved her in a widely reported and sexually charged law suit. After 1852 she became even more singular, in every sense. From that date on she never again enjoyed the support of a significant male figure—and dependence on such a figure was a prerequisite for female social respectability. She was estranged from her husband, and none of her clerical superiors willingly assumed this masculine role in her regard. No bishop or priest chose to associate himself directly with her congregation, or to support her unreservedly. Because she had, largely unwittingly, violated so many Victorian conventions and shibboleths, there hung about her constantly the whiff of scandal. The Roman Catholic bishops, intent upon establishing credentials of respectability for the Church in England, were understandably wary of her. Yet, *de rigueur*, every Victorian woman had to be dependent upon a man; and the bishops felt that they had to fulfil that role in the lives of Cornelia and the other early members of the Society. But the relationship was problematic almost from its inception—and its problems were rooted, at least in part, in gender assumptions and expectations.

In theory Cornelia subscribed to the same conventional dualistic view of humanity as the bishops. But in practice she could not always live it out. Her instinct, her integrity and her insight into embodied, incarnational spirituality led her sometimes to act out of a more holistic anthropology— one which she would have been hard pushed to articulate. So she came into conflict with the bishops (and with other male authority figures, such as schools' inspectors) at a level at which their differences were irresolvable, largely because they were not consciously or clearly articulated. That Cornelia sometimes conformed to expectations and sometimes did not must have further exacerbated male bewilderment and antagonism.

The Power of Cornelia's Sexuality

Paula Backscheider observes that women's bodies have always been "objects of [male] scrutiny, comment and evaluation."[42] Both the pro- and the anti-Cornelian myths agree that Cornelia was beautiful; and, of course, she was also sexually experienced. The bishops' awareness of this, and its significance in their dealings with her, are perhaps encoded in their tendency to speak of her as Mrs Connelly rather than as Mother Cornelia.

After their separation, Cornelia seems deliberately to have distanced herself from Pierce, never once, except in family correspondence, referring to him as anything other than Mr Connelly or the father of her children (though he continued to call her his wife). But, for the bishops, Pierce—and Cornelia's sexual relationship with him—hovered in "Mrs Connelly's" shadow. The Victorians had a horror of female sexual impropriety,[43] and any suggestion of it would have damaged not only Cornelia's reputation and that of her nascent Society, but also the whole Catholic Church in England, dogged as it was by popular misinformation and demands in parliament for the examination and regulation of nunneries.

In 1849 Wiseman apparently expressed concern that Pierce might possess documentary evidence of an ongoing sexual relationship with Cornelia. At much the same time Wiseman was failing to see the implications of establishing a "marine residence" for himself in a section of the convent building at St Leonards. In a letter, dated only "Tuesday," Cornelia reassures him:

> You may be quite easy, my dear Lord, as to my letters or that they could prove anything other than the affection of a sister to a brother. I do not believe I have ever written a letter to him that might not safely be brought before all our enemies ... and the very allusion to being in the confessional with him, is a want of delicacy that pains me more than I can express.[44]

Cornelia was certain of herself, her behaviour, her position. But that her husband was making such claims can only have heightened the wariness of

---

[42] Paula Backscheider, *Reflections on Biography* (Oxford: OUP, 1999), 130.

[43] Stereotypically among the Victorian middle classes, men might sow their wild oats, but women had to remain virginal.

[44] CC18:40.

the bishops towards her. Her physical attractiveness and sexual power, I suggest, had an effect on the celibate Victorian bishops that they would have found difficult to acknowledge. As recently as 1998 Gail Ramshaw wrote: "Sexual activity expresses and creates power in the self ... one way or other, sexual activity will change me."[45] After all, Cornelia had been sexually active, had borne children, and had struggled to reach a life-changing decision with her husband.

Cornelia could not fit the mould of the virginal, submissive, acquiescent woman religious. She was far from being "meek, subservient, other worldly ... lacking character and drive ... ineffectual and subordinate," as nineteenth-century women religious were stereotypically presumed to be.[46] Yet she often seems to have been genuinely puzzled by the reactions she provoked. When she knew she had displeased those in authority, even when she felt they had misunderstood or maligned her, her response was to withdraw into apology and protestations of obedience.[47] Not surprisingly, given Cornelia's straightforward assumption of authority on other occasions, the bishops doubted the sincerity of her submission. The robust directness and honesty of her preferred approach was so far from the gender stereotype that it seemed to them unfeminine and out of control. Wiseman, for instance, commented to Manning that Cornelia "needed a stronger hand than the Bishop of Southwark (at whom Mrs Con laughs and who seems afraid of her)."[48]

Gender assumptions were a contributory factor in her thorny relationships with these men, and restricted the development of her work. Some of these assumptions were accepted parts of social fabric (women's subservience and dependence, the inappropriateness of their pursuing intellectual activity or exercising authority, and so on). And Cornelia seems not always to have understood the finer points of negotiating these unwritten rules. But other issues, such as the bishops' response to Cornelia as intelligent, beautiful and sexually experienced, were more deeply hidden.

---

[45] Gail Ramshaw, *Under the Tree of Life: The Religion of a Feminist Christian* (New York: Continuum, 1998), 134.
[46] Mumm, *Stolen Daughters, Virgin Mothers*, ix.
[47] See, for instance, her letters to Bernard O'Reilly, Bishop of Liverpool, 19 October 1873 and 26 June 1877.
[48] D16:75.

Her life and work were influenced both by the fact that she was a woman, and by the fact that she was *this* woman.

Clerical Power

The pattern of male clerical power and female religious obedience which emerges from Cornelia's correspondence with ecclesiastics is a gender issue. Male religious were not subjected to the tight, minute and petty control by bishops and clergy which Cornelia and the Society not only endured but accepted as reasonable in spite of occasional expressions of frustration and irritation. Because so much of Cornelia's correspondence with Thomas Grant, Bishop of Southwark, is extant, we can acquire some idea of the control he exercised over the nuns at St Leonards, and over the whole Society. The letters illustrate the ways in which gender politics limited Cornelia's actions, and reveal something of her response to gender arrangements—a response which the dominant discourse of her life and her story otherwise conceals.

Susan Mumm speaks of "the assumption so dear to Victorians that unassisted women could never achieve anything worth doing."[49] Commenting explicitly on Anglican women's congregations, she says the bishops shared "the same essential distrust of women's psychological balance as ... those who argued that any structure headed by a woman was unnatural and intolerable."[50] Grant's correspondence with Cornelia suggests that he concurred unreservedly with his Anglican counterparts.

During the nineteen years that Grant was Cornelia's bishop, she deferred to his authority over a vast range of subjects: the appointment of chaplains, extraordinary confessors and retreat directors; the approbation of the rule; the acceptance of candidates for the Society, and their departure; nuns' dowries and financial arrangements generally; the expansion of the Society; the erection and design of new buildings at St Leonards; and every detail of the timetable, of the appointment of staff, and of the enrolment and behaviour of students in the training college and in the schools. Some of these matters were undoubtedly his concern as the local ordinary. But something of the suffocating nature of the gender-

---

[49] Mumm, *Stolen Daughters, Virgin Mothers*, 154.

[50] Mumm, *Stolen Daughters, Virgin Mothers*, 141.

specific control of women religious is revealed by letters that ask permission to repair the lunette from the monstrance, explain why children sit in particular benches in church, and accept that a bazaar to raise funds is forbidden.

Cornelia was not unaware of the pettiness of this control, and, for all her desire to conform and to obey, it was sometimes hard for her to accept it.

> We are very much in need of a small bake house and oven. It is a very little matter to teaze your Lordship in naming. Still it is "building" and I suppose that Nuns must not even build an oven without their Bishop's leave.—It is very comfortable <u>to ask</u> leave, but if—no I <u>will</u> not suppose it is teazing because your charity My Lord never minds trouble and you will not deprive us of the opportunity of practicing the Obedience that is <u>so</u> very sweet and profitable, and I am sure is ever dear to the perfection of the Bishop.[51]

Cornelia seems caught between her own need, as leader of her congregation, to make practical day-to-day decisions, and her desire to conform to a pattern of obedience which, the letter implies, she thought was petty. Hierarchical patterns of obedience are not explicitly gendered, and Cornelia certainly never perceived them as such, but they do appear, over and over again, to have curtailed her freedom in decision-making and leadership and to have been applied more rigorously because she was a woman.

Grant's letters show that he took the matter of his authority and the nuns' obedience extremely seriously, even when the issue at stake was apparently trivial. On one occasion he threatened those who failed to obey his instructions with dismissal from the Society, and on another with pain of mortal sin. Over the question of where the children sat in church Cornelia wrote, in an undated letter:

> It was I who gave leave for the children who had been ill to go into the empty benches on a week day for Mass, so I shall come under dismission and not the poor Sister who only obeyed.[52]

---

[51] CC11:28-29.
[52] CC15:53.

That the next sentence of her letter reads, "I hope your Lordship is quite well and not too much fatigued after all the kindness bestowed during your last visit," neatly conveys her determination to keep the matter in proportion.

The enforcement of clerical power in the most mundane of instances was not a foible of Grant's; Cornelia's correspondence with other bishops reveals the same assumptions of power and control in letter after letter. That Cornelia both retained her integrity as an intelligent woman, and remained loyal to the hierarchy (however much they perceived her as a thorn in the flesh), seems remarkable in the light of the pressure their control must have placed upon her. On 23 February 1874, for instance, she wrote to James Danell, Grant's successor in Southwark, about the nuns' mode of transport. The tone of his response, written on the letter in his own hand, seems both pompous and patronising, and perhaps explains the desire not to cross him which Cornelia's letter conveys:

> I heard indirectly last week that your Lordship did not like our Sisters going out in the Pony trap, which we have used occasionally during the last two years—If this is correct we part with it immediately—Yes, or no will be sufficient.
>
> Answer: I am pleased at your promised obedience to my strong wish that it should not be used in future.[53]

And it was not just bishops who exercised this authority over women religious. The convent chaplain in the early days of the Society also wielded a great deal of power and influence. Cornelia perceived the chaplain—and he perceived himself—as the bishop's representative to whom she owed obedience in ways which would be unthinkable to women religious today. The chaplains in Holy Child houses took part in the education of the sisters, had their say in community matters of all kinds (including the writing of the Constitutions) and were constantly consulted and deferred to. When their views were at variance with Cornelia's, the sisters experienced a conflict of obedience. All of this is entirely understandable in the Victorian context. And Cornelia did not have a thought-out response.

---

[53] CC17:6.

Sometimes she submitted her judgment to that of the chaplain; sometimes she resisted, and wrote letters to the bishop begging for (but never demanding) his removal.

Control and Containment of Women

Of more concern even than the power of male authority figures, especially for an apostolic order, were the strictures about enclosure, which again seem to be gender based, applied to the nuns because they were women. Physical enclosure, combined with close supervision of all their activities, restricted the freedom of women's congregations, and especially that of their leaders.[54] Cornelia's letter from Blackpool, dated 29 May 1866, reveals the sexual politics she sometimes engaged in with Grant:

> I am greatly obliged for your kind letter of the 25th and shall make it my duty not only to inform the Sacristans and Gate-Keeper of … the directions of your Lordship, but I will also have the notice printed and put up at the entrance in order to save unpleasant feelings and reproaches.
>
> Will your Lordship kindly inform me whether persons visiting the Blessed Sacrament when at the Convent during the time of Confessions ought to be refused? (Turned out.) Also whether Priests are included in the word "externs"—and whether Priests are still allowed to say Mass in the Chapel while the family he may be with is to be excluded.
>
> I fear being troublesome in asking these questions but as we are told there is danger of Mortal sin (!) in any inexactness I am forced to know exactly in all cases where we stand.[55]

There is about this whole letter an air of control, of careful wording, and of suppression of any emotional response. Cornelia is—politely—pointing out to Grant the practical implications of his demand. Her exclamation mark in the final sentence suggests she finds theologically questionable the notion that failure to carry out these minute regulations might constitute serious sin.

---

[54] The active women's congregations founded in the nineteenth century were anomalous. At this date the only women religious the Church recognised and legislated for were enclosed. The canons that had protected enclosed religious were inappropriate for apostolic women, and, when applied to them, made it difficult for them to exercise the ministries for which they had been founded.

[55] CC14:27.

Yet she had no formal theological training. The exclusion of women from the study of theology inhibited the independent thinking of nineteenth-century religious women, and ensured their submission to clerical authority. This, again, is a gender issue; Ruskin expressed the opinion that the one science it was dangerous for women to study was theology.[56] His assumption was shared by Wiseman, Cornelia's erstwhile supporter. When the St Leonards community inherited the extensive theological library of the Rev. John Jones, Wiseman appealed to Rome in the strongest terms in an effort to wrest it from their grasp. He complained to Cardinal Fransoni about the inappropriateness of a theological library becoming the property of "le fragili figlie di Eva": "The danger of that tree of knowledge to the fragile daughters of Eve is not yet sufficiently realised."[57]

Wiseman carried away the more up-to-date literature; Cornelia retained possession of many patristic texts and spiritual classics, and her personal notebooks testify to the fact that she used them. Nevertheless her limited knowledge of theology, and more explicitly of canon law, which had not yet been codified, forced her to rely on the judgment of clerics to ensure that the Society's Constitutions met the Roman criteria when she presented them for approbation.[58] Requesting permission to go to Rome, Cornelia acknowledged to Grant on 8 March 1869 that, in this matter of the Constitutions, she was very much a woman in a man's world. Her letter reveals not only her sense of inadequacy, but her internalisation of conventional gender stereotyping:

> I am afraid that I shall only fret myself and get into a puzzle of uncertainty, and annoy your Lordship in your present too many sufferings, if I go on thinking or writing about the Rules etc., which really ought not to fall upon a woman in any responsible sense, even before revision.[59]

---

[56] Mumm, *Stolen Daughters, Virgin Mothers*, 198.

[57] "… e che non abbastanza ancora si conosca il pericolo di quell' albero della scienza, alle fragili figlie di Eva."

[58] Later Cornelia relied on M l'Abbé Craisson's *Des Communautés religieuses à vœux simples: législation canonique et civile*. Her copy, containing numerous marginal annotations as well as a few pages of translation in her own hand, is extant. Cornelia urged all the superiors, especially those in the United States, to obtain and study this book.

[59] CC15:7.

In Rome she readily accepted the advice and supervision of Anselmo Knapen, a Franciscan, who acted as the Society's consultor. But his adaptation of the Constitutions, inadequately explained and presented, had far-reaching consequences for Cornelia and for the Society. And it is clear that he felt free to make changes without reference to her. (Which male founder would have tolerated that?) On 8 May 1870, back in St Leonards, Cornelia wrote to Grant in consternation about "the clause introduced into the Rules after our departure."[60]

Cornelia accepted that there were areas, like this matter of the Constitutions, in which it was difficult for women to act independently. But the tight control that Grant and Danell exercised over the nuns extended to the minutiae of daily living, and must have made the continued maintenance of an adult stance in relation to them difficult. That Cornelia, in spite of her inconsistencies, largely succeeded is worthy of note: it was not true of all women religious. Margaret Anne Cusack, founder of the Sisters of St Joseph of Peace, for instance, found clerical control so intolerable that she left her congregation in July 1888 and subsequently left the Church. And a congregation that Xavier Noble encountered in America took the opposite route of total capitulation and subservience. She wrote to Cornelia, 17 August 1862, expressing horror at "the extraordinary want of … independence of priestly government, oh dreadful, a Bishop or priest lord and master of the house!!"

Women's Social and Economic Dependence

Unlike the leaders of that congregation, Cornelia resolutely resisted any generalised infantilisation of members of the Society. To protect himself, Grant insisted that each sister who went to America should obtain the written consent of her parents or of some other responsible relative. Cornelia drew up the certificates as requested but did not fail to point out to him that "none of those going are under guardians being quite beyond minors."[61] On another occasion when he was delaying the clothing of a novice because her mother (a Protestant) had not given her consent, Cornelia wrote:

[60] CC15:32.
[61] CC13:48.

> Miss Thompson has done nothing but fret over your Lordship's doubt as to her Clothing .... The mere fact of her being 33 years of age is sufficient to act upon and if your Lordship were here you would not hesitate a moment in receiving her—therefore pray consider the matter settled.[62]

Almost always, as here, it was circumstance that pushed Cornelia into contravening the accepted norm of women's subservience to male authority. Sometimes, however, a principle was at stake. One such was the matter of the Society's economic independence, and the desire of its members to support themselves by working. Grant, who had been left with real financial difficulties after the division of the Westminster and Southwark dioceses, understandably feared that if the nuns' resources failed they would look to him as their ecclesial superior (and, arguably, the significant male figure in the life of the Society) for financial support which he would be unable to provide. For this reason, he continually tried to limit membership of the Society to women who had dowries; he resisted expenditure on buildings and the expansion of ministries; and he urged the investment of money for the support of old and infirm community members. On 9 September 1860, while asking for three sisters to be admitted to vows, Cornelia made clear that she was operating on a totally different principle, a principle at variance with normal Victorian gender assumptions:

> I should be very glad if we had thirty to offer your Lordship for vows instead of three, and I should willingly take the responsibility of their old age though in all probability they would never reach it ... I wish you would remember My Lord that we only want to <u>labour</u> for our support as mendicant orders beg, and above all as Our Blessed Lord himself laboured for thirty years. If we sink into making provision for our support, <u>not</u> imitating our Blessed Lord, we shall not be blessed .... This is what we wish to do if your Lordship is not averse to it.[63]

In spite of efforts such as this, the development of the Society was frequently determined (and restricted) by gender assumptions: the bishops—Victorian men, with Victorian assumptions about gender roles

---

[62] CC14:115.
[63] CC12:25.

and about men's responsibilities for women—struggled with the notion that the Society might have independent and autonomous government; that its members, by their own efforts, might maintain it financially; that they might accept whom they chose as potential members and expand the Society's works as they saw fit. The English hierarchy had been restored only in 1850, and the bishops were learning on the job, so to speak, and establishing a diocesan system on an *ad hoc* basis. Cornelia's desires for the Society, especially her attempts to gain pontifical status for it and to establish firm central government, came into conflict both with their desires for their dioceses, and with their assumptions about their responsibilities towards women religious.

The bishops wanted the Society to become a loose federation of diocesan houses, more amenable to their control and supervision. Bishops Goss and O'Reilly in Liverpool and Bishop Wood in Philadelphia all, to some extent, urged this view on the sisters. Danell in Southwark brought the matter to a head by declaring himself Bishop-Superior of the Institute, causing considerable ill feeling among his fellow bishops—ill feeling that was vented on Cornelia. The question of the Society's status was painful for Cornelia; and it was not resolved in her lifetime. This was another gender issue, arising, to some extent, out of the bishops' assumptions about women. They exercised not only spiritual but also material and patriarchal power over the women religious. The analogy with a husband's power in law over his wife and her property springs readily to mind.

From a Victorian point of view, the bishops' stance was understandable and valid. A group of women free to act independently was, at the very least, counter-cultural. But in her struggle against it Cornelia was not alone. Some congregations, like the Sisters of Mercy, had a structure that fitted more easily into the requirements of the bishops. Others, like the Society of the Sacred Heart, had faced similar problems in France earlier in the century—though Madeleine Sophie Barat was never without male champions.[64] The lack of any clerical protector made Cornelia particularly vulnerable.

---

[64] See Phil Kilroy, *Madeleine Sophie Barat: A Life* (Mahwah, NJ: Paulist, 2000).

Cornelia's Contravention of the Norms

To compound the problem, the bishops encountered Cornelia's self-confidence and her business-like assumption of authority in letter after letter. It was a vicious circle: because she had no man to fight her corner, she had to do it herself; because she fought her own corner she appeared to them unfeminine, arrogant, disobedient. There is no evidence to suggest that this was a conscious choice on Cornelia's part. If anything, the documentation reveals her conventionality. For instance, Mère Eugénie Milleret de Brou, founder of the Assumption sisters, with whom Cornelia stayed in Paris in 1846, commented, that Cornelia "aime à être gouvernée par des hommes."[65] Admittedly, Cornelia had little experience at this date of any male government other than Pierce's. Nevertheless, in moments of crisis her instinct seems to have been to bolster her resolve by placing herself under obedience to her (male) director or, once she had founded the Society, to the convent chaplain. At Derby she bound herself by a private vow not to see Pierce without the chaplain's consent. According to several Holy Child sources, she came to regret this decision and its consequences.

Her lack of consistency explains to some extent the problematic nature of her relationship with members of the hierarchy, and their general negativity towards her. When she challenged them, they were affronted; when she professed obedience, they were suspicious. Independence of thought was not an attitude which the bishops expected or found appropriate in women, and certainly not in women religious. In 1864 Cornelia noted among Wiseman's objections to the Constitutions: " ... in practice His Eminence had found the Sisters acting independently of him."[66] And Cornelia's letters, time after time, reveal an intelligent independence of thought which she did not shrink from expressing. To Grant she wrote, for instance, on the troubling subject of chaplains, on 17 March 1865:

> You know I always wish to have as far as possible what your Lordship wishes, and to express no wish regarding the Confessor you may choose to appoint, but at the same time I would be wrong if I did not frankly say that

---

[65] D5:118. "... likes to be governed by men."
[66] CC45:9.

we should much rather <u>not</u> have a Franciscan Father as Confessor at Mayfield.[67]

When Cornelia was in dispute with the parish at St Leonards about property, Grant, always fearful of scandal and adverse publicity, threatened that he would conduct no more clothings or professions for the community. This was a serious matter for the future of the Society, and a threat that he repeated on a number of occasions. He worried constantly that there might be too many novices, annotating one of Cornelia's letters: "Replied that the Novices may profess from year to year ... Rev. Mother being charged not to let the numbers of Novices grow beyond those really required for the Convent wants."[68] Once again we can see the power that the bishop had to curb the development and expansion of the congregation. Now, 21 October 1862, Cornelia responded to the bishop's threat with a straightforward confidence that, I suggest, would be unusual in correspondence with bishops even today:

> I took your letter received by the three o'clock post after having read it twice myself, and read it to Our Lady of Sorrows asking her in her own sweet meekness to listen to it—and the interior answer I got was "burn the letter and tell the Bishop to forget what he wrote and to come and tell you what more you can do than you have done."—I have burnt it my Lord and now will you come down and tell me what more I can do than I have done?[69]

Backscheider has observed that, in their relations with men, intelligence has been a mixed blessing for women.[70] The bishops' anti-Cornelian stance is understandable given her failure to conform to their (unarticulated and unexamined) assumptions and expectations. Equally understandable is the Society's myth of Cornelia as an obedient and dutiful daughter of the Church, which drew upon her view of events, her statements of intent, and the biographers' knowledge of her aspirations, hopes and intentions. The reality was more complex: Cornelia was constantly at the boundaries of a convention that she herself had nevertheless internalised. What can appear as

---

[67] CC14:6.
[68] CC12:28.
[69] CC13:81.
[70] Paula Backscheider, *Reflections on Biography* (Oxford: OUP, 1999), 131.

inconsistency is perhaps rather the confusion inherent in any prophetic beginning.

Cornelia as Mother

In the traditional presentation of Cornelia's life, there is often the impression of a gap between the first half of her life (her experience as wife and mother) and the second half (her experience as founder). The implication is that Cornelia had a series of vocations and that she left one behind as she embraced the next.[71] But neither she nor her contemporaries forgot about her marital status when she became a religious. Perhaps, therefore, a more organic reading of Cornelia's life is possible. For all that she experienced a painful dislocation in the loss of her husband and children, it may nevertheless be that she continued to develop as a mother (if not as a wife) during the period of her leadership of the Society. Her motherhood, and the myth and counter-myth attached to it, never fail to evoke a response in anyone who encounters Cornelia's story. This particular gender role, with all the power that clings to it, is of primary importance in any interpretation of her life.

Cornelia as Mother of her Children

Cornelia bore five children in just over eight years: her oldest child, Mercer, was born on 17 December 1832 and her youngest, Frank, on 29 March 1841. By the time Frank was born, two of his siblings were already dead. Mary Magdalen, born on 22 July 1839 in Grand Coteau, lived for only six weeks; the following February, John Henry, who had been born in Vienna, died from multiple burns. All the biographers, even those who are hazy about the details of the accident, agree that this death had a profound effect on Cornelia and on her spiritual growth.

Cornelia herself wrote very little about her children, and only a few of her letters to them are extant, but the evidence we have suggests that she enjoyed motherhood. Pierce, in a letter written sometime during 1839-1840, drew a (possibly idealized) picture of family life at Grand Coteau. In his description,

---

[71] Caritas McCarthy's study of Cornelia's spirituality, *The Spirituality of Cornelia Connelly: In God, For God, With God* (Lewiston and Queenston: Edwin Mellen, 1986), includes a lengthy section entitled "Through Successive Calls to Ultimate Vocation."

the "sweetest ... but the noisiest" children enjoy games round the piano after dinner whilst their "Mama lends an arm to the medley" and their "Papa [is forced] to be an involuntary sharer in the disturbance." Then they "all knelt together in our little Oratory" before the children went off to bed.[72] Less romantically, Cornelia, visiting Alton Towers whilst the children were left behind at Spetchley Park in 1843, is concerned when Frank falls ill:

> Mrs Berkeley ... says he is doing very well but we must be off at six tomorrow and trust in our good God that we shall find him well. We are too late for the rail train or we should have set off at once ... I am indeed more afraid of the Doctor than of the sickness as he is <u>not</u> homeopathic and I dread his taking calomel.[73]

Cornelia is anxious about Frank's illness; her responses to the deaths of Mary Magdalen and John Henry are shrouded in silence. Though Strub made a close analysis of Cornelia's terse entry in her notebook about her son,[74] we can only speculate on the depth of her sense of loss. She loved her children with passion, as her reaction to Pierce's removal of them demonstrates. A letter of hers to Pierce was quoted in the pamphlet *Case of the Rev. Pierce Connelly*:

> I have already told you I would see you when you bring back to my care my little girl, and <u>I will never</u> see you till then; unless God manifests his holy will through the command of the bishop.[75]

Cornelia added in the margin of her copy: "Yes, this was <u>my</u> will because he had broken his promise." Pierce's abduction of the children seems to have been motivated by his knowledge of her love for them. Wiseman told Lord Shrewsbury: "In one letter he [Pierce] tells Mrs C that he had carried off the children <u>as the only way to get hold of her through them</u>."[76]

The creators of the Society's pro-Cornelian myth knew that they must demonstrate the strength of her love for her children if they were to counter the contrary assertion that she was an unnatural mother who had

---

[72] D4:41-42.
[73] CC1:49.
[74] See chapter six.
[75] CC43:35.
[76] D6:14.

abandoned them. A story that exactly suited their purposes was recorded by Adeline Duval Mack, Cornelia's niece. She interviewed John McCloskey when he was a cardinal in New York and said that he told her:

> I can see Mrs Connelly approaching me clasping her hands and her beautiful eyes uplifted to my face. "Father McCloskey, is it necessary for Pierce Connelly to make this sacrifice and sacrifice me? I love my husband and my darling children. Why must I give them up? I love my religion and why cannot we remain happy, as the Earl of Shrewsbury's family? Why?"[77]

Doubt was raised about this story by James Walsh as long ago as 1959, but it remains part of the Society's mythology. Walsh categorizes Adeline Mack's statement as "long and rambling ... full of error and inaccuracy,"[78] and he makes clear that there are difficulties regarding both the dating of any encounter between Cornelia and Fr McCloskey and the opinions Mrs Mack asserts that the priest expressed. She says McCloskey remembered his response to Cornelia: "My heart was full of sympathy. I gave all the consolation in my power. I looked upon the action of the Pope as a mistake but I could not say so." Walsh comments:

> McCloskey was not in Rome during the period of Cornelia's second sojourn there .... If Cornelia ever had an interview with him, it was not in Rome .... In any case, it is highly unlikely that an ecclesiastic of his standing would commit himself to saying (especially to such an excitable witness), "I looked upon the action of the Pope as a mistake," particularly when the "action" referred to was a solemn decree of separation ...[79]

In spite of these difficulties, Flaxman retains the story, suggesting, in response to Walsh, that the encounter took place when the Connellys were on their first visit to Rome in 1836. McCloskey was in Rome then, but there is no other evidence from that visit of Cornelia agonizing over the loss of her children, and it is hard to see why at that time she would have anticipated separation from them. Furthermore, such an emotional outburst is out of character for the silent, reticent and self-controlled Cornelia whom the myth otherwise presents. For a feminist biographer,

---

[77] Quoted in Flaxman, *A Woman Styled Bold*, 45.
[78] Walsh, *The Vocation of Cornelia Connelly*, 12.
[79] Walsh, *The Vocation of Cornelia Connelly*, 13.

such self-contradiction would present no difficulty, but it sits uneasily in a more conventional hagiographical account.

A further problem for the pro-Cornelian myth-makers lies in her letters to her oldest son, Mercer, at school at Stonyhurst. A cache of letters survives, which suggests that Mercer valued them; but today the letters seem totally devoid of any understanding of his situation. Mercer, an adolescent whose father had become a priest and his mother a nun, was having his school fees paid by his parents' wealthy friends. And his mother failed to see how much this might affect his relationships with boys at Stonyhurst who knew his circumstances:

> How much I like Henry B he seems so frank and open. I asked him what there was between you & he assured me there was nothing at all—so you see my dear Boy it is your own imagination & not his—and you will profit by this my dear Merty I hope & get over all such useless thoughts, rather I should say <u>dangerous</u> thoughts since it is quite impossible for you ever to do your duty and be in the love of God, and of your neighbour while you give way to them .... The truth is dear Merty as I told you, while Henry Berkeley & the other good boys are labouring hard at the foundations of their buildings like persons of good sense you are building Castles in the air that will never be realised in any other way than to bring upon you a few more ferules before the end of the week.[80]

All Cornelia's letters to Mercer are in this vein. Her lack of intuitive sympathy for her son distances her from the present-day reader, and is particularly puzzling when contrasted with her concern for the children in the school at St Leonards. The letters to Mercer make good material for the anti-Cornelian myth. Pro-Cornelian writers offer the defence of different *mores*, arguing along the same lines as Judith Flanders:

> Child-rearing is one of those areas that has changed so radically in the last hundred years that it is almost impossible to look back, with our values now, without feeling that much of what happened then verged on the criminal.[81]

---

[80] CC1:27. "Ferules" refers to corporal punishment.
[81] Flanders, *A Circle of Sisters*, 131.

By chance, a letter survives from Cornelia to her sister-in-law, Elizabeth Murphy Bowen, written in November 1869, in which Cornelia expresses regret about Mercer:

> Nothing would induce me to advise you to send [your sons] to England for their education. The English boys are rough fighting boys & glory in combativenesses, in Colleges—and they get flogged too for naughtinesses, but at home with their Mothers and Sisters they are gentle as lambs and full of attention and politeness to their parents & Sisters. I always regretted having sent dear Mercer to an English College & would never have consented to sending Frank.[82]

Mercer died completely alienated from his mother and convinced of the rightness of his father's position. The two other children who survived to adulthood, Adeline and Frank, were also devoted to their father, with whom they lived until his death. Understandably, they thought of him as the more caring and supportive parent. Frank, on a rare visit to St Leonards, accused his mother of loving the nuns more than she loved him. Any account of Cornelia's life written today will have to acknowledge the damaging effect of their parents' choices on the Connelly children.

However, the separation was endlessly painful for Cornelia too. Aloysia Walker, one of her first companions, recalled Cornelia's reaction to separation from her children in 1846:

> It was from there [Birmingham] she sent her two elder children to school. Never shall I forget the struggle of that separation. It was, I think, one of the greatest sacrifices she had to make ... [83]

Cornelia's letters reveal not only how much she missed the children but also her efforts to maintain contact with them (and with Pierce), and her awareness of the criticisms of herself as an unnatural and deserting mother. As early as 1846, before the Society was established or separation from the children effected, she acknowledged the criticism of desertion that was being levelled against her. To her brother Ralph Peacock she wrote: " ... time and eternity eternity will prove if I have abandoned my duty to God

---

[82] CC1:86-87.
[83] D10:33.

and my dear children." [84] And she wrote to her sister, Adeline Duval, on 15 September 1851:

> I suppose you know that I know nothing about my dear children. I have several times sent letters to them and to Pierce which have been returned unopened.—But an anonymous letter was sent saying he was advised to take a wife—If it could be without sin by his vows being dissolved I should be very glad, but could he ever be happy again? Do pray for him, dear Addie, and my poor little ones. [85]

In another letter to Ralph Peacock she expressed her outrage at the loss of "my darling children, ever dearer to me than my own life." They were lost to her now, she said, as they had not been in 1846 and as she had never expected or intended that they should be. When she went to Derby:

> My dear children were as much under my eyes as if I had not left the world till their father broke his word and his promises and stole them away from me in a moment of excitement and unjust anger, may God forgive him. [86]

Four years later she was still struggling to come to terms with her anger and pain. In another letter to Ralph, on 18 November 1858, she wrote:

> I have nothing to tell you about my own darling children except that Pierce has taken them to Brussels without bringing them to see me or even letting me know of their departure—May God forgive him! Poor darlings! I little thought of their having to suffer in this way, while I can do nothing to help them except by prayer. [87]

It seems important to acknowledge that she was right: the children did suffer and, from their perspective, she was a less than satisfactory mother. All the biographers without exception defend Cornelia against this assertion: they rise stoutly to her defence and maintain that she was a good mother. And there is documentation, within limits, to support their claim. But the breakdown of her relationship with Pierce and her life as founder of the Society severely restricted her contact with and influence over the

---

[84] CC1:68.
[85] CC1:51.
[86] CC1:71.
[87] CC1:74-75.

children. After Frank was five and Adeline eleven their relationship with their mother effectively ceased. So, like much else in Cornelia's life, the question of how good a mother she was is debatable. That she wanted to be and tried to be is beyond question; that Frank at least thought she was not is also clear. But her detractors, from the nineteenth century until today, have judged her mothering and found it wanting. In the anti-Cornelian myth she is the archetypal unnatural mother.[88]

But what was Cornelia's own perspective? How did she cope with the loss of the children? In a letter to Pierce's brother, John, she explained that she had sacrificed her marriage for God, "AMDG":

> So you see it is not for nothing that I have given him to God. You may be sure this thought gives me much consolation and we ought to look for a greater share of the divine love in proportion as we are willing to sacrifice our natural happiness AMDG and look for even more in eternity.[89]

Other parts of this letter suggest that the sacrifice was not so easily effected, and that she did not anticipate that it would include the children. She could not easily abandon marriage and motherhood, and continued to think of herself as a wife and mother. Even as she looked to the founding of the Society she still saw the family unit as central to her life, saw herself primarily as Pierce's wife, Mercer's mother. An addendum to this letter reveals her underlying assumptions: the "we" she speaks of is not the Society but the Connelly family:

> We shall not leave Paris until August and then we go to Mrs Berkeley's until I decide under Father Mahone's direction upon my future movements, but you can send your letters for me to Pierce and he will send them to me wherever I may be. I trust that we may all see our dear country again but when God only knows and I do not think it will be likely to happen before Merty's education is finished.[90]

---

[88] This, of course, is a deeply gendered response to Cornelia's story. In spite of the fact that her children were wrested from her, she is accused of having abandoned them. Would a man, similarly placed, be castigated as an unnatural father?

[89] CC1:97.

[90] CC1:99.

To the end of her life her sense of family and the cost of her loss of contact with them were still fresh. In a letter to Dolores Wilkinson, extolling the privileges of religious life, she wrote, on 1 September 1876:

> Ah! This [religious life] is indeed a little foretaste of heaven which a thousand times repays our little secret acts of the day, which are also a pleasure in themselves; and again, are we not a thousand times repaid for our natural sacrifices of families and friends which will more or less cling to us humanly during our whole life to give us the merit of constant renewal.[91]

Spontaneous comments and asides such as this provide a glimpse of her ongoing sacrifice and suffering and are, therefore, a testimony to the value she placed on motherhood. Bellasis described Cornelia's loss of the children as "a cross without alleviation"[92]; and Cornelia is quoted as saying, "The remembrance of my children never leaves me."[93]

Perhaps because she was so isolated, family ties were extremely important to her. She ends a letter to her niece, Isabella Bowen, on 25 September 1872, "Ah! My dear Bella, I can only say that I love you as your own Mother and am ever yours in JC, CC." Yet she also recognised that such motherly love had its limits. To another niece, Cornelia Duval, she comments, on 27 January 1861(?), "none can ever quite equal a Mother's love."[94] With such evidence it is difficult to countenance the myth that demonizes Cornelia as an unnatural mother. Their parents' choices had painful consequences for the children; but there is little justification for branding Cornelia, or Pierce, as unloving or unnatural.

Cornelia as Spiritual and Founding Mother

As founder, Cornelia often called the members of the Society to motherliness and detailed for them what this involved. I suggest that the term "mother" carried specific meaning for Cornelia, derived from her experience of physical motherhood. She cannot have used it casually or unthinkingly because it connects the two parts of her experience,

---

[91] CC8:44-45.
[92] D73:213.
[93] D63:42.
[94] CC1:114; CC1:117.

motherhood and spiritual leadership. Such a connection continues to be affirmed today, not only in papal documents—*Mulieris dignitatem*[95] for instance—but in the writings of women themselves. Carol Wallace LaChance argues:

> Woman is potentially mother. Not only mother of physical offspring, but mother of life in all its facets—intellectual, emotional and spiritual .... To be mother is to be in touch with our true creative power whether we manifest that creativity in children, in work, in feeling, or in vision.[96]

Cornelia knew what it was to be mother. The anti-Cornelian myth sees her callously abandoning her children; the pro-Cornelian myth maintains that, separated from her children, she drew on and developed all that she had learned in the first half of her life to deepen and enrich the charism of her congregation. As founder, she continued to reflect on what mothering involved, and to articulate and model for the Society a style of mothering that called others to growth rather than confining them to endless childhood.

Any examination of Cornelia's living out of the role of spiritual and founding mother must examine the extent to which she integrated her earlier experiences into her changed circumstances. Did she learn from her mistakes or merely replicate them? Feminist biographers stress the importance of listening to women's private and personal discourse in order to retrieve "a portrait of gender arrangements that are invisible in the dominant discourse."[97] It would be satisfyingly neat if it were possible to demonstrate that an attitude to motherhood, to gender and to women's selfhood existed within the Society that was quite different from the prevailing public discourse. But what the documentation reveals, as with so much else in Cornelia's life, is not clear cut.

Religious Community: A Woman's World

In the nineteenth century a separate women's world existed, not just in convents but in society generally; it was almost entirely closed to men, but of great significance to women themselves. Virginia Woolf writes:

---

[95] John Paul II, Apostolic Letter (London: Catholic Truth Society, 1988).
[96] Carol Wallas LaChance, *The Way of the Mother: The Lost Journey of the Feminine* (Rockport, Ma: Element, 1991), xii.
[97] Long, *Telling Women's Lives*, 9.

> I tried to remember any case in the course of my reading where two women are represented as friends .... But almost without exception they are shown in their relation to men .... And how small a part of a woman's life is that; and how little can a man know even of that when he observes it through the black or rosy spectacles which sex puts upon his nose.[98]

Though the bishops exercised ecclesiastical jurisdiction, a religious congregation was a woman's world where the sisters were not primarily characterized by their relation to men. It has been suggested that nineteenth-century convents have a place "within the story of the advancement of women as an example of feminist practice," in spite of the fact that the religious themselves would not have understood or might even have rejected a feminist label:

> By feminist practice is meant "the association of women together for a feminist purpose ... the organization of a range of activities ... around the claims of women to determine different areas of their lives." Under this definition sisterhoods can be seen as firmly rooted in the feminist tradition, both by their fierce commitment to their women-created organisations and by their dedication to improving, or at least ameliorating, the lives of working-class women and their children.[99]

Convent records offer some evidence of the ways in which women related among themselves away from bi-polar gender conventions. In the Cornelian documentation a discourse can be heard between members of the Society that is quite different from the formal correspondence with the bishops. This glimpse into the female world of the convent confirms that the portrait of gender arrangements provided by the dominant discourse is less than the whole picture.

Women's Bodies

For instance, away from the world of male-female interaction, a quite different mode of thinking about women's bodies emerges. An unexpectedly open and healthy attitude to the body—an attitude devoid of prudery or guilt or embarrassment—seems to have been the norm in the

---

[98] Virginia Woolf, *A Room of One's Own* (London: Grafton Books, 1987 [1929]), 97.
[99] Mumm, *Stolen Daughters, Virgin Mothers*, xi.

Society. Menstruation is a good indicator of women's general health, and members of the Society were apparently not reticent about discussing it. Cornelia wrote to Catherine Tracey, on 20 October 1873:

> I am so thankful to our Good God that you are getting well & the monthly epoch is all right. I hope you kept to your bed the first day, and that you will do so throughout the winter as this is the best safety.[100]

Cornelia's letters to early members of the Society are shot through with practical concern about health. And they in their turn offered advice to her. When Xavier Atkinson passed on a suggestion about the benefits of Turkish baths, Cornelia commented, "I do not think it would be very religious, but if I am not better soon I shall try hot baths <u>at home</u>."[101]

Yet within Cornelia's response, there lurks an anxiety about convention, even though there was greater openness within this woman's world. Cornelia's unusual breadth of experience did not render her completely free from stereotypical attitudes to gender and sexuality. Indeed, in some of her writings, the tone of platitudinous Victorian moralising is marked. In the 1860s, in the Rules for the Schools of the Society of the Holy Child Jesus, for instance, she adds a rider to the first rule: "A woman without piety and virtue is a disgrace to her sex."[102]

But other writings reveal a refreshing freedom from the unthinkingly conventional. The Customal, a document that offers a gloss on the daily life of the nuns, frequently highlights Cornelia's understanding of human nature and her healthy attitude to relationships. In one section, for instance, she inserts a telling addendum to that centuries-old tradition of religious life that warned against "particular friendships." She did not challenge the received wisdom, but pointed out that "particular aversions" were equally dangerous: "Believe me there are two great rocks you must avoid, *viz.*— <u>aversions</u> and particular friendships, both are very dangerous and destructive."[103]

---

[100] CC8:15.
[101] CC6:5.
[102] CC37:10.
[103] CC44:51.

This sentence is typical of the particular mix of the conventional and the unconventional that is constantly encountered in Cornelia's writings. It also affirms the healthy, clear-sighted attitude she seems to have had to human relationships and sexuality, in spite of the prevailing *Zeitgeist* and the contemporary dubious theology of the relative merits of marriage and celibacy. It is noteworthy, given Cornelia's personal history, that no disparagement of marriage or recoiling from sexual activity is to be found in any of her writings. In one letter only—to her niece Bella Bowen—she advocates religious life rather than marriage, and then on the purely practical grounds that in religion a woman as delicate as Bella would be spared the life-endangering experience of giving birth:

> Ah what is life! To marry and die and leave children for others to be unkind to or something like this .... You must come and be a nun my darling ... and do not give yourself to be any man's slave to die and leave a family. You are not strong enough to bear such a sad lot.[104]

Possibly Cornelia is remembering her own fears of dying in childbirth. Bella was not unduly influenced by her aunt: she married just the same.

A Woman-Affirming Environment[105]

The life of the early Society, as Cornelia constructed it, seems to have been a blend of conformity to convention and the exercise of a more unconventional, womanly style. The government structures offer a good example of her approach. The existing biographies describe a hierarchical model of government that gave power to those in authority and exacted obedience from their "subjects." And, for those expecting to find it, there is plenty of evidence for this in the documentation. Cornelia valued obedience highly; she often suggested that the will of God could be found through acceptance of rightly ordered authority, through obedience to the hierarchy of the Church. As founder she was careful to emphasize the importance of submission to the power of the bishops. Sometimes the language in which she expresses herself seems, to a modern reader, extravagant to the point of distastefulness: "Ah! God is very very good to

---

[104] CC1:113.

[105] The phrase is Susan Mumm's. See Mumm, *Stolen Daughters, Virgin Mothers*, 10.

us, and our Bishops are full of the Charity of true fathers, when we are humble little children."[106] But the authenticity of her sentiment is clear. To Agatha Deacy, one of the superiors in the USA, she wrote:

> I want to hear that the Bishop and priests are pleased with your efforts, and then I shall be at ease and know you are working in docility and obedience to those whom God has placed over us.[107]

Yet, alongside this pattern of orthodox submission to "those whom God has placed over us," which was applied to leaders within the Society as well to bishops, it is equally possibly to find in the documentation substantial evidence of a countervailing attitude of independence and personal empowerment. An explicitly feminist presentation and interpretation of Cornelia's life might choose to emphasize these aspects of her vision and practice precisely because they bolster current feminist preference, just as the earlier biographers selected the material that affirmed their own world-view within the convent subculture. But the documentation seems to reveal something more complex—a "both … and" rather than an "either … or" approach. Cornelia both accepted and challenged current social assumptions and practices. This can be categorized as inconsistency; or it can be read as her understandable inability to see beyond those assumptions and practices whilst inchoately knowing that they were not quite right, at least for a women's group.

The evidence of the documentation is that Cornelia established a government structure for the Society reflecting the hierarchical pattern that was normative both in the Church and in Victorian society generally, while also promoting community solidarity in discussion and decision-making. This approach was more remarkable in the convent culture of the nineteenth century than it would be today. Though it transgressed current social norms, it seems to have been based on the spirituality of discernment, which was central to Cornelia's style of government, rather than on any conscious rebellion against accepted custom. Cornelia was convinced of the value of each person and of each person's ability to think things through for herself.

---

[106] CC46B:51.
[107] CC46:13.

It is hard to exaggerate how different life in the Society was from the subservient and subordinated experience of many women in Victorian Britain. The convent at St Leonards was a shared space where the members dreamed up a communal vision for the Society, where they were united by a common project. But, as their number grew, Cornelia recognised the increasing importance of appropriate lines of authority and obedience. So there was a hierarchical structure of government; but her letters constantly show that it functioned in a very different way from that of the bishops in their dioceses, a way that would now be considered consonant with feminist practice. Cornelia insisted that the lines of obedience should not be fudged, but she also consulted and took advice from the community, delegating a good deal of real responsibility. She expressed confidence in the abilities and decision-making skills of individual sisters, and allowed them considerable freedom to express and act upon their own judgment.

Aware of her capacity to influence others, Cornelia consciously tried to leave them free. To an unidentified sister she wrote: "I will not say what I think about it because I want to leave you to God's inspirations and to your fidelity to the same."[108]

The difference between this approach and the prevailing attitude of the bishops in Cornelia's own regard scarcely needs underlining. Cornelia's letters reveal a practice of shared decision-making within the Society which would have been quite foreign to the bishops: "I have consulted our Community regarding the inclosed proposal [and] we have decided ... "; "the final decision of the Community is contrary to your plans"; "it is a growing conviction of our Community ... "; "I answer for the Community .... The general wish of the Community is to withdraw."[109] And, lest this be considered merely rhetorical, there is extensive evidence of her involving individual sisters in decision-making and of her leaving quite significant decisions to them. It must be remembered that, for the most part, the members of the Society were inexperienced: superiors were commonly in their early twenties. But they were to decide what was best locally—"No, I had no intention of writing myself. You must do all those local matters from the

---

[108] CC8:69.
[109] CC3:41; CC3:46; CC4:15; CC5:20.

Convent."[110] They might even decide on the suitability of candidates for the Society and take steps to incorporate them. In 1856 in a letter discussing the pupil teachers in Preston with Lucy Woolley, Cornelia writes: "If <u>you now wish to give any the hood</u> you may do so, and keep them with you until you come down here yourself."[111]

Perhaps Cornelia sometimes came to regret the independence she encouraged in others when it resulted in outcomes of which she did not approve. Emily Bowles and Lucy Woolley, two of the most gifted of the early members of the Society, were given significant responsibility for the communities and ministries in Lancashire, from which Cornelia herself was furthest removed. They had real authority delegated to them and were free to exercise their judgment about individuals and situations without constant reference to Cornelia. Lucy especially acquitted herself well, establishing a network of successful schools in Preston. But ultimately both women left the Society when their differences with Cornelia became insurmountable. Cornelia's reaction to their departures underlines the friendship and mutuality that was part of the Society's government structure: she experienced a sense of personal betrayal because these women had been her friends (not just dissatisfied subordinates) and she had assumed, wrongly, that they would always share the same viewpoint. It is easy to draw a parallel between the breakdown of Cornelia's relationship with these two oldest spiritual "children" and her failure to understand and support Mercer. Once again, her mothering was perceived as less than good enough.

However, Cornelia's confidence in others, and her desire that they should make important decisions for themselves, were not restricted to the most senior or most gifted members of the Society. When Bessie Gray, Sister de Loyola, was caught up in a financial dispute with her family, Cornelia maintained, in a long correspondence with Grant, the rightness both of Bessie's independent decision-making and of her own insistence on leaving her free. On 13 October 1860 she wrote to Grant:

[110] CC6:202.
[111] CC8:51.

Sister de Loyola is acting for herself with her lawyers. If the Codicil is proved invalid by the previous settlement she will be safe, but if not she must <u>choose for herself </u>either to obtain a Bond from her Brothers and Sisters to secure her rights during her lifetime, or to abandon her religious life. We cannot my Lord be answerable for her loss of property in any future events. There is plenty of time to weigh all matters thoroughly, and she is quite capable and willing to act for herself.[112]

Bessie subsequently left the Society, but Cornelia did not regret the approach she had adopted. She explained to Grant: "I kept myself free from any other advice than that of following her director's decision" (11 August 1861) and "I do know that I never advised her to a less perfect life nor have I any thing to reproach myself with in the sad course she has taken. I did my utmost to prevent her taking any unadvised step ... " (5 May 1862).[113]

Mumm suggests that one of the attractions of religious life for nineteenth-century women was that it enabled them "to participate in the government of a semi-democratic institution."[114] "In a world that seemed materialistic, godless and male," religious life "validated the worth of women, their abilities and their labour." The "inventive and evolving community structures gave women independence, autonomy and control over their lives; they provided a nurturing woman-affirming environment ... religious communities empowered women."[115] The documentation that survives about life at St Leonards and in the early Society suggests that, for the Holy Child sisters as for other women religious, convent life offered an opportunity to live at one remove from the sexual scripts and gender stereotypes prevailing in the public sphere. An examination of their lifestyle reveals the influence of Cornelia's experience of physical motherhood on the charism of the Society.

Mother: A Society Term

After the Society was established, Cornelia's maternal feelings found an easy outlet among the pupils in the schools, and she urged on the sisters a

---

[112] CC12:41.

[113] CC12:94-95; CC13:21.

[114] Mumm, *Stolen Daughters, Virgin Mothers*, xii.

[115] Mumm, *Stolen Daughters, Virgin Mothers*, 9-10.

motherly attitude to the children. In the *Book of Studies*, among the Common Rules for the Mistresses of the Schools, she stipulated that the mistresses "must regard [their pupils] as the children of God ... and they should cherish a truly maternal love for them."[116] In a book of educational directives she drew out the practical implications of being motherly, illustrating the humane and psychologically healthy approach which she consistently advocated. During recreation, she wrote:

> They shall watch over them as mothers and enter into conversation with them from time to time—not confining themselves to pious subjects alone but mingling amusement and instruction in such a manner as will recreate them.[117]

An entry in the commonplace book reveals something more of the quality of this motherliness. It is not to satisfy any need in the individual sister, but to be for the good of the children. Thus the nuns will exercise a "motherly watchfulness over the children without self-seeking or coddling tenderness."[118] Perhaps Cornelia had experienced "self-seeking" and "coddling tenderness" in herself when she was with the pupils? In her circumstances it would hardly have been surprising. But instinct and experience convinced her of the self-giving, even sacrificial, dimension of mother love, and it was this ideal that she held up before the community.

Cornelia's exploration of motherly authority was not, however, confined to relationships in the schools. Occasionally she used the image of motherliness in an unexpected context, revealing how easily that particular comparison sprang to her mind. In June 1872, for instance, in a notebook entry on "dealing with ourselves and conquering our <u>faults</u> and <u>tempers</u>," she suggested that "We should treat ourselves ... as a kind and judicious Mother would treat a rebellious child."[119]

Of greater significance is her frequent use of the term "mother" in her discussion of leadership and authority within the Society itself. Motherhood

---

[116] CC37:79.
[117] CC35:21. Immediately prior to this Cornelia suggested that during recreations the sisters should "give themselves up to the children ... becoming little children with them ...."
[118] CC23:23.
[119] CC22:17.

was not merely something she had experienced physically, but was an approach to living that could be empowering for others. She might conceivably have treated those who entered the Society as substitute children, being a good ten years older than most of them. Instead, she called them to motherhood too, and in her directives spelt out for them what that meant:

> In the government of her subjects, a Superior should resemble a Mother, that is, she should be filled with the spirit of charity, compassion and solicitude for those whom God has confided to her care as so many Spiritual children. Without this true maternal love, very little is to be done or looked for. ...
>
> A Superior must be a <u>Mother to all</u>, and a Mother of <u>mildness</u> and of strength at the same time. God alone with our own co-operation can make us what we ought to be.[120]

That members of the Society came to expect motherliness from their superiors is borne out by Berchmans Carey's choice of image when she wrote to Danell, on 25 February 1874, complaining of Cornelia's treatment of the house sisters:

> Dear Revd Father ... it is a relief to open my heart to someone & you are our only refuge on earth, as our Mth General has become a Stepmother to some of us.[121]

This letter is evidence that, as the Society grew larger, the homely intimacy and easy relationships that had characterized the early years at St Leonards could no longer be sustained, and some at least in the Society viewed superiors as remote, even alien. Cornelia's response seems to have been to reinforce the motherly aspect of authority. In a book of Notes for Superiors she wrote:

> In the Old Book of the Sacred Heart Devotions there was a prayer containing these words "Have Mercy Oh Lord on our Superiors and enemies." The form has been changed in the books now in use, but there is still a tendency among people to class Superiors and enemies.—How do we regard our Superiors? We ought to look upon them as our Mothers and

---

[120] CC55:33, CC41:22.
[121] D54:79.

treat them with honour and reverence, and also with tenderness and affection.—Are we afraid of them? We ought not to fear our Superiors. No good can come of it and if a character has once be[en] thoroughly cowed it is almost impossible to rise up from it.[122]

And in the Society Customal she wrote of the need for a "maternal spirit" among superiors, so that obedience could be "easy and unconstrained" rather than "burdensome":

> When a Superior gives an order or imposes a charge, she should do it sweetly and kindly, more in the form of a request than a command; for acting in this maternal spirit, she produces a sensible impression on the minds of her subjects, and renders their obedience easy and unconstrained. Whereas to command with severity and to preserve a distance of manner creates fear and distrust in their minds and renders every command burdensome, however light it may be in itself.[123]

In religious communities today the notion of the superior as mother is extremely suspect. Many women's congregations have ceased to use the title "mother" largely because it placed those using it in a dependent, even infantile, position.[124] If the superiors act as mothers, the other members of the community are, by analogy, being treated as children. But personal discernment lay at the heart of the Society's spirituality, and consequently immature dependence on others was discouraged. So whatever Cornelia understood by motherly authority, it cannot have been intended to reduce members of the community to the status of children.

Today the association between motherhood and spiritual leadership is problematic. But it had real importance for Cornelia and the early Society. It was associated with the humane, healthy, homely nature of leadership and authority within the congregation, in contradistinction to the more rigid hierarchical models which were imposed elsewhere. As a paradigm for power in a women's group in the nineteenth century it was both enlightened and liberating.

---

[122] CC46:15.

[123] CC55:48.

[124] Women religious are not alone in struggling with the concept of motherhood. In the summer of 1999 the Catholic Women's Network called their conference "Motherness" in case some might think "we would lapse into sentimentality about motherhood ...." (Editorial, *Network*, 60 [Autumn 1999].)

Other Aspects, Themes, Questions

In this chapter it has only been possible to examine the major roles in Cornelia's life—wife, mother, founder—and to indicate how some significant themes (gender, power, motherhood) might be explored and re-presented in a feminist context. These roles and themes are offered as examples only, illustrating the importance of ongoing spiritual and biographical reinterpretation. Any number of other aspects of Cornelia's story might be reread in a similar way. Cornelia's debt to the spirituality of Francis de Sales, her spirituality of suffering, and the person of Pierce and his perspective on events, all of which have been touched upon in the preceding pages, are just some of the themes that might profitably be revisited.

Francis de Sales

Aspects of Cornelia's charism are known to derive directly from de Sales, notably her insistence on the need to "begin again with the most sweet and holy and loving Child Jesus—a humbled God—walking with Him step by step in the ways of the child."[125] But the all-pervading nature of de Sales' influence has not been fully explored, though even a cursory glance at his spiritual teaching indicates how influential it was for Cornelia.

Wendy Wright highlights Salesian characteristics that are immediately recognisable as formative of Cornelia's spirituality. She speaks of his interest in "the whole person," and his conviction that "a free and loving human response to the divine call was essential to an authentic spiritual orientation." This, together with his understanding of "the hidden life" and of the importance of "gentleness (*douceur*)," led to his call for "radical interior self-denial" without "rigorous exterior mortification." He encouraged not "excessive austerity" but "interior asceticism [rooted in] the ordinary means available in everyday life: a simple surrender of the will to the specifics of the circumstances in which one found oneself"; an "utter abandonment to the will of God … realised in the ordinary facts of everyday life." In Jane Frances de Chantal he confirmed "maternal tenderness" and "motherly attentiveness," by which he meant "not only

---

[125] CC47:3.

solicitude in a general way but an affectionate allowance for those under her care." "It was required that faults be noted and that advancement in virtue be cultivated, [but] the way in which this would be undertaken must never be so judgmental that those under tutelage would be discouraged or intimidated." [126]

Wright believes that his approach—"maternal tenderness, freedom from authoritarianism, urging toward interior asceticism, insistence on fidelity to the Rule, patience with the 'difficult' but good-hearted, high expectations of the 'advanced'"—is particularly suitable for a women's group. And it seems that Cornelia recognised this too, and that his *douceur* encouraged in her a gentle interpretation of Ignatius. But the suggestion here is only that a fuller study of de Sales' influence would enhance our understanding of Cornelia's spirituality and charism.

Spirituality of Suffering

Unlike Cornelia's heritage from de Sales, her spirituality of suffering has frequently been examined and held up for admiration and imitation. Indeed, it is not possible to tell her story without addressing her response to what she herself called her "most unusual sufferings." [127] But, once more, the issue at stake is one of cultural assumption and interpretation. The way in which the spirituality of suffering is presented in convent culture—the notion that "holiness is to be nailed with Christ to the Cross" [128]—is explicitly repudiated by many women theologians today. The relevance of Cornelia's approach to suffering must be re-examined. It may have suited her and served her within her nineteenth-century context, and it may even, perhaps, have deepened her relationship with God; but we must ask whether women today would find her approach empowering and liberating, merely demeaning, or even downright harmful? The suggestion here is that Cornelia's life experiences, her silences, her terse entries in her spiritual notebooks, her written prayers, her personal resolutions, her advice to others, her desires for the Society and its Constitutions must all be re-

---

[126] Wendy M. Wright, "St Jane de Chantal's Guidance of Women" (paper presented to the American Academy for the Study of Religion, December 1984).

[127] CC 45:12.

[128] Walsh, *The Vocation of Cornelia Connelly*, 9.

examined in the light of this question. It may then be possible to assert that Cornelia has a contribution to make to the current theological debate about suffering, and especially about "women's passive compliance with suffering."[129]

Pierce Connelly

In this study, attention has frequently been drawn to the presentation of Pierce in the biographies. A fundamental disjunction has been apparent: how is the claim for Cornelia's wisdom and maturity to be squared with her choice of, and continuing love for, a man whom the biographers unreservedly disparage? What has been gained and what lost by his demonization? What other interpretations of Pierce and of his marriage to Cornelia are possible?

An "accurate" portrayal of Pierce is probably even less likely than of Cornelia, because all the information we have is coloured by his rejection of Roman Catholicism. But whilst "facts" are beyond retrieval, different interpretations, informed by current psychological theory, are still possible. A recent study of middle-class masculinity in Victorian England suggests that relationships between husbands and wives were often more complex than the accepted conventions about the Connellys' marriage allow. A marriage which has been explored in some detail—that of Edward Benson (who became Archbishop of Canterbury) and his wife, Mary—is reminiscent of the Connellys' in many respects, and perhaps throws a different light upon Pierce's behaviour:

> Edward's need for comfort and reassurance was intense. Like many others he came to terms with his dependence by constructing his wife as mother … Mary would gather him to her breast, intuit his unarticulated needs and regulate the emotional equilibrium of the household … Victorian men were more drawn than most to the appeal of the wife-mother. But at the same time Mary never lost her character of child-wife …. The greater a man's dependence on his wife for counsel and comfort, the greater the strain on his sense of masculine self-sufficiency, and the greater the temptation to compensate for this by the arbitrary exercise of domestic authority. Husbands negotiated this contradiction between dependence and dominance by relating to their wives in quite distinct modes. When

---

[129] Kristina M. Rankka, *Women and the Value of Suffering* (Collegeville, Mn: Liturgical, 1998), 153.

asserting his authority the husband acted as a patriarch; in turning to his wife for support his conduct was more like that of a child towards his mother .... In the American context this syndrome has been dubbed the "patriarchal child."[130]

Was Pierce perhaps a quintessential "patriarchal child" and Cornelia correspondingly an angelic wife-mother?[131] The very question highlights one of the difficulties of applying a hermeneutics of suspicion to the presentation of Pierce and attempting to read against the grain of the biographies: any retrieval of a different Pierce will modify the view of Cornelia. Ultimately it may be necessary to accept that a different reading of the marriage and of Pierce is not possible. But a more liberal and less condemnatory approach to him is surely called for, especially since Buckle hints that the condemnation of Pierce by his contemporaries (even by members of the Society) was not universal:

> Mother Teresa knew all as she was intimately acquainted with the family of the Connellys and she had a great opinion of Mr Connelly's talent, fervour and good disposition till the fatal separation ... Mother Teresa laid all the blame on Miss Bowles who misrepresented the whole affair ... Mother Teresa acted throughout as the affectionate friend of all parties and ... saw Mr Connelly several times before he left England and tried to conciliate him.[132]

Cornelia's response to the gender assumptions of her time was not always conscious, let alone consistent; it cannot be categorized as heroic or perfect. But, somehow, it does seem to have been largely healthy. Even the aspects of socialised gender control that most constrained her and curtailed her activity were not totally fruitless, as she struggled to respond with as much integrity as she could muster.

---

[130] John Tosh, *A Man's Place: Masculinity and the Middle-Class Home in Victorian England* (New Haven and London: Yale UP, 1999), 71.

[131] Flaxman comments (*A Woman Styled Bold*, 117) that Cornelia "was a wife whose love of her husband was often maternal."

[132] D78:25, 26.

Chapter Nine

OUTCOMES AND CONCLUSIONS

At the beginning of this book, I asked how far the biographers' personal preferences and the concerns of the moment might have influenced the construction of their texts. Did the biographies of Cornelia Connelly reflect different spiritualities, different assumptions about holiness and about women? Were the biographers, consciously or unconsciously, using Cornelia's story to promote and validate a particular model of religious life, a particular view of the Society? Did the Society experience the need for a new biography, a different telling of the founder's story, each time it entered a new phase of its existence? And, finally, would a biography written today, rooted in current biographical strategies and in the principles underlying contemporary Christian feminist spirituality, provide a substantially different reading of the story?

Cornelia's story cannot be presented free from conscious and unconscious interpretation and bias. The positionality of the biographers, the context out of which they were writing, and their purpose in presenting the life, have determined their perspective on Cornelia, their construction of her story. Writing this book has helped me to arrive at a clearer understanding of the biographers' standpoints, a more informed reading of their texts, and a fairer assessment of their presentation of Cornelia. It has heightened my awareness of how Cornelia's story intermeshes with the contexts and value systems of her biographers: in reading the one, we absorb the other. In my last chapter, I have drawn on both pro- and anti-Cornelian myths to explore the interrelated themes of gender and power and their significance in Cornelia's story, in order to illustrate what a thematic approach to her life might reveal.

It would be contrary to the whole tenor of this book to come to a definitive conclusion. Its purpose has been to open rather than to close, to ask questions rather than to provide solutions. As Carla Ricci has written:

I am not putting forward conclusions as though they were final destinations and so, necessarily, closures to the reflections .... If these are at this moment *points of arrival* thanks to the dynamic of research, they are also, in a process of creative projection, *points of departure*, the beginnings of other ways into the interior of an open-ended process which in its course will be able to look at them in new contexts of research and analysis.[1]

Nevertheless, this book raises topics which are of importance in Cornelian scholarship, and which will have to be taken into consideration by any future biographer. It calls attention to issues of specific relevance to such biographers: the potential, and the limitations, of the original source materials; the continuing influence of changes in the self-perception of women religious on how the life of a religious founder is narrated; and the problems associated with an idealized or configured life. It suggests that thematic and specialist studies of particular aspects, incidents and short periods in Cornelia's life would be of value in themselves, as well as having significance for any future full-length biography.

The Documentation

Once the cause of Cornelia's canonisation was introduced, her congregation spent more than ten years searching for and collating her extant public and private writings. Easy access to this documentation separates all post-1980 studies of Cornelia from previous readings of her life. These source materials have introduced a new rigour and professionalism into Cornelian studies, providing the tools for a serious historical scholarship that is very different from the earlier fairly amateur, explicitly in-house, loving accounts of the life of the Reverend Mother Foundress.

However, the documentation remains provisional. In spite of the historical commissioners' claim that their information concerning Cornelia had been exhaustively researched and presented, new material continues to come to light. For instance, the Oxford archives have recently acquired documents about the Duchess of Leeds, Cornelia's most significant benefactor, and an account of Maria Joseph Buckle's early life written by

---

[1] Carla Ricci, *Mary Magdalene and Many Others—Women Who Followed Jesus* (Tunbridge Wells: Burns and Oates, 1994), 196.

Xavier Gwynn in the 1940s. And Erin Brown, a descendant of one of Cornelia's slaves who is researching her ancestry, argues that Cornelia did not free her slaves when she left Grand Coteau, as the pro-Cornelian myth-makers have wanted to believe. She had them baptized as Catholics, but it is extremely unlikely that she taught them to read or write, as tradition within Cornelia's congregation has maintained at least since the 1920s. The existing biographies make only passing reference to this aspect of Cornelia's life in the southern states of the USA. For the official Society biographers, Cornelia's slave ownership was either an embarrassment to be played down, or a fact that was not of primary importance to their narratives. But today, when there is a major interest in the underside of history—in the history of people who did not have power—it is an aspect of Cornelia's life which requires fuller exploration. We must expect new aspects of other issues to be raised in a similar way in the future.

An important question which needs to be asked of the carefully collated documentation is whether it enables us to get closer to Cornelia than the biographies do, and to hear her own voice for ourselves. Occasionally, in unsent letters recorded in the letter book, there are flashes of passion and anger, and outbursts of resentment and irritation; but otherwise it appears that Cornelia was instinctively discreet, and exercised a good deal of self-censorship even in her most personal letters. When Wiseman was fearful of sexual scandal in the 1850s, she was able to reassure him with the utmost confidence that her letters to Pierce would provide no evidence: "You may be quite easy, my dear Lord ... I do not believe I have ever written a letter to him that might not safely be brought before all our enemies."[2] Cornelia's reticence in all personal matters, and the paucity of her private notes, mean that it is her public persona that is more immediately recoverable from the documentation: Cornelia the administrator, the educator, the religious superior.

Any future biographer will have to select from the primary sources and interpret them, just as previous biographers have done, but it is doubtful whether anyone will come closer to authenticity using the same methods. If, however, a different approach were to be taken to the documentation, it is

---

[2] CC18:40.

possible that some new insights might be arrived at. Detailed analysis of Cornelia's language, her rhetoric, her preferred imagery and theological emphases could well be fruitful avenues for further research.

The Biographers

Although the documentation is important, it is not all-encompassing. Cornelia's biographers (including Wadham) have written within a reiterative and partially oral Holy Child tradition, a tradition that has its own parameters and is curiously ahistorical. Whatever their conscious intentions, the biographers examined here now seem to have had a dual objective. On the one hand, they repeat the received version of Cornelia's story, defending and justifying her actions, personality and holiness not only uncritically but with something verging on missionary zeal. On the other hand, their texts spring out of the moment in which they were written, and reinforce the values and attitudes that were current within the Society at that time.

Cornelia's pre-Vatican II biographers presumed that the value systems within which they were writing were unchanging, even unchangeable. They had no reason to question their assumptions about holiness or canonisation, about gender, religious life, perfection, mortification or suffering. They interpreted Cornelia's life from within the framework of their assumptions, and, consciously and unconsciously, they used her story to reinforce specific views and values. The two post-Vatican II authors (Strub and Flaxman) were more alert to change; they used the sources in a more sophisticated way and had a better sense of historical context; but, beneath the surface of their texts, many of the rhetorical and devotional patterns of the earlier biographers are still discernible. Their own context (the modern world, the post-Vatican II Church) is reflected in their concern to present an "accurate" picture of Cornelia.

All the biographers rely heavily on Buckle's master narrative, and they are caught up in the creation of a pro-Cornelia myth which counters the contrary myth of Cornelia's detractors. Buckle set out, quite consciously, to defend Cornelia against the hostile opinions of her contemporaries and, in so doing, she established a myth of the perfect Cornelia, which was accepted and reinforced by later biographers.

Yet, in spite of the power of Buckle's original construction, the Cornelias of the biographies differ to a surprising degree. Their differences reflect the needs and preoccupations current within the Society when each biography was written. "Biography," it has recently been asserted, "is simply part of our desire to colonise the past with the obsessions of our present."[3]

Buckle valued obedience and struggled with Cornelia's non-conformity; Bellasis was a dutiful spiritual daughter at the feet of the founding mother;[4] Gompertz' Cornelia was the ideal of the Holy Child sister;[5] and Bisgood's portrayal was of a calm, self-controlled and silent woman, a model of convent culture. The resistance of James Walsh and the Society to Wadham's presentation of Cornelia, as a woman struggling to come to terms with her husband's choices, was based on their assumptions about holiness, and on their consequent need to defend Cornelia against any suggestion that she was less than perfect. Strub was the first to question this approach, and, by 1990, Flaxman's insights were so far removed from Buckle's that her presentation of a passionate, compelling and bold Cornelia praised and admired the very qualities that Buckle had sought to minimise or excuse. And yet, in other ways, she had not moved very far from the first biographer's claim that all of Cornelia's actions and decisions could be justified as those of a saint.

The significance of the selection and interpretation of data is demonstrated by the fact that each of these different portrayals of Cornelia is supported by substantial use of the same primary source materials.

A New Life for Each New Age

Though Cornelia's biographers were consciously engaged in writing an account of the beloved foundress, developments in their presentation of the story also reflect changes in the self-perception of women religious. As changes occurred, a need was experienced for a new telling of the story through which the biographers could, consciously and unconsciously,

---

[3] Adrian Hamilton, "Drowning in a Sea of Salacious Biographies," *The Independent* (26 November 2002), 21.

[4] Alison Weber observes, "Detachment from one's biological family was a prerequisite virtue for the novice, but ... it was frequently replaced with affection for the mother foundress." (*Teresa of Avila*, 156.)

[5] Her approach is redolent of the spirituality of religious life encapsulated in the works of Columba Marmion (See, for example, *Christ the Ideal of the Monk* [St Louis: Herder, 1926].)

validate the present through their construction of the past. Whereas Buckle, writing shortly after Vatican I, sought to construct Cornelia's life around a model of obediential holiness, Flaxman, a quarter of a century after Vatican II, highlighted Cornelia's dynamism and independence. Today a postmodern biographer would be less exercised by the need to choose and defend a particular emphasis, and could present an imperfect, inconsistent, self-contradictory Cornelia, who was sometimes silent and submissive, sometimes passionate and peremptory. And a postmodern member of Cornelia's congregation, reflecting current developments in religious life, might warm to such a presentation.

Cornelia is, however, more than a construct, and each succeeding generation cannot have unlimited freedom to reinvent her. This is particularly important if she is being presented, not only as a fascinating nineteenth-century woman, but as a continuing model for other Christians. There is a theological reality at the heart of her story (God's relationship with her, God's dealings with her in the extraordinary vicissitudes of her life) which remains constant, although it has to be realised once again by each generation. We undertake historical research into Cornelia's life, and reread her texts, in order to discover fresh insights into this theological reality. Any Cornelian biography must draw on those insights and develop them in the presentation of the life story.

In an unarticulated way, the existing biographies fulfil this function. The biographies of the founder carry more than the story of one woman; their pages contain a presentation and justification of the Society's understanding and current living of its charism. As the Society's self-perception has changed, the older biographies have been perceived as corresondingly inadequate, both for the Society's members and for a wider readership.

Changes in Women's Religious Life

The first two biographies of Cornelia, those by Buckle and Bellasis, belong to a phase in the development of women's religious life in Britain identified by Susan O'Brien[6] as occurring roughly between 1890 and 1914, when the

---

[6] O'Brien, "Women Religious."

long nineteenth century drew to a close. During this period, O'Brien says, women's congregations were no longer at the cutting edge of change as they had been earlier, but were retrenching, looking inwards towards the Church rather than outwards towards social and political engagement. And the biographies reflect this focus: Cornelia is a saint more because of her personal perfection and her obedience to the hierarchy than because of her ministerial activity.

The biographies by Gompertz, Wadham and Bisgood were written during O'Brien's next phase, from World War I to the mid-1960s. This period, which saw such radical changes in social behaviour and expectations, was characterized within religious life by increasing institutionalisation and uniformity:

> Catholicism had a timeless feel about it. Could it ever have been different? It felt so solid, sure, and self-contained …. Women religious seem to have shared this same world view. The future held small adjustments but there were no major changes foreseen or wanted.[7]

This static and confident Roman Catholic viewpoint is reflected in all of these biographies, with Gompertz and Bisgood especially presuming the unchangeability of convent culture. They both read Cornelia's life from this perspective, and deliberately use her story to reinforce convent values.

Strub and Flaxman belong in O'Brien's post-Vatican II phase, *c.*1965-1990. "This was a chaotic period … there was a great deal of experimentation, but … without a clear vision of what the needs were, of what women religious could and should be, and of what they, as women, could become."[8] In such a context, the old, certain presentation of Cornelia would no longer serve; as convent culture was increasingly discarded, so was its version of Cornelia's story.

Problems of the Idealized Life: The "Perfect Nun"

The discourse of the "perfect nun"—a woman who, by means of self-denial, mortification and suffering, has reached a plateau of unvarying

---

[7] O'Brien, "Women Religious," 12-13.
[8] O'Brien, "Women Religious," 13.

perfection—is problematic for any biographer today. She is also an unsatisfactory and unacceptable role model for contemporary Christians, not merely because the equation of sanctity with perfection is no longer credible, but because the perfect or idealized wife, mother or religious is perceived as unreal. Cornelia's biographers all struggled to square their knowledge of her limitations with their own need to present her as perfect, because they conflated perfection and holiness. As has been demonstrated, this led them into a series of explanations and justifications, into trying to gloss over her mistakes or minimise them—in short, into presenting a less than full picture of Cornelia the human being.

And this is true, not just of the pre-Vatican II biographies, but of the works of Strub and Flaxman too. The primary emphasis in their writing continues to be on a Cornelia who is immune to the moral complexities of ordinary life, rather than having to negotiate them. Strub's claim is made in extravagant language:

> At Grand Coteau Cornelia's spiritual physiognomy became what it was to remain until her death. The inner face which she turned toward God became as distinctive and clearly defined as her beautiful profile. Age and life served only to accentuate the most marked of her soul's features. She remained interiorly consistent with the person she had become at Grand Coteau, meeting the incoherence and absurdity of much that was to befall her with the inner coherence of her unequivocal "yes" to God.[9]

Although this was written as recently as 1987, it strikes as alien a note as anything in Buckle.

Today, when Cornelia's human failings present no problems biographically or theologically, the stress on perfection in the biographies serves only to distance their subject from the reader. The struggle with the construct of perfection, which so exercised earlier biographers, no longer concerns those of the present day. It is now possible, without being in any way iconoclastic, to present Cornelia's holiness alongside and through her inadequate, sometimes mistaken, responses to unforeseen events, and through her own imperfect choices and decisions (her refusal to see Pierce in the parlour in Derby, for instance, which she herself came to regret).

---

[9] Strub, *Informatio*, 103.

Today, accepting responsibility for one's mistakes is acknowledged as a healthy part of the human condition; so an honest presentation of Cornelia's struggles with difficult situations can make her a more attractive and accessible model for present-day Christians.

A Way Forward

As this overview shows, all biographies are necessarily written from within a specific context and value system. And so, a final question must be addressed: does our own moment need a substantially different reading of the story, and can it produce one?

The postmodern biographer recognises the importance of context; instead of striving for what now seems the unattainable goal of an agenda-free, objective, neutral, definitive presentation of a life, the biographer today deliberately calls attention to his or her own agenda, positionality and relationship with the subject. It is openly acknowledged that the biography is being written by *this* person, within *this* context, and is focusing specifically on *these* issues and addressing *these* questions.

In the light of this biographical development, and with an awareness of the theological need for a rereading that is not a reinvention, I suggest that a new biographer might abandon the conventionally chronological, and focus on some of the dominant themes that emerge in Cornelia's life. It might be easier to address what her story has to say about questions that are of interest today in a specific, detailed study of a particular aspect of her experience. There the context and assumptions of the biographer, and the insights of the theologian, could become helpful tools rather than stumbling blocks. This approach—the examination of specific themes or periods—has recently been proposed by Michael Holroyd as a way forward in biography:

> In the future, I believe, we will have fewer birth-to-death lives, and more selective ones, focusing on a relationship, a year from which some composition springs; or simply portraits-in-miniature of people who were not famous …. The great pioneering biographies are not for imitation, but for more imaginative use: in their power to suggest how we may incorporate

techniques from other branches of literature, and open new territory by finding original methods of collaborating with our friends, the dead.[10]

The danger inherent in the thematic approach, which must be guarded against in any biography and particularly in one with a spiritual focus, is that it leaves room for the narrator to side-step those aspects of the subject's life and choices that do not fit in with current interests and pre-occupations. In Cornelia's case, the temptation would be to ignore the dimensions of her spirituality that are problematic for us—her strong emphasis on mortification and self-denial, for instance, or her unquestioning acceptance of hierarchical structures. But similar omissions and sleights of hand are equally possible in the chronological biography. And the thematic approach has a number of advantages. It enables a fuller exploration of particular aspects of the life story, allowing all the contradictory facets to be presented. It frees the life from a restricting linear presentation, and from "tidying up"; in Cornelia's case, this would mean avoiding the construction of her life as if everything in it led up to her assumption of the role of "mother foundress." And without the pressure to demonstrate perfection, it leaves room for self-contradictions, inconsistencies, complexity and ambiguity.

In my last chapter, I have highlighted the impact of gender and power on Cornelia's life. Any number of other aspects of her life and spirituality await similar re-examination, and a postmodern writer, freed from the reiterative tradition and from the pressure to shape Cornelia's life according to the mould of the earlier biographers, might be able to address them differently. Every new moment will ask its own questions. A future biographer might explore Cornelia's spiritual language, or her well-developed views on art and the impact of visual piety. Her sense of self, her self-perception and self-representation, disentangled from her living of gender roles and from our own preconceptions of "the nun," would be of real interest to women today. The spirituality, psychology and anthropology underlying her educational philosophy might be evaluated from within its current application in African schools. Cornelia might be set more firmly within the context of the lives and stories of other early members of the

---

[10] Michael Holroyd, "Our Friends, the Dead," *The Guardian* (1 June 2002), review section, 42.

Society, rather than being isolated from them and elevated above them. The possibilities are endless.

Any new full-length biography will clearly need to move beyond the frame of the earliest authors who were writing explicitly for Cornelia's spiritual daughters and producing a biography for the nuns. Convents have sustained and encouraged generations of vibrant women; and convent writers like Buckle and Bellasis, Gompertz and Bisgood, Strub and Flaxman have made a significant contribution in the field of women's spiritual biography. But today, something more is needed. Cornelia, struggling within the limitations of her own personality and her own culture, has relevance for a wider Christian readership who are looking for encouragement in their own difficult lives. This book offers the future biographer a heightened consciousness of the reiterative convent-centred tradition that has dominated Cornelian scholarship; and it challenges the biographer to rearticulate Cornelia's story for readers who are hungry to connect with their foremothers' spiritual passion.

BIBLIOGRAPHY

Primary Sources

Autograph letters and other documents, Archives of the Society of the Holy Child Jesus, Oxford.

The Writings of the Servant of God Cornelia Connelly, compiled in typescript and photocopy from manuscripts and printed texts for the apostolic process of her beatification and canonisation, 58 volumes, Archives of the Society of the Holy Child Jesus, Oxford. (Referred to as CC.)

Documentation Presented by the Historical Commission for the Beatification and Canonisation of the Servant of God, Cornelia Connelly, Foundress of the Society of the Holy Child Jesus, 87 volumes, Archives of the Society of the Holy Child Jesus, Oxford. (Referred to as D.)

Positio: Documentary Study for the Canonisation Process of the Servant of God Cornelia Connelly (née Peacock) 1809-79, Sacred Congregation for the Causes of Saints, Prot. No. 953, Southwark, 3 volumes, Archives of the Society of the Holy Child Jesus, Oxford. These volumes contain selected documents from the sources listed above, *Writings* (CC) and *Documentation* (D), as well as a commentary.

Bellasis, Mary Francis, *Life of the Mother Foundress, SHCJ*, unpublished typescript, completed 1919, Archives of the Society of the Holy Child Jesus, Oxford. (D72-75.)

Bisgood, Marie Thérèse, *Cornelia Connelly: A Study in Fidelity* (London: Burns & Oates, 1963).

Buckle, Maria Joseph, *Materials Collected for a Life of Cornelia Connelly*, unpublished typescript, completed 1886, Archives of the Society of the Holy Child Jesus, Oxford. (D63-67.)

——, *Personal Recollections*, unpublished typescript, Archives of the Society of the Holy Child Jesus, Oxford. (D78.)

Flaxman, Radegunde, *A Woman Styled Bold: The Life of Cornelia Connelly 1809-1879* (London: Darton, Longman and Todd, 1991).

Gompertz, Mary Catherine ["A Member of the Society"], *The Life of Cornelia Connelly, 1809-1879* (London: Longman, Green & Co., 1922).

Strub, Elizabeth Mary, *Informatio, Positio for the Canonisation Process of the Servant of God, Cornelia Connelly (née Peacock) 1809-1879*, Sacred Congregation for the Causes of Saints, Prot. No. 953 (Rome: SHCJ, 1987).

Wadham, Juliana, *The Case of Cornelia Connelly* (London: Collins, 1956).

Secondary Sources

Alpern, Sara, Joyce Antler, Elisabeth Israels Perry and Ingrid Winther Scobie, eds., *The Challenge of Feminist Biography: Writing the Lives of Modern American Women* (Urbana and Chicago: University of Illinois Press, 1992).

Atkinson, Clarissa W., "'Your Servant, My Mother': The Figure of St Monica in the Ideology of Christian Motherhood," in C. W. Atkinson and others, eds., *Immaculate and Powerful: The Female in Sacred Image and Social Reality* (Boston: Beacon, 1995).

Backscheider, Paula, *Reflections on Biography* (Oxford: OUP, 1999).

Bellasis, Edward, *Memorials of Mr Serjeant Bellasis* (London: Burns, Oates and Washbourne, 1923 [1893]).

Brueggeman, Walter, *The Bible and Postmodern Imagination: Texts Under Negotiation* (London: SCM, 1993).

Burke, Peter, "How to Become a Counter-Reformation Saint," in David M. Luebke, ed., *The Counter-Reformation: The Essential Readings* (London: Blackwell, 1999).

Bynum, Carolyn Walker, "Religious Women in the Later Middle Ages," in Jill Raitt, ed., *Christian Spirituality II: High Middle Ages and Reformation* (London: SCM, 1988).

Carr, Anne E., "The New Vision of Feminist Theology," in Catherine Mowry LaCugna, ed., *Freeing Theology*.

Chopp, Rebecca S. and Sheila Greeve Davaney, eds., *Horizons in Feminist Theology: Identity, Tradition, and Norms* (Minneapolis: Fortress, 1997).

Christ, Carol P. and Judith Plaskow, eds., *WomanSpirit Rising: A Feminist Reader in Religion* (New York: HarperCollins, 1992 [1979]).

Curran, Patricia, *Grace Before Meals: Food Ritual and Body Discipline in Convent Culture* (Urbana and Chicago: University of Illinois Press, 1989).

Daly, Mary, *Gyn/Ecology: The Metaethics of Radical Feminism* (London: Women's Press, 1991 [1979]).

Dowd Hall, Jacquelyn, "Lives Through Time: Second Thoughts on Jessie Daniel Ames," in Alpern and others, *The Challenge of Feminist Biography*.

Edel, Leon, *Writing Lives: Principia Biographia* (New York and London: W. W. Norton & Company, 1984 [1959]).

Fiorenza, Elisabeth Schüssler, *Bread Not Stone: The Challenge of Feminist Biblical Interpretation* (Boston: Beacon, 1984).

———, *Discipleship of Equals* (London: SCM, 1993).

Fiorenza, Francis Schüssler and John P. Galvin, eds., *Systematic Theology: Roman Catholic Perspectives,* 2 (Minneapolis: Fortress, 1991).

Flanders, Judith, *A Circle of Sisters* (London: Viking, 2001).

Flint, Kate, *The Woman Reader, 1837-1914* (Oxford: Clarendon, 1993).

Fromm, Gloria G., ed., *Essaying Biography: A Celebration for Leon Edel* (Hawaii: University of Hawaii Press, 1986).

Garrison, Dee, "Two Roads Taken: Writing the Biography of Mary Heaton Vorse," in Alpern and others, eds., *The Challenge of Feminist Biography*.

Hall, Jacquelyn Dowd, "Lives Through Time: Second Thoughts on Jessie Daniel Ames," in Alpern and others, eds., *The Challenge of Feminist Biography*.

Hamer, Edna, *Elizabeth Prout 1820-1864: A Religious Life for Industrial England* (Bath: Downside Abbey, 1994).

Harding, Sandra, "Is There a Feminist Method?" in Sandra Harding, ed., *Feminism and Methodology* (Bloomington and Indianapolis: Indiana UP; Milton Keynes: Open UP, 1987).

van Heijst, Annelies, *Longing for the Fall*, translated by Henry Jansen (Kampen: Kok Pharos, 1995).

Heilbrun, Carolyn G., *Writing a Woman's Life* (New York: Ballantine Books, 1988).

Hines, Mary E., "Community for Liberation," in Catherine Mowry LaCugna, ed., *Freeing Theology*.

Hinsdale, Mary Ann, "Heeding the Voices: An Historical Overview," in Ann O'Hara Graff, ed., *In the Embrace of God: Feminist Approaches to Theological Anthropology* (Maryknoll, NY: Orbis, 1995).

Holmes, Richard, *Sidetracks: Explorations of a Romantic Biographer* (London: HarperCollins, 2000).

Holroyd, Michael, "Our Friends, the Dead," *The Guardian*, review section (1 June 2002).

Johnson, Elizabeth A., "Saints and Mary," in Fiorenza and Galvin, eds., *Systematic Theology*.

——, *Friends of God and Prophets: A Feminist Theological Reading of the Communion of Saints* (London: SCM, 1998).

Jones, Serene, "Women's Experience between a Rock and a Hard Place: Feminist, Womanist, and *Mujerista* Theologies in North America," in Chopp and Davaney, eds., *Horizons in Feminist Theology*.

Kilroy, Phil, *Madeleine Sophie Barat: A Life* (Mahwah, NJ: Paulist, 2000).

Kinast, Robert L., *What Are They Saying About Theological Reflection?* (New York and Mahwah: Paulist, 2000).

LaChance, Carol Wallas, *The Way of the Mother: The Lost Journey of the Feminine* (Rockport, Ma: Element, 1991).

LaCugna, Catherine Mowry, ed., *Freeing Theology: The Essentials of Theology in Feminist Perspective* (New York: HarperSanFrancisco, 1993).

Langland, Elizabeth, *Nobody's Angels: Middle-Class Women and Domestic Ideology in Victorian Culture* (Ithaca and London: Cornell UP, 1995).

Long, Judy, *Telling Women's Lives: Subject, Narrator, Reader, Text* (New York: New York UP, 1999).

Maitland, Sara, "Saints for Today," *The Way*, 36/4 (October 1996).

Manguel, Alberto, *A History of Reading* (London: HarperCollins Flamingo, 1996).

McCarthy, Caritas, *The Spirituality of Cornelia Connelly: In God, For God, With God* (Lewiston and Queenston: Edwin Mellen, 1986).

McClelland, V. Alan and Michael Hodgetts, eds., *From Without the Flaminian Gate: 150 Years of Roman Catholicism in England and Wales,* (London: Darton, Longman and Todd, 1999).

McClendon, James W., *Biography as Theology: How Life Stories Can Remake Today's Theology* (Philadelphia: Trinity Press International, 1990 [1974]).

McDonald, Helen, SHCJ, "Cornelia's Life in the South," unpublished paper, completed 2003.

McLaughlin, Eleanor L., "The Christian Past: Does It Hold a Future for Women?" in Christ and Plaskow, eds., *WomanSpirit Rising.*

Molinari, Paul, SJ, "Commitment to Love: A Reply to Cornelia Connelly's Critics," *Homiletic and Pastoral Review* 64 (October 1963), 21-29.

Mumm, Susan, *Stolen Daughters, Virgin Mothers: Anglican Sisterhoods in Victorian Britain* (London and New York: Leicester UP, 1999).

Murphy, Anne, SHCJ, "Old Catholics, New Converts, Irish Immigrants: A Reassessment of Catholicism in England in the Nineteenth Century," *Cherwell Papers*, 1/3 (San Diego: 1993).

Nagel, Paul C., *The Adams Women: Abigail and Louisa Adams, Their Sisters and Daughters* (Cambridge, Ma: Harvard UP, 1999 [1987]).

Navone, John, SJ, *Seeking God in Story* (Collegeville, Mn: Liturgical, 1990).

Newsome, David, *The Victorian World Picture* (London: John Murray, 1997).

O'Brien, Susan, "Women Religious: Historical Past—Future Perspectives," unpublished paper, given at the Assembly of the British Province of the Sisters of Notre Dame, August 1994.

———, "Religious Life for Women," in McClelland and Hodgetts, eds., *From Without the Flaminian Gate*.

Press, Margaret, "Sanctity, Images and Stories," *The Way*, 36/4 (October 1996).

Ramshaw, Gail, *Under the Tree of Life: The Religion of a Feminist Christian* (New York: Continuum, 1998).

Rankka, Kristina M., *Women and the Value of Suffering* (Collegeville, Mn: Liturgical, 1998).

Ricci, Carla, *Mary Magdalene and Many Others: Women Who Followed Jesus* (Tunbridge Wells: Burns & Oates, 1994).

Richter, Harvena, "The Biographer as Novelist," in Fromm, ed., *Essaying Biography*.

Rudnick, Lois, "The Male Identified Woman and Other Anxieties: The Life of Mabel Dodge Luhan," in Alpern and others, eds., *The Challenge of Feminist Biography*.

Ruether, Rosemary Radford, *Sexism and God Talk* (London: SCM, 1983).

Saiving, Valerie, "The Human Situation: A Feminine View," in Christ and Plaskow, eds., *WomanSpirit Rising*.

Schulenburg, Janet Tibbets, *Forgetful of Their Sex: Female Sanctity and Society, Ca. 500-1000* (Chicago and London: University of Chicago Press, 1998).

Suenens, Léon-Joseph, Cardinal, *The Nun in the World* (London: Burns & Oates, 1962).

Sheldrake, Philip, *Spirituality and History* (London: SPCK, 1991).

Sklar, Kathryn Kish, "Coming to Terms with Florence Kelley: The Tale of a Reluctant Biographer," in Alpern and others, eds., *The Challenge of Feminist Biography*.

Strub, Elizabeth Mary, "James Walsh, Cornelia Connelly and the Society of the Holy Child Jesus," *Letters and Notices*, 87/391 (Christmas 1986), 185-197.

——, *Ignatius, the Spiritual Exercises and Cornelia: A Retreat By All Means* (San Diego: Society of the Holy Child Jesus, 1996).

Stuart, Elizabeth, *Spitting at Dragons: Towards a Feminist Theology of Sainthood* (London: Mowbray, 1996).

Sweet, Matthew, *Inventing the Victorians* (London: Faber, 2001).

Symonds, Richard, *Far Above Rubies: The Women Uncommemorated in the Church of England* (Leominster: Gracewing, 1993).

Taylor, Thérèse, *Bernadette of Lourdes* (London: Burns and Oates, 2003)

Tosh, John, *A Man's Place: Masculinity and the Middle-Class Home in Victorian England* (New Haven and London: Yale UP, 1999).

Walsh, James, SJ, *The Vocation of Cornelia Connelly* (The Month, 1959).

Ware, Susan, "Unlocking the Porter-Dewson Partnership: A Challenge for the Feminist Biographer," in Alpern and others, eds., *The Challenge of Feminist Biography*.

Weber, Alison, *Teresa of Avila and the Rhetoric of Femininity* (Princeton: Princeton UP, 1990).

Wilson, A. N., *The Victorians* (London: Hutchinson, 2002).

Woodward, Kenneth, *Making Saints: Inside the Vatican: Who Become Saints, Who Do Not, and Why ...* (London: Chatto and Windus, 1991).

Woolf, Virginia, *A Writer's Diary* (New York: Harcourt Brace, 1954).

——, *A Room of One's Own* (London: Grafton Books, 1987 [1929]).

——, "The Art of Biography," in *The Crowded Dance of Modern Life: Selected Essays: Volume Two* (London: Penguin, 1993).

Wright, Wendy M., "St Jane de Chantal's Guidance of Women," paper presented to the American Academy for the Study of Religion, December 1984.

Wyschogrod, Edith, *Saints and Postmodernism* (Chicago and London: University of Chicago Press, 1990).

Young, Pamela Dickey, *Feminist Theology/Christian Theology: In Search of a Method* (Minneapolis, Mn: Fortress, 1990).

INDEX

A full index of the events of Cornelia's life is not offered here. Many references to aspects of Cornelia's life are to be found under the names of each of her biographers.